Professional Examinations

GW00722506

Paper F7 (INT)

Financial Reporting

EXAM KIT

ACCA OFFICIAL PUBLISHER

KAPLAN

PUBLISHING

British Library Cataloguing-in-Publication Data

A catalogue record for this book is available from the British Library.

Published by:
Kaplan Publishing UK
Unit 2, The Business Centre
Molly Millars Lane
Wokingham
Berkshire
RG41 2QZ

ISBN 978 1 84710 486 1

© Kaplan Financial Limited, December 2007

Printed and bound in Great Britain by William Clowes Ltd, Beccles, Suffolk

Acknowledgements

The past ACCA exam questions are the copyright of the Association of Chartered Certified Accountants. The original answers to the questions from June 1994 onwards were produced by the examiners themselves and have been adapted by Kaplan Publishing.

We are grateful to the Chartered Institute of Management Accountants and the Institute of Chartered Accountants in England and Wales for permission to reproduce past exam questions. The answers have been prepared by Kaplan Publishing.

KAPLAN PUBLISHING

CONTENTS

Section

5   Download December 2007 exam questions and answers from the ACCA website: www.accaglobal.com/students.

INDEX TO QUESTIONS AND ANSWERS

SYLLABUS AND EXAM FORMAT

Format of the exam

Number of marks

Five compulsory questions:

Three questions (25 marks each)	75
Question 4	15
Question 5	10
	———
Total time allowed: 3 hours	100
	———

Aim

To develop knowledge and skills in understanding and applying accounting standards and the theoretical framework in the preparation of financial statements of entities, including groups and how to analyse and interpret those financial statements.

Objectives

On successful completion of this paper candidates should be able to:

- discuss and apply a conceptual framework for financial reporting

- discuss a regulatory framework for financial reporting

- prepare and present financial statements which conform with international accounting standards

- account for business combinations in accordance with international accounting standards

- analyse and interpret financial statements.

KAPLAN PUBLISHING

Position of the paper in the overall syllabus

The Financial Reporting syllabus assumes knowledge acquired in Paper F3, *Financial Accounting*, and develops and applies this further and in greater depth.

The syllabus begins with the conceptual framework of accounting with reference to the qualitative characteristics of useful information and the fundamental bases of accounting introduced in the Paper F3 syllabus within the Knowledge module. It then moves into a detailed examination of the regulatory framework of accounting and how this informs the standard setting process.

The main areas of the syllabus cover the reporting of financial information for single companies and for groups in accordance with generally accepted accounting practice and relevant accounting standards.

Finally, the syllabus covers the analysis and interpretation of information from financial reports.

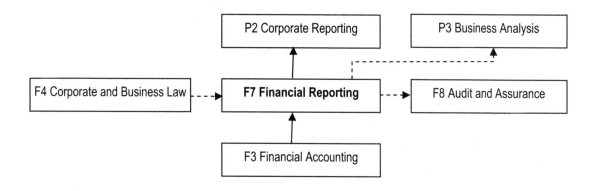

Syllabus content

A   A conceptual framework for financial reporting

1.   The need for a conceptual framework

2.   Understandability, relevance, reliability and comparability

3.   Recognition and measurement

4.   The legal versus the commercial view of accounting

5.   Alternative models and practices

6.   The concept of 'faithful representation' ('true and fair view')

B   A regulatory framework for financial reporting

1.   Reasons for the existence of a regulatory framework

2.   The standard setting process

3.   Specialized, not-for-profit, and public sector entities

C   Financial statements

1.   Cash flow statements

2.   Tangible non-current assets

3.   Intangible assets

4.   Inventory

5.   Financial assets and financial liabilities

6.   Leases

7.   Provisions, contingent liabilities and contingent assets

8.   Impairment of assets

9.   Taxation

10. Regulatory requirements relating to the preparation of financial statements

11. Reporting financial performance

D   Business combinations

1.   The concept and principles of a group

2.   The concept of consolidated financial statements

3. Preparation of consolidated financial statements including an associate

E   Analysing and interpreting financial statements

1. Limitations of financial statements

2. Calculation and interpretation of accounting ratios and trends to address users' and stakeholders' needs

3. Limitations of interpretation techniques

4. Specialized, not-for-profit, and public sector entities

Excluded topics

The following topics are specifically excluded from the syllabus:

*   partnership and branch financial statements
*   preparing group financial statements involving more than one subsidiary
*   piecemeal acquisitions, disposal of subsidiaries and group reconstructions
*   foreign currency translation/consolidations, hedging, hyperinflationary economies
*   financial statements of banks and similar financial institutions
*   group cash flows
*   schemes of reorganization/reconstruction
*   company/share valuation
*   derivative financial instruments
*   accounting for retirement benefit costs/plans
*   share based payments
*   International Financial Reporting Standard Exposure Drafts and Discussion Drafts/Papers.

Key areas of the syllabus

The key topic areas are as follows:

Accounting principles and concepts, accounting theory

*   Framework for the Preparation and Presentation of Financial Statements.
*   Revenue recognition.
*   Substance over form.

Preparation of financial statements of companies limited by liability

*   Presentation of financial statements.
*   Accounting and disclosure requirements of International Accounting Standards/International Financial Reporting Standards.

Preparation of consolidated financial statements

*   Definitions of subsidiaries: exclusions from consolidation.
*   Simple groups.

Analysis and interpretation of financial statements

*   Preparation of reports for various user groups.
*   Preparation and analysis of cash flow statements.

Other topic areas

Note: These may be examined as part of a question within the above key areas or as a substantial part of a separate optional question:

- accounting for leases
- construction contracts
- earnings per share
- impairment of assets, provisions
- non-current assets held for sale and discontinued operations
- goodwill and other intangible assets.

Approach to examining the syllabus

The syllabus is assessed by a three-hour paper-based examination.

All questions are compulsory. It will contain both computational and discursive elements. Some questions will adopt a scenario/case study approach.

Question 1 will be a 25-mark question on the preparation of group financial statements and/or extracts thereof, and may include a small discussion element. Computations will be designed to test an understanding of principles.

Question 2, for 25 marks, will test the reporting of non-group financial statements. This may be from information in a trial balance or by restating draft financial statements.

Question 3, for 25 marks, is likely to be an appraisal of an entity's performance and may involve cash flow statements.

Questions 4 and 5 will cover the remainder of the syllabus and will be worth 15 and 10 marks respectively.

An individual question may often involve elements that relate to different subject areas of the syllabus. For example, the preparation of an entity's financial statements could include matters relating to several accounting standards.

Questions may ask candidates to comment on the appropriateness or acceptability of management's opinion or chosen accounting treatment. An understanding of accounting principles and concepts and how these are applied to practical examples will be tested.

Questions on topic areas that are also included in Paper F3 will be examined at an appropriately greater depth in this paper.

Candidates will be expected to have an appreciation of the need for specified accounting standards and why they have been issued. For detailed or complex standards, candidates need to be aware of their principles and key elements.

Additional information

Candidates need to be aware that questions involving knowledge of new examinable regulations will not be set until at least six months after the last day of the month in which the regulation was issued.

ANALYSIS OF PILOT PAPER

June 2007

Q1   Consolidation (25 marks)

(a)   A discussion question in which you are asked to explain the treatment in the consolidated financial statements of investments in:

- 80% of the ordinary shares of another company

- 50% of loan notes issued by another company

- 40% of the ordinary shares of another company.

(b)   You are asked to prepare a consolidated balance sheet for a group including one subsidiary and one associate. Complications include:

- the mid-year acquisition of both investments

- a fair value adjustment

- unrealized profit in inventory

- the impairment of:

    – goodwill arising on acquisition of the subsidiary

    – the investment in the associate.

Q2   Company financial statements (25 marks)

You are presented with a trial balance and five additional notes and asked to produce:

(a)   an income statement

(b)   a statement of changes in equity

(c)   a balance sheet.

The technical issues which must be dealt with are:

- An upwards revaluation of land and buildings and resulting revision of depreciation

- An upwards revaluation of investments

- Accounting for a new finance lease

- Accounting for income tax for the year and a movement on the deferred tax provision.

Q3　Performance appraisal – ratios/cash flow (25 marks)

You are provided with the income statement and balance sheet for a listed company for one year, together with background information and a number of ratios calculated for the previous year.

You are required to:

(a)　Calculate the same ratios for the current year

(b)　Analyse the performance and position of the company in the current year as compared to the previous year

(c)　Explain how your approach to performance appraisal would differ for a not-for-profit organization.

Q4　Conceptual/regulatory framework – IASs

(a)　You are asked to explain

- Relevance

- Reliability

- Comparability

And explain how they make financial information useful.

(b)　You are required to explain 3 accounting issues and identify which of the Framework's qualitative characteristics are relevant. The issues are:

- The inception of a finance lease

- A change in accounting policy

- The usefulness of historical cost accounting.

Q5　Conceptual/regulatory framework – IASs

(a)　You are asked to describe the issues of revenue and profit recognition in relation to construction contracts.

(b)　You are provided with information regarding two construction contracts and asked to calculate amounts to be disclosed in the balance sheet and income statement at the end of the first year.

REVISION GUIDANCE

Planning your revision

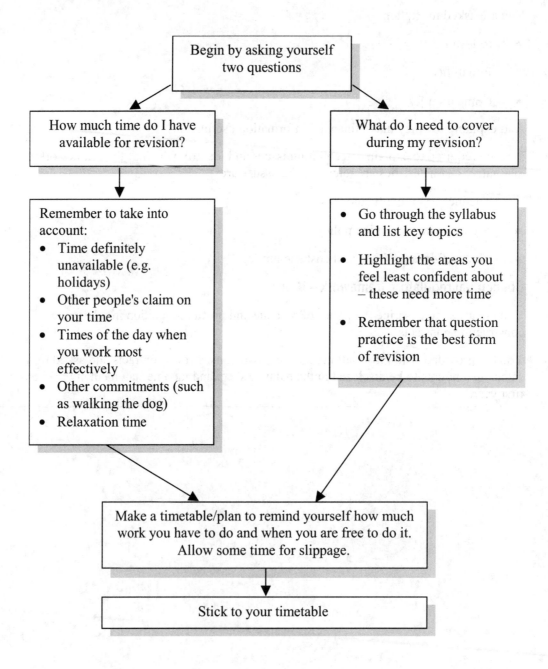

Begin by asking yourself two questions

How much time do I have available for revision?

What do I need to cover during my revision?

Remember to take into account:
- Time definitely unavailable (e.g. holidays)
- Other people's claim on your time
- Times of the day when you work most effectively
- Other commitments (such as walking the dog)
- Relaxation time

- Go through the syllabus and list key topics
- Highlight the areas you feel least confident about – these need more time
- Remember that question practice is the best form of revision

Make a timetable/plan to remind yourself how much work you have to do and when you are free to do it. Allow some time for slippage.

Stick to your timetable

KAPLAN PUBLISHING

Revision techniques

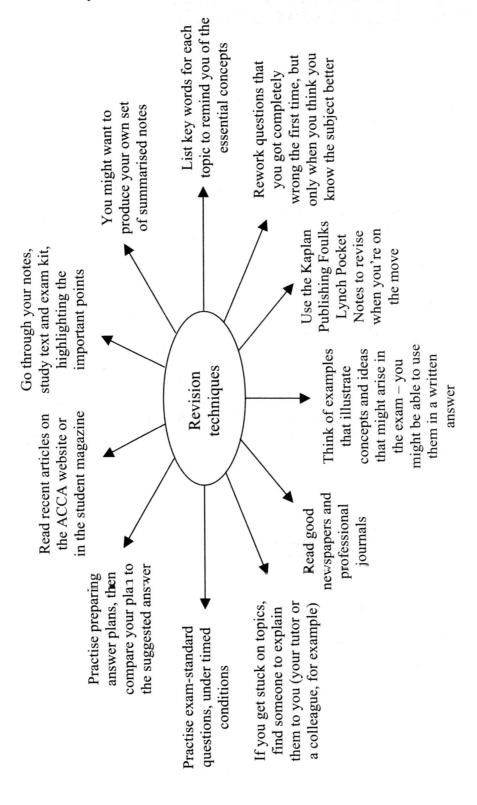

You might want to produce your own set of summarised notes

List key words for each topic to remind you of the essential concepts

Rework questions that you got completely wrong the first time, but only when you think you know the subject better

Go through your notes, study text and exam kit, highlighting the important points

Use the Kaplan Publishing Foulks Lynch Pocket Notes to revise when you're on the move

Read recent articles on the ACCA website or in the student magazine

Revision techniques

Think of examples that illustrate concepts and ideas that might arise in the exam – you might be able to use them in a written answer

Practise preparing answer plans, then compare your plan to the suggested answer

Read good newspapers and professional journals

Practise exam-standard questions, under timed conditions

If you get stuck on topics, find someone to explain them to you (your tutor or a colleague, for example)

EXAM TECHNIQUES

- Use the allocated **15 minutes reading and planning time** at the beginning of the exam to read the questions and begin planning your answers.

- You might want to spend the first few minutes of the exam **reading through the questions**.

- Where you have a **choice of question**, decide which questions you will do.

- Unless you know exactly how to answer the question, spend some time **planning** your answer.

- **Divide the time** you spend on questions in proportion to the marks on offer. One suggestion is to allocate 1.8 minutes to each mark available, so a 10-mark question should be completed in 18 minutes.

- Spend the last **five minutes** reading through your answers and **making any additions or corrections**.

- If you **get completely stuck** with a question, leave space in your answer book and **return to it later.**

- Stick to the question and **tailor your answer** to what you are asked. Pay particular attention to the verbs in the question.

- If you do not understand what a question is asking, **state your assumptions**. Even if you do not answer in precisely the way the examiner hoped, you should be given some credit, if your assumptions are reasonable.

- You should do everything you can to make things easy for the marker. The marker will find it easier to identify the points you have made if your **answers are legible**.

- **Essay questions**: Your essay should have a clear structure. It should contain a brief introduction, a main section and a conclusion. Be concise. It is better to write a little about a lot of different points than a great deal about one or two points.

- **Computations:** It is essential to include all your workings in your answers. Many computational questions require the use of a standard format: company income statement, balance sheet and cash flow statement for example. Be sure you know these formats thoroughly before the exam and use the layouts that you see in the answers given in this book and in model answers.

- **Case studies**: To write a good case study, first identify the area in which there is a problem, outline the main principles/theories you are going to use to answer the question, and then apply the principles/theories to the case.

- **Reports, memos and other documents**: Some questions ask you to present your answer in the form of a report or a memo or other document. So use the correct format – there could be easy marks to gain here.

KAPLAN PUBLISHING

UPDATE

REVISED VERSION OF IAS 1 *PRESENTATION OF FINANCIAL STATEMENTS*

The revised version of IAS 1 issued in 2007 introduces:

(a)   a number of new terms; and

(b)   new presentations of financial performance.

This has an effect in this Exam Kit on the presentation of financial statements and the way certain bookkeeping entries are described.

The **new terms** used in this Exam Kit are set out below alongside the previous terms:

Previous term	New IAS 1 term
– Balance sheet	– Statement of financial position
– Income statement	– Statement of comprehensive income
– Cash flow statement	– Statement of cash flows (including in title of IAS 7)
– Balance sheet date	– End of reporting period/reporting period end
– After the balance sheet date	– After the reporting period (including in title of IAS 10)
– Equity holders (in analysis of profit for year between parent shareholders and the minority interest, for example)	– Owners
– Credited to/debited to/charged in/ included in the income statement	– Recognised in profit or loss

Previously the statements of performance were:

(a)   an income statement, finishing with profit for the year

(b)   a statement of changes in equity which:

    (i)   had a section which presented gains/losses recognised directly in equity, e.g. revaluation gains on non-current assets

    (ii)   summed the total of such gains/losses with the profit for the year ('profit or loss') to arrive at the total recognised income and expense for the year

    (iii)   then adjusted for prior period errors, changes of accounting policies and transactions with equity holders (such as new share issues and dividends paid) and transfers between revaluation reserve and retained earning (such as revaluation surplus realised through excess depreciation charges).

The new IAS 1 requires the presentation of all items of income or expense (i.e. the items referred to in (b) (i) and (ii) above) recognised in the period in one of two permissible formats:

- a single statement of comprehensive income; or

- an income statements and a second statement beginning with profit or loss (from the income statement) and displaying components of other comprehensive income.

This Kit adopts the single statement of comprehensive income.

A statements of changes in equity is still required, but it will only include items referred to in (b) (iii) above.

For the present it is acceptable in the exams to use the previous terminology and statements of performance, but the questions and answers in this Exam Kit have all been adjusted to use the new IAS 1 terminology and formats.

Section 1

PRACTICE QUESTIONS

A CONCEPTUAL FRAMEWORK FOR FINANCIAL REPORTING

1 IASB FRAMEWORK

(a) The IASB's *Framework for the preparation and presentation of financial statements* (Framework) sets out the concepts that underlie the preparation and presentation of financial statements that external users are likely to rely on when making economic decisions about an enterprise.

Required:

Explain the purpose and authoritative status of the Framework. **(5 marks)**

(b) Of particular importance within the Framework are the definitions and recognition criteria for assets and liabilities.

Required:

Define assets and liabilities and explain the important aspects of their definitions. Explain why these definitions are of particular importance to the preparation of an entity's statement of financial position and statement of comprehensive income.

(8 marks)

(c) Peterlee is preparing its financial statements for the year ended 31 March 20X6. The following items have been brought to your attention:

(i) Peterlee acquired the entire share capital of Trantor during the year. The acquisition was achieved through a share exchange. The terms of the exchange were based on the relative values of the two companies obtained by capitalising the companies' estimated future cash flows. When the fair value of Trantor's identifiable net assets was deducted from the value of the company as a whole, its goodwill was calculated at $2.5 million. A similar exercise valued the goodwill of Peterlee at $4 million. The directors wish to incorporate both the goodwill values in the companies' consolidated financial statements. **(4 marks)**

(ii) During the year Peterlee acquired an iron ore mine at a cost of $6 million. In addition, when all the ore has been extracted (estimated in 10 years time) the company will face estimated costs for landscaping the area affected by the mining that have a present value of $2 million. These costs would still have to be incurred even if no further ore was extracted. The directors have proposed that an accrual of $200,000 per year for the next ten years should be made for the landscaping. **(4 marks)**

(iii) On 1 April 20X5 Peterlee issued an 8% $5 million convertible loan at par. The loan is convertible in three years time to ordinary shares or redeemable at par in cash. The directors decided to issue a convertible loan because a non-convertible loan would have required an interest rate of 10%. The directors intend to show the loan at $5 million under non-current liabilities. The following discount rates are available:

	8%	10%
Year 1	0.93	0.91
Year 2	0.86	0.83
Year 3	0.79	0.75

(4 marks)

Required:

Describe (and quantify where possible) how Peterlee should treat the items in (i) to (iii) in its financial statements for the year ended 31 March 20X6 commenting on the directors' views where appropriate.

The mark allocation is shown against each of the three items above.

(Total: 25 marks)

2   ANGELINO

(a) Recording the substance of transactions, rather than their legal form, is an important principle in financial accounting. Abuse of this principle can lead to profit manipulation, non-recognition of assets and substantial debt not being recorded on the statement of financial position.

Required:

Describe how the use of off balance sheet financing can mislead users of financial statements.

Note: your answer should refer to specific user groups and include examples where recording the legal form of transactions may mislead them.   **(9 marks)**

(b) Angelino has entered into the following transactions during the year ended 30 September 20X6:

(i) In September 20X6 Angelino sold (factored) some of its trade receivables to Omar, a finance house. On selected account balances Omar paid Angelino 80% of their book value. The agreement was that Omar would administer the collection of the amounts receivable and remit a residual amount to Angelino depending upon how quickly individual customers paid. Any balance uncollected by Omar after six months will be refunded to Omar by Angelino.

(5 marks)

(ii) On 1 October 20X5 Angelino owned a freehold building that had a carrying amount of $7.5 million and had an estimated remaining life of 20 years. On this date it sold the building to Finaid for a price of $12 million and entered into an agreement with Finaid to rent back the building for an annual rental of $1.3 million for a period of five years. The auditors of Angelino have commented that in their opinion the building had a market value of only $10 million at the date of its sale and to rent an equivalent building under similar terms to the agreement between Angelino and Finaid would only cost $800,000 per annum. Assume any finance costs are 10% per annum.   **(6 marks)**

(iii)   Angelino is a motor car dealer selling vehicles to the public. Most of its new vehicles are supplied on consignment by two manufacturers, Monza and Capri, who trade on different terms.

Monza supplies cars on terms that allow Angelino to display the vehicles for a period of three months from the date of delivery or when Angelino sells the cars on to a retail customer if this is less than three months. Within this period Angelino can return the cars to Monza or can be asked by Monza to transfer the cars to another dealership (both at no cost to Angelino). Angelino pays the manufacturer's list price at the end of the three month period (or at the date of sale if sooner). In recent years Angelino has returned several cars to Monza that were not selling very well and has also been required to transfer cars to other dealerships at Monza's request.

Capri's terms of supply are that Angelino pays 10% of the manufacturer's price at the date of delivery and 1% of the outstanding balance per month as a display charge. After six months (or sooner if Angelino chooses), Angelino must pay the balance of the purchase price or return the cars to Capri. If the cars are returned to the manufacturer, Angelino has to pay for the transportation costs and forfeits the 10% deposit. Because of this Angelino has only returned vehicles to Capri once in the last three years.   **(5 marks)**

Required:

Describe how the above transactions and events should be treated in the financial statements of Angelino for the year ended 30 September 20X6. Your answer should explain, where relevant, the difference between the legal form of the transactions and their substance.

Note: The mark allocation is shown against each of the three transactions above.

(Total: 25 marks)

3   REVENUE RECOGNITION

Revenue recognition is the process by which companies decide when and how much income should be recognized in profit or loss. It is a topical area of great debate in the accounting profession. The IASB looks at revenue recognition from conceptual and substance points of view. There are occasions where a more traditional approach to revenue recognition does not entirely conform to the IASB guidance; indeed neither do some International Accounting Standards.

Required:

(a)   Explain the implications that the IASB's *Framework for the Preparation and Presentation of Financial Statements* (Framework) and the application of substance over form have on the recognition of income in profit or loss. Give examples of how this may conflict with traditional practice and some accounting standards.   **(6 marks)**

(b)   Derringdo sells goods supplied by Gungho. The goods are classed as A grade (perfect quality) or B grade, having slight faults. Derringdo sells the A grade goods acting as an agent for Gungho at a fixed price calculated to yield a gross profit margin of 50%. Derringdo receives a commission of 12.5% of the sales it achieves for these goods. The arrangement for B grade goods is that they are sold by Gungho to Derringdo and Derringdo sells them at a gross profit margin of 25%. The following information has been obtained from Derringdo's financial records:

	$000
Inventory held on premises 1 April 20X2	
– A grade	2,400
– B grade	1,000
Goods from Gungho plc year to 31 March 20X3	
– A grade	18,000
– B grade	8,800
Inventory held on premises 31 March 20X3	
– A grade	2,000
– B grade	1,250

Required:

Prepare the statement of comprehensive income extracts for Derringdo for the year to 31 March 20X3 reflecting the above information. **(5 marks)**

(c) Derringdo acquired an item of plant at a gross cost of $800,000 on 1 October 20X2. The plant has an estimated life of 10 years with a residual value equal to 15% of its gross cost. Derringdo uses straight-line depreciation on a time apportioned basis. The company received a government grant of 30% of its cost price at the time of its purchase. The terms of the grant are that if the company retains the asset for four years or more, then no repayment liability will be incurred. If the plant is sold within four years a repayment on a sliding scale would be applicable. The repayment is 75% if sold within the first year of purchase and this amount decreases by 25% per annum. Derringdo has no intention to sell the plant within the first four years. Derringdo's accounting policy for capital based government grants is to treat them as deferred credits and release them to profit or loss over the life of the asset to which they relate.

Required:

(i) Discuss whether the company's policy for the treatment of government grants meets the definition of a liability in the IASB's *Framework*. **(3 marks)**

(ii) Prepare extracts of Derringdo's financial statements for the year to 31 March 20X3 in respect of the plant and the related grant:

– applying the company's policy;

– in compliance with the definition of a liability in the *Framework*.

Your answer should consider whether the sliding scale repayment should be used in determining the deferred credit for the grant. **(6 marks)**

(d) Derringdo sells carpets from several retail outlets. In previous years the company has undertaken responsibility for fitting the carpets in customers' premises. Customers pay for the carpets at the time they are ordered. The average length of time from a customer ordering a carpet to its fitting is 14 days. In previous years, Derringdo had not recognized a sale in profit or loss until the carpet had been successfully fitted as the rectification costs of any fitting error would be expensive. From 1 April 20X2 Derringdo changed its method of trading by sub-contracting the fitting to approved contractors. Under this policy the sub-contractors are paid by Derringdo and they (the sub-contractors) are liable for any errors made in the fitting. Because of this Derringdo is proposing to recognize sales when customers order and pay for the goods, rather than when they have been fitted. Details of the relevant sales figures are:

	$000
Sales made in retail outlets for the year to 31 March 20X3	23,000
Sales value of carpets fitted in the 14 days to 14 April 20X2	1,200
Sales value of carpets fitted in the 14 days to 14 April 20X3	1,600

Note: the sales value of carpets fitted in the 14 days to 14 April 20X2 are not included in the annual sales figure of $23 million, but those for the 14 days to 14 April 20X3 are included.

Required:

Discuss whether the above represents a change of accounting policy, and, based on your discussion, calculate the amount that you would include in revenue for carpets in the year to 31 March 20X3. **(5 marks)**

(Total: 25 marks)

4 HISTORIC COST

Over the years there have been many attempts by national and international standard setters to find an accepted method of dealing with the reporting of the effects of price changes.

There have been two main methods put forward by various accounting standard bodies for reporting the effects of price changes. One method is based on the movements in general price inflation and is referred to as a General (or Current) Purchasing Power Approach, the other method is based on specific price changes of goods and assets and is generally referred to as a Current Cost Approach. Some bodies have also suggested an approach which combines features of each method.

Required:

(i)   Explain the limitations of (pure) historic cost accounts when used as a basis for assessing the performance of an enterprise. You should give an example of how each of three different user groups may be misled by such information. **(8 marks)**

(ii) Describe the advantages and criticisms of General Purchasing Power and Current Cost Accounting. **(7 marks)**

(Total: 15 marks)

5 CREATIVE ACCOUNTING

The principle of recording the substance or economic reality of transactions rather than their legal form lies at the heart of the *Framework for the Preparation and Presentation of Financial Statements* (Framework) and several International Accounting Standards. The development of this principle was partly in reaction to a minority of public interest companies entering into certain complex transactions. These transactions sometimes led to accusations that company directors were involved in 'creative accounting'.

Required:

(i)   Explain, with relevant examples, what is generally meant by the term 'creative accounting'. **(5 marks)**

(ii) Explain why it is important to record the substance rather than just the legal form of transactions and describe the features that may indicate that the substance of a transaction is different from its legal form. **(5 marks)**

(Total: 10 marks)

6 S

(a) You are the management accountant of S. During the most recent financial year (ended 31 March 20X8), the company has entered into a factoring arrangement with F. The main terms of the agreement are as follows:

(1) On the first day of every month S transfers (by assignment) all its trade receivables to F, subject to credit approval by F for each amount transferred by S.

(2) At the time of transfer of the receivables to F, S receives a payment from F of 70% of the gross amount transferred. The payment is debited by F to a factoring account which is maintained in the books of F.

(3) Following transfer of the amounts receivable, F collects payments from trade receivables and performs any necessary follow-up work.

(4) After collection by F, the cash received from the customer is credited to the factoring account in the books of F.

(5) F handles all aspects of the collection of the receivables of S in return for a monthly charge of 1% of the total value of the debts transferred at the beginning of that month. The amount is debited to the factoring account in the books of F.

(6) Any amounts not collected by F within 90 days of transfer are regarded by F as irrecoverable and re-assigned to S. The cash previously advanced by F in respect of irrecoverable amounts is recovered from S. The recovery is only possible out of the proceeds of other receivables which have been assigned to S. For example, if, in a particular month, S assigned trade receivables having a value of $10,000 and an amount of $500 was identified as irrecoverable, then the amounts advanced by F to S would be $6,650 [70% × $10,000 – 70% × $500].

(7) On a monthly basis, F debits the factoring account with an interest charge which is calculated on a daily basis on the balance on the factoring account.

(8) At the end of every quarter, F pays over to S a sum representing any credit balance on its factoring account with S at that time.

Required:

Write a memorandum to the Board of Directors of S which outlines how the receivables factoring arrangement will be reported in the financial statements of S. **(10 marks)**

7 FLOW

On 1 April 20X7, Flow sold a freehold property to another company, River. Flow had purchased the property for $500,000 on 1 April 20W8 and had charged total depreciation of $60,000 for the period 1 April 20W8 to 31 March 20X7.

River paid $850,000 for the property on 1 April 20X7, at which date its true market value was $550,000.

From 1 April 20X7 the property was leased back by Flow on a ten-year operating lease for annual rentals (payable in arrears) of $100,000. A normal annual rental for such a property would have been $50,000.

Required:

Show the journal entries which Flow will make to record:

- its sale of the property to River on 1 April 20X8;
- the payment of the first rental to River on 31 March 20X9.

Justify your answer with reference to appropriate International Accounting Standards.

(10 marks)

8 BLFB

You are the management accountant of BLFB. BLFB imports timber which it uses to manufacture and sell a large range of furniture products. BLFB makes up financial statements to 30 June each year.

On 1 June 20X9, BLFB purchased for $40 million a large quantity of timber from an overseas supplier. The timber was intended to be used in the manufacture of a large quantity of high-quality furniture. Before manufacturing such furniture, it is necessary to keep the new timber in controlled conditions for at least five years from the date of purchase.

On 1 July 20X9, BLFB sold the timber to Southland Bank for $45 million. The timber was physically retained by BLFB under the controlled conditions that were necessary to render the timber suitable for use. At the date of the sale on 1 July 20X9, BLFB signed an agreement to re-purchase the timber from Southland Bank on 30 June 20Y4 for a price of $66.12 million. Responsibility for the security and condition of the timber remained with BLFB.

Your assistant, who is responsible for preparing the draft financial statements for the year ended 30 June 20Y0, has shown the transaction as a sale of $45 million and recorded a profit of $5 million.

Required:

(a) Write a memorandum to your assistant that:

    (i) describes what is meant by the 'substance' of a transaction and how to determine 'substance'; and **(6 marks)**

    (ii) explains why transactions should be accounted for according to their substance. **(6 marks)**

(b) (i) Prepare all the journal entries that should have been made in the financial statements of BLFB for the year ended 30 June 20Y0 in order to account correctly for the sale of timber to Southland Bank. **(6 marks)**

    (ii) Explain fully how the entries you have made comply with the requirement to account for the transaction according to its substance. You should also explain why the treatment suggested by your assistant is incorrect. **(7 marks)**

(Total: 25 marks)

9   LMN

(a)   The IASB's *Framework for the preparation and presentation of financial statements* has a section on recognition in financial statements.

Required:

Explain the *Framework*'s recognition criteria in general and in particular how assets, liabilities, income and expenses are to be recognized in financial statements.

(5 marks)

(b)   LMN trades in motor vehicles, which are manufactured and supplied by their manufacturer, IJK. Trading between the two entities is subject to a contractual agreement, the principal terms of which are as follows:

- LMN is entitled to hold on its premises at any one time up to 80 vehicles supplied by IJK. LMN is free to specify the ranges and models of vehicle supplied to it. IJK retains legal title to the vehicles until such time as they are sold to a third party by LMN.

- While the vehicles remain on its premises, LMN is required to insure them against loss or damage.

- The price at which vehicles are supplied is determined at the time of delivery; it is not subject to any subsequent alteration.

- When LMN sells a vehicle to a third party, it is required to inform IJK within three working days. IJK submits an invoice to LMN at the originally agreed price; the invoice is payable by LMN within 30 days.

- LMN is entitled to use any of the vehicles supplied to it for demonstration purposes and road testing. However, if more than a specified number of kilometres are driven in a vehicle, LMN is required to pay IJK a rental charge.

- LMN has the right to return any vehicle to IJK at any time without incurring a penalty, except for any rental charge incurred in respect of excess kilometres driven.

Required:

Discuss the economic substance of the contractual arrangement between the two entities in respect of the recognition of inventory and of sales.   **(10 marks)**

(Total: 15 marks)

10   DCB

DCB is a manufacturing and trading entity with several overseas operations. One of its subsidiaries, GFE, operates in a country which experiences relatively high rates of inflation in its currency, the crown. Most entities operating in that country voluntarily present two versions of their financial statements: one at historical cost, and the other incorporating current cost adjustments. GFE complies with this accepted practice.

Extracts from the statement of comprehensive income adjusted for current costs for the year ended 30 September 20X5 are as follows:

	Crowns 000	Crowns 000
Historical cost operating profit		750
Current cost of sales adjustments:		
Cost of sales adjustment	(65)	
Depreciation adjustment	(43)	
Loss on net monetary position	(16)	
		(124)
Current cost operating profit		626

Required:

(a) Explain the defects of historical cost accounting in times of increasing prices.

(4 marks)

(b) Explain how EACH of the three current cost accounting adjustments in GFE's financial statements contributes to the maintenance of capital. **(6 marks)**

(Total: 10 marks)

A REGULATORY FRAMEWORK FOR FINANCIAL REPORTING

11   IASCF

Historically financial reporting throughout the world has differed widely. The International Accounting Standards Committee Foundation (IASCF) is committed to developing, in the public interest, a single set of high quality, understandable and enforceable global accounting standards that require transparent and comparable information in general purpose financial statements. The various pronouncements of the IASCF are sometimes collectively referred to as International Financial Reporting Standards (IFRS) GAAP.

Required:

(a) Describe the functions of the various internal bodies of the IASCF, and how the IASCF interrelates with other national standard setters. **(10 marks)**

(b) Describe the IASCF's standard setting process including how standards are produced, enforced and occasionally supplemented. **(10 marks)**

(c) Comment on whether you feel the move to date towards global accounting standards has been successful. **(5 marks)**

(Total: 25 marks)

12   CONCEPTUAL FRAMEWORK

In 1989 the forerunner to the current IASB, the IASC, issued its *Framework for the preparation and presentation of financial statements*. This document is part of the overall conceptual framework within which the current IASB works.

Required:

(a) Describe what is meant by a conceptual framework. **(3 marks)**

(b) Explain the main reasons for having a conceptual framework **(8 marks)**

(c) Explain the purpose of the *Framework for the preparation and presentation of financial statements.* **(8 marks)**

(d) Discuss the extent to which IFRS are relevant to not-for-profit entities. **(6 marks)**

(Total: 25 marks)

13 USERS AND QUALITIES

The *Framework for the preparation and presentation of financial statements* indicates the overall purpose of financial statements and considers the various users of these financial statements. It also gives much detail about the qualitative characteristics of financial statements which make them useful.

Required:

(a) Explain the overall objective of financial statements. **(2 marks)**

(b) Discuss the information needs of the different types of users of financial statements considered in the *Framework.* **(8 marks)**

(c) Discuss the qualitative characteristics which make information useful to users of the financial statements. **(12 marks)**

(d) Explain why in practice a balance is often required between the various characteristics. **(3 marks)**

(Total: 25 marks)

FINANCIAL STATEMENTS

14 BROADOAK

The broad principles of accounting for property, plant and equipment involve distinguishing between capital and revenue expenditure, measuring the cost of assets, determining how they should be depreciated and dealing with the problems of subsequent measurement and subsequent expenditure. IAS 16 *Property, Plant and Equipment* has the objective of improving consistency in these areas.

Required:

(a) Explain:

   (i) how the initial cost of an item of property, plant and equipment should be measured, and

   (4 marks)

   (ii) the circumstances in which subsequent expenditure on those assets should be capitalized. **(3 marks)**

(b) Explain IAS 16's requirements regarding the revaluation of property, plant and equipment and the accounting treatment of surpluses and deficits on revaluation and gains and losses on disposal. **(8 marks)**

(c) (i) Broadoak has recently purchased an item of plant from Plantco, the details of this are:

	$	$
Basic list price of plant		240,000
trade discount applicable to Broadoak		12.5% on list price
Ancillary costs:		
shipping and handling costs		2,750
estimated pre-production testing		12,500
maintenance contract for three years		24,000
site preparation costs		
electrical cable installation	14,000	
concrete reinforcement	4,500	
own labour costs	7,500	26,000

Broadoak paid for the plant (excluding the ancillary costs) within four weeks of order, thereby obtaining an early settlement discount of 3%.

Broadoak had incorrectly specified the power loading of the original electrical cable to be installed by the contractor. The cost of correcting this error of $6,000 is included in the above figure of $14,000.

The plant is expected to last for 10 years. At the end of this period there will be compulsory costs of $15,000 to dismantle the plant and $3,000 to restore the site to its original use condition.

Required:

Calculate the amount at which the initial cost of the plant should be measured. (Ignore discounting.) **(5 marks)**

(ii) Broadoak acquired a 12-year lease on a property on 1 October 19W9 at a cost of $240,000. The company policy is to revalue its properties to their market values at the end of each year. Accumulated amortization is eliminated and the property is restated to the revalued amount. Annual amortization is calculated on the carrying values at the beginning of the year. The market values of the property on 30 September 20X0 and 20X1 were $231,000 and $175,000 respectively. The existing balance on the revaluation reserve at 1 October 19W9 was $50,000. This related to some non-depreciable land whose value had not changed significantly since 1 October 19W9.

Required:

Prepare extracts of the financial statements of Broadoak (including the movement on the revaluation reserve) for the years to 30 September 20X0 and 20X1 in respect of the leasehold property. **(5 marks)**

(Total: 25 marks)

15   ELITE LEISURE AND ADVENT

(a)   Elite Leisure is a private limited liability company that operates a single cruise ship. The ship was acquired on 1 October 19W5. Details of the cost of the ship's components and their estimated useful lives are:

Component	Original cost ($million)	Depreciation basis
Ship's fabric (hull, decks etc)	300	25 years straight-line
Cabins and entertainment area fittings	150	12 years straight-line
Propulsion system	100	useful life of 40,000 hours

At 30 September 20X3 no further capital expenditure had been incurred on the ship.

In the year ended 30 September 20X3 the ship had experienced a high level of engine trouble which had cost the company considerable lost revenue and compensation costs. The measured expired life of the propulsion system at 30 September 20X3 was 30,000 hours. Due to the unreliability of the engines, a decision was taken in early October 20X3 to replace the whole of the propulsion system at a cost of $140 million. The expected life of the new propulsion system was 50,000 hours and in the year ended 30 September 20X4 the ship had used its engines for 5,000 hours.

At the same time as the propulsion system replacement, the company took the opportunity to do a limited upgrade to the cabin and entertainment facilities at a cost of $60 million and repaint the ship's fabric at a cost of $20 million. After the upgrade of the cabin and entertainment area fittings it was estimated that their remaining life was five years (from the date of the upgrade). For the purpose of calculating depreciation, all the work on the ship can be assumed to have been completed on 1 October 20X3. All residual values can be taken as nil.

Required:

Calculate the carrying amount of Elite Leisure's cruise ship at 30 September 20X3 and prepare extracts in respect of it from Elite Leisure's statement of comprehensive income for the year ended 30 September 20X4 and its statement of financial position at that date. Your answer should explain the treatment of each item.   **(12 marks)**

(b)   Advent is a publicly listed company.

Details of Advent's non-current assets at 1 October 20X3 were:

	Land and buildings $m	Plant $m	Telecommunications licence $m	Total $m
Cost/valuation	280	150	300	730
Accumulated depreciation/amortization	(40)	(105)	(30)	(175)
Net book value	240	45	270	555

The following information is relevant:

(i)   The land and building were revalued on 1 October 19W8 with $80 million attributable to the land and $200 million to the building. At that date the estimated remaining life of the building was 25 years. A further revaluation was not needed until 1 October 20X3 when the land and building were valued at $85 million and $180 million respectively. The remaining estimated life of the building at this date was 20 years.

(ii) Plant is depreciated at 20% per annum on cost with time apportionment where appropriate. On 1 April 20X4 new plant costing $45 million was acquired. In addition, this plant cost $5 million to install and commission. No plant is more than four years old.

(iii) The telecommunications licence was bought from the government on 1 October 20X2 and has a 10 year life. It is amortized on a straight line basis. In September 20X4, a review of the sales of the products related to the licence showed them to be very disappointing. As a result of this review the estimated recoverable amount of the licence at 30 September 20X4 was estimated at only $100 million.

There were no disposals of non-current assets during the year to 30 September 20X4.

Required:

(i) Prepare statement of financial position extracts of Advent's non-current assets as at 30 September 20X4 (including comparative figures), together with any disclosures required (other than those of the accounting policies) under current International Financial Reporting Standards. **(9 marks)**

(ii) Explain the usefulness of the above disclosures to the users of the financial statements. **(4 marks)**

(Total: 25 marks)

16 WILDERNESS GROUP

(a) The main objective of IAS 36 *Impairment of assets* is to prescribe the procedures that should ensure that an entity's assets are included in its statement of financial position at no more than their recoverable amounts. Where an asset is carried at an amount in excess of its recoverable amount, it is said to be impaired and IAS 36 requires an impairment loss to be recognized.

Required:

(i) Define an impairment loss explaining the relevance of fair value less costs to sell and value in use; and state how frequently assets should be tested for impairment; **(6 marks)**

Note: your answer should NOT describe the possible indicators of an impairment.

(ii) Explain how an impairment loss is accounted for after it has been calculated. **(5 marks)**

(b) The assistant financial controller of the Wilderness group, a public listed company, has identified the matters below which she believes may indicate an impairment to one or more assets:

(i) Wilderness owns and operates an item of plant that cost $640,000 and had accumulated depreciation of $400,000 at 1 October 20X4. It is being depreciated at $12\frac{1}{2}$% per annum on cost. On 1 April 20X5 (exactly half way through the year) the plant was damaged when a factory vehicle collided into it. Due to the unavailability of replacement parts, it is not possible to repair the plant, but it still operates, albeit at a reduced capacity. Also it is expected that as a result of the damage the remaining life of the plant from the date of the damage will be only two years. Based on its reduced capacity, the estimated present value of the plant in use is $150,000. The plant has a current disposal value of $20,000 (which will be nil in two years' time), but Wilderness has been offered a trade-in value of $180,000 against a replacement machine which has a cost of $1 million (there would be no disposal costs for the replaced plant). Wilderness is reluctant to replace the plant as it is worried about the long-term demand for the product produced by the plant. The trade-in value is only available if the plant is replaced.

Required:

Prepare extracts from the statement of financial position and statement of comprehensive income of Wilderness in respect of the plant for the year ended 30 September 20X5. Your answer should explain how you arrived at your figures. **(7 marks)**

(ii) On 1 April 20X4 Wilderness acquired 100% of the share capital of Mossel, whose only activity is the extraction and sale of spa water. Mossel had been profitable since its acquisition, but bad publicity resulting from several consumers becoming ill due to a contamination of the spa water supply in April 20X5 has led to unexpected losses in the last six months. The carrying amounts of Mossel's assets at 30 September 20X5 are:

	$000
Brand (Quencher – see below)	7,000
Land containing spa	12,000
Purifying and bottling plant	8,000
Inventories	5,000
	———
	32,000
	———

The source of the contamination was found and it has now ceased.

The company originally sold the bottled water under the brand name of 'Quencher', but because of the contamination it has rebranded its bottled water as 'Phoenix'. After a large advertising campaign, sales are now starting to recover and are approaching previous levels. The value of the brand in the statement of financial position is the depreciated amount of the original brand name of 'Quencher'.

The directors have acknowledged that $1.5 million will have to be spent in the first three months of the next accounting period to upgrade the purifying and bottling plant.

Inventories contain some old 'Quencher' bottled water at a cost of $2 million; the remaining inventories are labelled with the new brand 'Phoenix'. Samples of all the bottled water have been tested by the health authority and have been passed as fit to sell. The old bottled water will have to be relabelled at a cost of $250,000, but is then expected to be sold at the normal selling price of (normal) cost plus 50%.

Based on the estimated future cash flows, the directors have estimated that the value in use of Mossel at 30 September 20X5, calculated according to the guidance in IAS 36, is $20 million. There is no reliable estimate of the fair value less costs to sell of Mossel.

Required:

Calculate the amounts at which the assets of Mossel should appear in the consolidated statement of financial position of Wilderness at 30 September 20X5. Your answer should explain how you arrived at your figures. **(7 marks)**

(Total: 25 marks)

17   LINNET   — Redo)))

(a)   (i)   Linnet is a large public listed company involved in the construction industry. Accounting standards normally require construction contracts to be accounted for using the percentage (stage) of completion basis. However under certain circumstances they should be accounted for using the completed contracts basis.

Required:

Discuss the principles that underlie each of the two methods and describe the circumstances in which their use is appropriate.   **(6 marks)**

(ii)   Linnet is part way through a contract to build a new football stadium at a contracted price of $300 million. Details of the progress of this contract at 1 April 20X3 are shown below:

	$ million
Cumulative revenue invoiced	150
Cumulative cost of sales to date	112
Profit to date	38

The following information has been extracted from the accounting records at 31 March 20X4:

	$ million
Total progress payment received for work certified at 29 Feb 20X4	180
Total costs incurred to date (excluding rectification costs below)	195
Rectification costs	17

Linnet has received progress payments of 90% of the work certified at 29 February 20X4. Linnet's surveyor has estimated the sales value of the further work completed during March 20X4 was $20 million.

At 31 March 20X4 the estimated remaining costs to complete the contract were $45 million.

The rectification costs are the costs incurred in widening access roads to the stadium. This was the result of an error by Linnet's architect when he made his initial drawings.

Linnet calculates the percentage of completion of its contracts as the proportion of sales value earned to date compared to the contract price.

All estimates can be taken as being reliable.

Required:

Prepare extracts of the financial statements for Linnet for the above contract for the year to 31 March 20X4.   **(11 marks)**

(b)   Linnet also manufactures and sells high quality printing paper. The auditor has drawn the company's attention to the sale of some packs of paper on 20 April 20X4 at a price of $45 each. These items were included in closing inventory on 31 March 20X4 at their manufactured cost of $48 each. Further investigations revealed that during the inventory count on 31 March 20X4 a quantity of packs of A3-size paper had been damaged by a water leak. The following week the company removed the damage by cutting the paper down to A4 size (A4 size is smaller than A3). The paper was then repackaged and put back into inventory. The cost of cutting and repackaging was $4 per pack. The normal selling price of the paper is $75 per pack for the A3 and $50 per pack for the A4, however on 12 April 20X4 the company reduced the selling prices of all its paper by 10% in response to similar price cuts by its competitors.

Securiprint, one of the customers that bought some of the 'damaged' paper, had used it to print some share certificates for a customer. Securiprint informed Linnet that these share certificates had been returned by the customer because they contained marks that were not part of the design. Securiprint believes the marks were part of a manufacturing flaw on the part of Linnet and is seeking compensation.

Required:

Discuss the impact the above information may have on the draft financial statements of Linnet for the year to 31 March 20X4. **(8 marks)**

(Total: 25 marks)

18 BOWTOCK

(a) (i) IAS 12 *Income Taxes* details the requirements relating to the accounting treatment of deferred tax.

Required:

Explain why it is considered necessary to provide for deferred tax and briefly outline the principles of accounting for deferred tax contained in IAS 12 *Income Taxes*. **(5 marks)**

(ii) Bowtock purchased an item of plant for $2,000,000 on 1 October 20X0. It had an estimated life of eight years and an estimated residual value of $400,000. The plant is depreciated on a straight-line basis. The tax authorities do not allow depreciation as a deductible expense. Instead a tax expense of 40% of the cost of this type of asset can be claimed against income tax in the year of purchase and 20% per annum (on a reducing balance basis) of its tax base thereafter. The rate of income tax can be taken as 25%.

Required:

In respect of the above item of plant, calculate the deferred tax charge/credit in Bowtock's statement of comprehensive income for the year to 30 September 20X3 and the deferred tax balance in the statement of financial position at that date. **(6 marks)**

Note: work to the nearest $000.

(b) Bowtock has leased an item of plant under the following terms:

Commencement of the lease was 1 January 20X2

Term of lease five years

Annual payments in advance $12,000

Cash price and fair value of the asset – $52,000 at 1 January 20X2

Implicit interest rate within the lease (as supplied by the lessor) 8% per annum (to be apportioned on a time basis where relevant).

The company's depreciation policy for this type of plant is 20% per annum on cost (apportioned on a time basis where relevant).

Required:

Prepare extracts of the statement of comprehensive income and statement of financial position for Bowtock for the year to 30 September 20X3 for the above lease.

(5 marks)

(c)   (i)   Explain why events occurring after the reporting date may be relevant to the financial statements of the previous period.   **(4 marks)**

      (ii)   At 30 September 20X3 Bowtock had included in its draft statement of financial position inventory of $250,000 valued at cost. Up to 5 November 20X3, Bowtock had sold $100,000 of this inventory for $150,000. On this date new government legislation (enacted after the year end) came into force which meant that the unsold inventory could no longer be marketed and was worthless.

           Bowtock is part way through the construction of a housing development. It has prepared its financial statements to 30 September 20X3 in accordance with IAS 11 *Construction Contracts* and included a proportionate amount of the total estimated profit on this contract. The same legislation referred to above (in force from 5 November 20X3) now requires modifications to the way the houses within this development have to be built. The cost of these modifications will be $500,000 and will reduce the estimated total profit on the contract by that amount, although the contract is still expected to be profitable.

           Required:

           Assuming the amounts are material, state how the information above should be reflected in the financial statements of Bowtock for the year ended 30 September 20X3.   **(5 marks)**

           (Total: 25 marks)

19 MULTIPLEX

The following transactions and events have arisen during the preparation of the draft financial statements of Multiplex for the year to 31 March 20X0:

(a)   On 1 April 19W9 Multiplex issued $80 million 8% convertible loan stock at par. The stock is convertible into equity shares, or redeemable at par, on 31 March 20X4, at the option of the stockholders. The terms of conversion are that each $100 of loan stock will be convertible into 50 equity shares of Multiplex. A finance consultant has advised that if the option to convert to equity had not been included in the terms of the issue, then a coupon (interest) rate of 12% would have been required to attract subscribers for the stock. Interest is paid in arrears on 31 March each year.

     The value of $1 receivable at the end of each year at a discount rate of 12% are:

Year	$
1	0.89
2	0.80
3	0.71
4	0.64
5	0.57

Required:

Calculate the statement of comprehensive income finance charge for the year to 31 March 20X0 and the statement of financial position extracts at 31 March 20X0 in respect of the issue of the convertible loan stock.   **(5 marks)**

(b)   On 1 January 20X0 Multiplex acquired the whole of Steamdays, a company that operates a scenic railway along the coast of a popular tourist area. The summarized statement of financial position at fair values of Steamdays on 1 January 20X0, reflecting the terms of the acquisition was:

	$000
Goodwill	200
Operating licence	1,200
Property – train stations and land	300
Rail track and coaches	300
Two steam engines	1,000
Purchase consideration	3,000

The operating licence is for ten years. It was renewed on 1 January 20X0 by the transport authority and is stated at the cost of its renewal. The carrying values of the property and rail track and coaches are based on their value in use. The engines are valued at their net selling prices.

On 1 February 20X0 the boiler of one of the steam engines exploded, completely destroying the whole engine. Fortunately no one was injured, but the engine was beyond repair. Due to its age a replacement could not be obtained. Because of the reduced passenger capacity the estimated value in use of the whole of the business after the accident was assessed at $2 million.

Passenger numbers after the accident were below expectations even after allowing for the reduced capacity. A market research report concluded that tourists were not using the railway because of their fear of a similar accident occurring to the remaining engine. In the light of this the value in use of the business was re-assessed on 31 March 20X0 at $1.8 million. On this date Multiplex received an offer of $900,000 in respect of the operating licence (it is transferable). The realizable value of the other net assets has not changed significantly.

Required:

Calculate the carrying value of the assets of Steamdays (in Multiplex's consolidated statement of financial position) at 1 February 20X0 and 31 March 20X0 after recognising the impairment losses. **(6 marks)**

(c) On 1 January 20X0 the Board of Multiplex approved a resolution to close the whole of its loss-making engineering operation. A binding agreement to dispose of the assets was signed shortly afterwards. The sale will be completed on 10 June 20X0 at an agreed value of $30 million. The costs of the closure are estimated at:

– $2 million for redundancy/retrenchment

– $3 million in penalty costs for non-completion of contracted orders

– $1.5 million for associated professional costs

– losses on the sale of the net assets and liabilities, whose book value at 31 March 20X0 was $66 million and $20 million respectively

– operating losses for the period from 1 April 20X0 to the date of sale are estimated at $4.5 million.

Multiplex accounts for its various operations on a divisional basis.

Required:

Advise the directors on the correct treatment of the closure of the engineering division. **(5 marks)**

(d) Multiplex is in the intermediate stage of a construction contract for the building of a new privately owned road bridge over a river estuary. The original details of the contract are:

Approximate duration of contract:	3 years
Date of commencement:	1 October 19W8
Total contract price:	$40 million
Estimated total cost:	$28 million

An independent surveyor certified the value of the work in progress as follows:
- on 31 March 19W9 — $12 million
- on 31 March 20X0 — $30 million (including the $12 million in 19W9)

Total costs incurred at:
- 31 March 19W9 — $9 million
- 31 March 20X0 — $28.5 million (including the $9 million in 19W9)

Progress billings at 31 March 20X0 were $25 million

On 1 April 19W9 Multiplex agreed to a contract variation that would involve an additional fee of $5 million with associated additional estimated costs of $2 million.

The costs incurred during the year to 31 March 20X0 include $2.5 million relating to the replacement of some bolts which had been made from material that had been incorrectly specified by the firm of civil engineers who were contracted by Multiplex to design the bridge. These costs were not included in the original estimates, but Multiplex is hopeful that they can be recovered from the firm of civil engineers. The advice to Multiplex from its lawyers is that there is about a 60% chance of success.

Multiplex calculates profit on construction contracts using the percentage of completion method. The percentage of completion of the contract is based on the value of the work certified to date compared to the total contract price.

Required:

Prepare the statement of comprehensive income and statement of financial position extracts in respect of the contract for the year to 31 March 20X0 only. **(9 marks)**

(Total: 25 marks)

20 TORRENT

(a) Torrent is a large publicly listed company whose main activity involves construction contracts. Details of three of its contracts for the year ended 31 March 20X6 are:

Contract	Alpha	Beta	Ceta
Date commenced	1 April 20X4	1 October 20X5	1 October 20X5
Estimated duration	3 years	18 months	2 years
	$m	$m	$m
Fixed contract price	20	6	12
Estimated costs at start of contract	15	7.5 (note (iii))	10
Costs to date:			
at 31 March 20X5	5	Nil	Nil
at 31 March 20X6	12.5 (note (ii))	2	4
Estimated costs at 31 March 20X6 to complete	3.5	5.5 (note (iii))	6
Progress payments received at 31 March 20X5 (note (i))	5.4	Nil	Nil
Progress payments received at 31 March 20X6 (note (i))	12.6	1.8	Nil

Notes

(i) The company's normal policy for determining the percentage completion of contracts is based on the value of work invoiced to date compared to the contract price. Progress payments received represent 90% of the work invoiced. However, no progress payments will be invoiced or received from contract Ceta until it is completed, so the percentage completion of this contract is to be based on the cost to date compared to the estimated total contract costs.

(ii) The cost to date of $12.5 million at 31 March 20X6 for contract Alfa includes $1 million relating to unplanned rectification costs incurred during the current year (ended 31 March 20X6) due to subsidence occurring on site.

(iii) Since negotiating the price of contract Beta, Torrent has discovered the land that it purchased for the project is contaminated by toxic pollutants. The estimated cost at the start of the contract and the estimated costs to complete the contract include the unexpected costs of decontaminating the site before construction could commence.

Required:

Prepare extracts of the statement of comprehensive income and statement of financial position for Torrent in respect of the above construction contracts for the year ended 31 March 20X6 **(12 marks)**

(b) (i) The issued share capital of Savoir, a publicly listed company, at 31 March 20X3 was $10 million. Its shares are denominated at 25 cents each. Savoir's profits attributable to its ordinary shareholders for the year ended 31 March 20X3 were also $10 million, giving an earnings per share of 25 cents.

Year ended 31 March 20X4

On 1 July 20X3 Savoir issued eight million ordinary shares at full market value. On 1 January 20X4 a bonus issue of one new ordinary share for every four ordinary shares held was made. Profits attributable to ordinary shareholders for the year ended 31 March 20X4 were $13,800,000.

Year ended 31 March 20X5

On 1 October 20X4 Savoir made a rights issue of shares of two new ordinary shares at a price of $1.00 each for every five ordinary shares held. The offer was fully subscribed. The market price of Savoir's ordinary shares immediately prior to the offer was $2.40 each. Profits attributable to ordinary shareholders for the year ended 31 March 20X5 were $19,500,000.

Required:

Calculate Savoir's earnings per share for the years ended 31 March 20X4 and 20X5 including comparative figures. **(9 marks)**

(ii) On 1 April 20X5 Savoir issued $20 million 8% convertible loan stock at par. The terms of conversion (on 1 April 20X8) are that for every $100 of loan stock, 50 ordinary shares will be issued at the option of loan stockholders. Alternatively the loan stock will be redeemed at par for cash. Also on 1 April 20X5 the directors of Savoir were awarded share options on 12 million ordinary shares exercizable from 1 April 20X8 at $1.50 per share. The average market value of Savoir's ordinary shares for the year ended 31 March 20X6 was $2.50 each. The income tax rate is 25%. Profits attributable to ordinary shareholders for the year ended 31 March 20X6 were $25,200,000. The share options have been correctly recorded in the statement of comprehensive income.

Required:

Calculate Savoir's basic and diluted earnings per share for the years ended 31 March 20X6 (comparative figures are NOT required).

You may assume that both the convertible loan stock and the directors' options are dilutive. **(4 marks)**

(Total: 25 marks)

21 QRS

The directors of QRS, a listed entity, have met to discuss the business's medium to long term financing requirements. Several possibilities were discussed, including the issue of more shares using a rights issue. In many respects this would be the most desirable option because the entity is already quite highly geared. However, the directors are aware of several recent cases where rights issues have not been successful because share prices are currently quite low and many investors are averse to any kind of investment in shares.

Therefore, the directors have turned their attention to other options. The finance director is on sick leave, and so you, her assistant, have been given the task of responding to the following note from the Chief Executive:

'Now that we've had a chance to discuss possible financing arrangements, the directors are in agreement that we should structure our issue of financial instruments in order to be able to classify them as equity rather than debt. Any increase in the gearing ratio would be unacceptable. Therefore, we have provisionally decided to make two issues of financial instruments as follows:

1   An issue of non-redeemable preferred shares to raise $4 million. These shares will carry a fixed interest rate of 6%, and because they are shares they can be classified as equity.

2   An issue of 6% convertible bonds, issued at par value, to raise $6 million. These bonds will carry a fixed date for conversion in four years' time. Each $100 of debt will be convertible at the holder's option into 120 $1 shares. In our opinion, these bonds can actually be classified as equity immediately, because they are convertible within five years on terms that are favourable to the holder.

Please confirm that these instruments will not increase our gearing ratio should they be issued.'

Note: You determine that the market rate available for similar non-convertible bonds is currently 8%.

Required:

Explain to the directors the accounting treatment, in respect of debt/equity classification, required by IAS 32 *Financial Instruments:Presentation* for each of the proposed issues, advising them on the acceptability of classifying the instruments as equity.

Your explanation should be accompanied by calculations where appropriate.

Present value factors at 8% for each of the following four years are:

Year 1   0.926

Year 2   0.857

Year 3   0.794

Year 4   0.735 **(10 marks)**

22 PX

During its financial year ended 31 December 20X4, an entity, PX, entered into the transactions described below:

In November 20X4, having surplus cash available, PX made an investment in the securities of a listed entity. The directors intend to realize the investment in March or April 20X5, in order to fund the planned expansion of PX's principal warehouse.

PX lent one of its customers, DB, $3,000,000 at a variable interest rate pegged to average bank lending rates. The loan is scheduled for repayment in 20X9, and PX has provided an undertaking to DB that it will not assign the loan to a third party.

PX added to its portfolio of relatively small investments in the securities of listed entities. PX does not plan to dispose of these investments in the short term.

Required:

In accordance with IAS 39 *Financial Instruments: Recognition and Measurement*:

(i) identify the appropriate classification of these three categories of financial asset and briefly explain the reason for each classification; **(6 marks)**

(ii) explain how the financial assets should be measured in the financial statements of PX at 31 December 20X4. **(4 marks)**

(Total: 10 marks)

23 TALL

You are the management accountant of Tall. The company is planning a number of acquisitions in 20Y0 and so you are aware that additional funding will be needed. Today's date is 30 November 20X9. On 1 October 20X9 Tall raised additional funding as follows:

- Tall issued 15 million $1 bonds at par. The bonds pay no interest but are redeemable on 1 October 20Y4 at $1.61 – the total payable on redemption being $24.15m. As an alternative to redemption, bondholders can elect to convert their holdings into $1 equity shares on the basis of one equity share for every bond held. The current price of a $1 share is $1.40 and it is reckoned that this will grow by at least 5 per cent per annum for the next five years.

- Tall issued 10 million $1 preference shares at $1.20 per share, incurring issue costs of $100,000. The preference shares carry no dividend and are redeemable on 1 October 20Y5 at $2.35 per share – the total payable on redemption being $23.5m.

Your assistant is unsure how to reflect the additional funding in the financial statements of Tall. He expresses the opinion that both of the new capital instruments should logically be reflected in the equity section of the statement of financial position. He justifies this by saying that:

- the preference shares are legally shares and so equity is the appropriate place to present them;

- the bonds and the preference shares seem to have very similar terms of issue and it is quite likely that the bonds will become shares in five years' time, given the projected growth in the equity share price.

He has no idea how to show the finance costs of the capital instruments in the statement of comprehensive income. He is aware that IAS 39 *Financial Instruments:Recognition and Measurement* is the relevant accounting standard, but is unaware of its details.

Required:

(a)　Write a memorandum to your assistant which evaluates the comments he has made regarding the presentation of the financial instruments and explains the correct treatment where necessary. Your memorandum should refer to the provisions of relevant accounting standards. **(4 marks)**

(b)　Explain and evaluate the relevant provisions of IAS 39 regarding the computation of the finance cost of capital instruments such as bonds and preference shares. You are not required to compute the finance costs for either of the instruments mentioned in this question. **(6 marks)**

(Total: 10 marks)

24　TRIANGLE

Triangle, a public listed company, is in the process of preparing its draft financial statements for the year to 31 March 20X5. The following matters have been brought to your attention:

(i)　On 1 April 20X4 the company brought into use a new processing plant that had cost $15 million to construct and had an estimated life of ten years. The plant uses hazardous chemicals which are put in containers and shipped abroad for safe disposal after processing. The chemicals have also contaminated the plant itself which occurred as soon as the plant was used. It is a legal requirement that the plant is decontaminated at the end of its life. The estimated present value of this decontamination, using a discount rate of 8% per annum, is $5 million. The financial statements have been charged with $1.5 million ($15 million/10 years) for plant depreciation and a provision of $500,000 ($5 million/10 years) has been made towards the cost of the decontamination. **(8 marks)**

(ii)　On 15 May 20X5 the company's auditors discovered a fraud in the material requisitions department. A senior member of staff who took up employment with Triangle in August 20X4 had been authorising payments for goods that had never been received. The payments were made to a fictitious company that cannot be traced. The member of staff was immediately dismissed. Calculations show that the total amount of the fraud to the date of its discovery was $240,000 of which $210,000 related to the year to 31 March 20X5. (Assume the fraud is material.) **(5 marks)**

(iii)　The company has contacted its insurers in respect of the above fraud. Triangle is insured for theft, but the insurance company maintains that this is a commercial fraud and is not covered by the theft clause in the insurance policy. Triangle has not yet had an opinion from its lawyers. **(4 marks)**

(iv)　On 1 April 20X4 Triangle sold maturing inventory that had a carrying value of $3 million (at cost) to Factorall, a finance house, for $5 million. Its estimated market value at this date was in excess of $5 million. The inventory will not be ready for sale until 31 March 20X8 and will remain on Triangle's premises until this date. The sale contract includes a clause allowing Triangle to repurchase the inventory at any time up to 31 March 20X8 at a price of $5 million plus interest at 10% per annum compounded from 1 April 20X4. The inventory will incur storage costs until maturity. The cost of storage for the current year of $300,000 has been included in trade receivables (in the name of Factorall). If Triangle chooses not to repurchase the inventory, Factorall will pay the accumulated storage costs on 31 March 20X8. The proceeds of the sale have been debited to the bank and the sale has been included in Triangle's revenue. **(8 marks)**

Required:

Explain how the items in (i) to (iv) above should be treated in Triangle's financial statements for the year to 31 March 20X5 in accordance with current international accounting standards. Your answer should quantify the amounts where possible.

The mark allocation is shown against each of the four matters above.

(Total: 25 marks)

25 PARTWAY

(a) (i) State the definition of both non-current assets held for sale and discontinued operations and explain the usefulness of information for discontinued operations. **(4 marks)**

Partway is in the process of preparing its financial statements for the year ended 31 October 20X6. The company's main activity is in the travel industry mainly selling package holidays (flights and accommodation) to the general public through the Internet and retail travel agencies. During the current year the number of holidays sold by travel agencies declined dramatically and the directors decided at a board meeting on 15 October 20X6 to cease marketing holidays through its chain of travel agents and sell off the related high-street premises. Immediately after the meeting the travel agencies' staff and suppliers were notified of the situation and an announcement was made in the press. The directors wish to show the travel agencies' results as a discontinued operation in the financial statements to 31 October 20X6. Due to the declining business of the travel agents, on 1 August 20X6 Partway expanded its Internet operations to offer car hire facilities to purchasers of its Internet holidays.

The following are extracts from Partway's statement of comprehensive income results – years ended:

	Internet	*31 October 20X6* *Travel agencies*	*Car hire*	*Total*	*31 October 20X5* *Total*
	$000	$000	$000	$000	$000
Revenue	23,000	14,000	2,000	39,000	40,000
Cost of sales	(18,000)	(16,500)	(1,500)	(36,000)	(32,000)
Gross profit/(loss)	5,000	(2,500)	500	3,000	8,000
Operating costs	(1,000)	(1,500)	(100)	(2,600)	(2,000)
Profit/(loss) before tax	4,000	(4,000)	400	400	6,000

The results for the travel agencies for the year ended 31 October 20X5 were: revenue $18 million, cost of sales $15 million and operating expenses of $1.5 million.

Required:

(ii) Discuss whether the directors' wish to show the travel agencies' results as a discontinued operation is justifiable. **(4 marks)**

(iii) Assuming the closure of the travel agencies is a discontinued operation, prepare the extracts from the statement of comprehensive income of Partway for the year ended 31 October 20X6 together with its comparatives. Show the required analysis of the discontinued operations. **(6 marks)**

(b)   (i)   Describe the circumstances in which an entity may change its accounting policies and how a change should be applied. **(5 marks)**

The terms under which Partway sells its holidays are that a 10% deposit is required on booking and the balance of the holiday must be paid six weeks before the travel date. In previous years Partway has recognized revenue (and profit) from the sale of its holidays at the date the holiday is actually taken. From the beginning of November 20X5, Partway has made it a condition of booking that all customers must have holiday cancellation insurance and as a result it is unlikely that the outstanding balance of any holidays will be unpaid due to cancellation. In preparing its financial statements to 31 October 20X6, the directors are proposing to change to recognising revenue (and related estimated costs) at the date when a booking is made. The directors also feel that this change will help to negate the adverse effect of comparison with last year's results (year ended 31 October 20X5) which were better than the current year's.

Required:

(ii)   Comment on whether Partway's proposal to change the timing of its recognition of its revenue is acceptable and whether this would be a change of accounting policy. **(6 marks)**

(Total: 25 marks)

26   SITUATIONS

You have been asked to advise on a number of accounting problems which are each given separately below.

(a)   XY recently acquired a new subsidiary, AB. Upon undertaking the fair value exercise in respect of AB the following issues arose:

(i)   At the date of acquisition a customer had brought a legal action against AB. The outcome of the case was uncertain at the date of acquisition, but it was considered possible that AB would be found liable to pay compensation to the customer. The individual financial statements of AB drawn up at the date of acquisition did not include any amount payable in respect of the legal case.

(ii)   The group will need to spend approximately $100 million in order to integrate the new subsidiary into the existing operation.

Explain how each of the above issues will affect the net assets of AB to be included in the initial calculation of goodwill on consolidation. **(3 marks)**

(b)   B issued new interest bearing borrowings to finance a construction project on the following terms:

- The new borrowings had a nominal value of $50 million.

- The borrowings carried an annual interest rate of 4%.

- The costs of issuing the borrowings totalled $600,000. This comprised under-writing fees relating to the issue of $500,000 and fees of $100,000 payable for general advice on which of a number of sources of finance should be pursued.

- The borrowings were theoretically repayable at $60 million after five years. However, the borrowings contained an option to convert into ordinary shares after five years as an alternative to repayment. At the date of issue, the directors of B were reasonably certain that the investors would choose the conversion option.

Calculate the total financing cost relating to these borrowings. **(3 marks)**

(c)   At its year end, 31 March 20X5, entity JBK held 60,000 shares in a listed entity, X. The shares were purchased on 11 February 20X5 at a price of 85¢ per share. The market value of the shares on 31 March 20X5 was 87.5¢. The investment is categorized as held-for-trading.

Explain how this investment would be treated both at initial acquisition of the investment and when subsequently remeasured on 31 March 20X5.   **(3 marks)**

(d)   PQR holds several investments in subsidiaries. In December 20X5, it acquired 100% of the ordinary share capital of STU. PQR intends to exclude STU from consolidation in its group financial statements for the year ended 28 February 20X6, on the grounds that it does not intend to retain the investment in the longer term.

Explain, with reference to the relevant International Financial Reporting Standard, the conditions relating to exclusion of this type of investment from consolidation.

(3 marks)

(e)   On 1 January 20X6, EFG issued 10,000 5% convertible bonds at their par value of $50 each. The bonds will be redeemed on 1 January 2011. Each bond is convertible at the option of the holder at any time during the five-year period. Interest on the bond will be paid annually in arrears.

The prevailing market interest rate for similar debt without conversion options at the date of issue was 6%.

Explain how this financial instrument should be recognized in the financial statements of EFG at the date of issue and calculate any relevant amounts.

Discount factor at 6% for year 5 is 0.747 and the cumulative discount factor for years 1 to 5 is 4.212.   **(3 marks)**

(Total: 15 marks)

27   WINGER

The following trial balance relates to Winger at 31 March 20X0:

	$000	$000
Revenue (note (i))		358,450
Cost of sales	185,050	
Distribution costs	28,700	
Administration expenses	15,000	
Lease rentals (note (ii))	20,000	
Loan note interest paid	2,000	
Interim dividends	12,000	
Property at cost (note (iii))	200,000	
Plant and equipment at cost	154,800	
Depreciation 1 April 19W9 – plant and equipment		34,800
Development expenditure (note (iv))	30,000	
Profit on disposal of non-current assets		45,000
Trade accounts receivable	55,000	
Inventories – 31 March 20X0	28,240	
Cash and bank	10,660	
Trade accounts payable		29,400
Taxation – over provision in year to 31 March 19W9		2,200
Ordinary shares of 25c each		150,000
8% Loan notes (issued 19W7, redeemable 20X5)		50,000
Retained earnings 1 April 19W9		71,600
	741,450	741,450

The following notes are relevant:

(i)   Included in revenue is $27 million, which relates to sales made to customers under sale or return agreements. The expiry date for the return of these goods is 30 April 20X0. Winger has charged a mark-up of 20% on cost for these sales.

(ii)   A lease rental of $20 million was paid on 1 April 19W9. It is the first of five annual payments in advance for the rental of an item of equipment that has a cash purchase price of $80 million. The auditors have advised that this is a finance lease and have calculated the implicit interest rate in the lease as 12% per annum. Leased assets should be depreciated on a straight-line basis over the life of the lease.

(iii)   On 1 April 19W9 Winger acquired a new property at a cost of $200 million. For the purpose of calculating depreciation only, the asset has been separated into the following elements:

Separate asset	Cost $000	Life
Land	50,000	freehold
Heating system	20,000	10 years
Lifts	30,000	15 years
Building	100,000	50 years

The depreciation of the elements of the building should be calculated on a straight-line basis. The new property replaced an existing building that was sold on the same date for $95 million. It had cost $50 million and had a carrying value of $80 million at the date of sale. The profit on this property has been calculated on the original cost. It had not been depreciated on the basis that the depreciation charge would not be material.

Plant and machinery is depreciated at 20% on the reducing balance basis.

(iv)   The figure for development expenditure in the list of account balances represents the amounts deferred in previous years in respect of the development of a new product. Unfortunately, during the current year, the Government has introduced legislation which effectively bans this type of product. As a consequence of this the project has been abandoned. The directors of Winger are of the opinion that writing off the development expenditure, as opposed to its previous deferment, represents a change of accounting policy and therefore wish to treat the write-off as a prior period adjustment.

(v)   A provision for income taxes for the year to 31 March 20X0 of $15 million is required.

Required:

(a)   Prepare the statement of comprehensive income of Winger for the year to 31 March 20X0.   **(9 marks)**

(b)   Prepare a statement of financial position as at 31 March 20X0 in accordance with International Accounting Standards as far as the information permits.   **(11 marks)**

(c)   Discuss the acceptability of the company's previous policy in respect of non-depreciation of property.   **(5 marks)**

(Total: 25 marks)

28 ALLGONE

The following trial balance relates to Allgone at 31 March 20X3:

	$000	$000
Revenue (note (i))		236,200
Purchases	127,850	
Operating expenses	12,400	
Loan note interest paid	2,400	
Preference dividend	2,000	
Land and buildings – at valuation (note (ii))	130,000	
Plant and equipment – cost	84,300	
Software – cost 1 April 20W9	10,000	
Stock market investments – valuation 1 April 20X2 (note (iii))	12,000	
Depreciation 1 April 20X2 – plant and equipment		24,300
Depreciation 1 April 20X2 – software		6,000
Extraordinary item (note (iv))	32,000	
Trade receivables	23,000	
Inventory – 1 April 20X2	19,450	
Bank		350
Trade payables		16,200
Ordinary shares of 25c each		60,000
10% Irredeemable preference shares		20,000
12% Loan note (issued 1 July 20X2, redeemable 20X8))		40,000
Deferred tax		3,000
Revaluation reserve (relating to land and buildings and the investments)		45,000
Retained earnings – 1 April 20X2		4,350
	455,400	455,400

The following notes are relevant:

(i) Revenue includes $8 million for goods sold in March 20X3 for cash to Funders, a merchant bank. The cost of these goods was $6 million. Funders has the option to require Allgone to repurchase these goods within one month of the year-end at their original selling price plus a facilitating fee of $250,000.

The inventory at 31 March 20X3 was counted at a cost value of $8.5 million. This includes $500,000 of slow moving inventory that is expected to be sold for a net $300,000.

(ii) Non-current assets:

On 1 April 20X2 Allgone revalued its land and buildings. The details are:

	Cost 1 April 19W7	Valuation 1 April 20X2
	$000	$000
Land	20,000	25,000
Building	80,000	105,000

The building had an estimated life of 40 years when it was acquired and this has not changed as a result of the revaluation. Depreciation is on a straight-line basis. The surplus on the revaluation has been added to the revaluation reserve, but no other movements on the revaluation reserve have been recorded.

Plant and equipment is depreciated at 20% per annum on the reducing balance basis.

Software is depreciated straight line over a five-year life.

(iii) The investment represents 7.5% of the ordinary share capital of Wondaworld. This investment is classified as an available-for-sale financial asset and the revaluation reserve at 1 April 20X2 contained a surplus of $5 million for previous revaluations of the investment. The stock market price of Wondaworld ordinary shares was $2.50 each on 1 April 20X2 and by 31 March 20X3 this had fallen to $2.25.

(iv) The extraordinary item is a loss incurred due to a fraud relating to the company's investments. A senior employee of the company, who left in January 20X2, had diverted investment funds into his private bank account. The fraud was discovered by the employee's replacement in April 20X2. It is unlikely that any of the funds will be recovered. Allgone has now implemented tighter procedures to prevent such a fraud recurring. The company has been advised that this loss will not qualify for any tax relief.

(v) The directors have estimated the provision for corporation tax for the year to 31 March 20X3 at $11.3 million. The deferred tax provision at 31 March 20X3 is to be adjusted to reflect the tax base of the company's net assets being $16 million less than carrying values. The rate of income tax is 30%. The movement on deferred tax should be charged to the statement of comprehensive income.

Required:

In accordance with International Accounting Standards and International Financial Reporting Standards as far as the information permits, prepare:

(a) the statement of comprehensive income of Allgone for the year to 31 March 20X3; and **(7 marks)**

(b) the statement of changes in equity for the year to 31 March 20X3; and **(5 marks)**

(c) the statement of financial position as at 31 March 20X3. **(13 marks)**

Notes to the financial statements are not required. **(Total: 25 marks)**

29 TOURMALET

The following extracted balances relate to Tourmalet at 30 September 20X3:

	$000	$000
Ordinary shares of 20 cents each		50,000
Retained earnings at 1 October 20X2		47,800
Revaluation reserve at 1 October 20X2		18,500
6% Redeemable preference shares 20X5 (redeemable 20X8)		30,000
Trade payables		35,300
Tax		2,100
Land and buildings – at valuation (note (iii))	150,000	
Plant and equipment – cost (note (v))	98,600	
Investment property – valuation at 1 October 20X2 (note (iv))	10,000	
Depreciation 1 October 20X2 – land and buildings		9,000
Depreciation 1 October 20X2 – plant and equipment		24,600
Trade receivables	31,200	
Inventory – 1 October 20X2	26,550	
Bank	3,700	
Revenue (note (i))		313,000
Investment income (from properties)		1,200
Purchases	158,450	
Distribution expenses	26,400	
Administration expenses	23,200	
Interim preference dividend	900	
Ordinary dividend paid	2,500	
	531,500	531,500

The following notes are relevant:

(i)   Revenue includes $50 million for an item of plant sold on 1 June 20X3. The plant had a book value of $40 million at the date of its sale, which was charged to cost of sales. On the same date, Tourmalet entered into an agreement to lease back the plant for the next five years (being the estimated remaining life of the plant) at a cost of $14 million per annum payable annually in arrears. An arrangement of this type is deemed to have a financing cost of 12% per annum. No depreciation has been charged on the item of plant in the current year.

(ii)   The inventory at 30 September 20X3 was valued at cost of $28.5 million. This includes $4.5 million of slow moving goods. Tourmalet is trying to sell these to another retailer but has not been successful in obtaining a reasonable offer. The best price it has been offered is $2 million.

(iii)   On 1 October 19W9, Tourmalet had its land and buildings revalued by a firm of surveyors at $150 million, with $30 million of this attributed to the land. At that date the remaining life of the building was estimated to be 40 years. These figures were incorporated into the company's books. There has been no significant change in property values since the revaluation. $500,000 of the revaluation reserve will be realized in the current year as a result of the depreciation of the buildings.

(iv)   Details of the investment property are:

Value – 1 October 20X2 $10 million

Value – 30 September 20X3 $9.8 million

The company adopts the fair value method in IAS 40 *Investment Property* of valuing its investment property.

(v)   Plant and equipment (other than that referred to in note (i) above) is depreciated at 20% per annum on the reducing balance basis. All depreciation is to be charged to cost of sales.

(vi)   The above balances contain the results of Tourmalet's car retailing operations which ceased on 31 December 20X2 due to mounting losses. The results of the car retailing operation, which is to be treated as a discontinued operation, for the year to 30 September 20X3 are:

	$000
Sales	15,200
Cost of sales	16,000
Operating expenses	3,200

The operating expenses are included in administration expenses in the trial balance.

Tourmalet is still paying rentals for the lease of its car showrooms. The rentals are included in operating expenses. Tourmalet is hoping to use the premises as an expansion of its administration offices. This is dependent on obtaining planning permission from the local authority for the change of use, however this is very difficult to obtain. Failing this, the best option would be early termination of the lease which will cost $1.5 million in penalties. This amount has not been provided for.

(vii)   The balance on the taxation account in the trial balance is the result of the settlement of the previous year's tax charge. The directors have estimated the provision for income tax for the year to 30 September 20X3 at $9.2 million.

Required:

(a)   Comment on the substance of the sale of the plant and the directors' treatment of it.

(5 marks)

(b)   Prepare the statement of comprehensive income; and   **(17 marks)**

(c)   Prepare a statement of changes in equity for Tourmalet for the year to 30 September 20X3 in accordance with current International Accounting Standards.   **(3 marks)**

Note: A statement of financial position is NOT required. Disclosure notes are NOT required.

(Total: 25 marks)

30   HARRINGTON

Reproduced below are the draft financial statements of Harrington, a public company, for the year to 31 March 20X5:

Statement of comprehensive income – Year to 31 March 20X5		$000
Revenue (note (i))		13,700
Cost of sales (note (ii))		(9,200)
Gross profit		4,500
Operating expenses		(2,400)
Loan note interest paid (refer to statement of financial position)		(25)
Profit before tax		2,075
Income tax expense (note (vi))		(55)
Profit for the period		2,020

Statement of financial position as at 31 March 20X5

	$000	$000
Property, plant and equipment (note (iii))		6,270
Investments (note (iv))		1,200
		7,470
Current assets		
Inventory	1,750	
Trade receivables	2,450	
Bank	350	4,550
Total assets		12,020
Equity and liabilities:		
Ordinary shares of 25c each (note (v))		2,000
Reserves:		
Share premium		600
Retained earnings – 1 April 20X4	2,990	
– Year to 31 March 20X5	2,020	
– dividends paid	(500)	4,510
		7,110
Non-current liabilities		
10% loan note (issued 20X2)	500	
Deferred tax (note (vi))	280	780
Current liabilities		
Trade payables		4,130
		12,020

The company policy for ALL depreciation is that it is charged to cost of sales and a full year's charge is made in the year of acquisition or completion and none in the year of disposal.

The following matters are relevant:

(i)   Included in revenue is $300,000 being the sale proceeds of an item of plant that was sold in January 20X5. The plant had originally cost $900,000 and had been depreciated by $630,000 at the date of its sale. Other than recording the proceeds in sales and cash, no other accounting entries for the disposal of the plant have been made. All plant is depreciated at 25% per annum on the reducing balance basis.

(ii)   On 31 December 20X4 the company completed the construction of a new warehouse. The construction was achieved using the company's own resources as follows:

	$000
Purchased materials	150
Direct labour	800
Supervision	65
Design and planning costs	20

Included in the above figures are $10,000 for materials and $25,000 for labour costs that were effectively lost due to the foundations being too close to a neighbouring property. All the above costs are included in cost of sales. The building was brought into immediate use on completion and has an estimated life of 20 years (straight-line depreciation).

(iii)   Details of the other property, plant and equipment at 31 March 20X5 are:

	$000	$000
Land at cost		1,000
Buildings at cost	4,000	
Less accumulated depreciation at 31 March 20X4	(800)	3,200
Plant at cost	5,200	
Less accumulated depreciation at 31 March 20X4	(3,130)	2,070
		6,270

At the beginning of the current year (1 April 20X4), Harrington had an open market basis valuation of its properties (excluding the warehouse in note (ii) above). Land was valued at $1.2 million and the property at $4.8 million. The directors wish these values to be incorporated into the financial statements. The properties had an estimated remaining life of 20 years at the date of the valuation (straight-line depreciation is used). Harrington makes a transfer to realized profits in respect of the excess depreciation on revalued assets.

Note: depreciation for the year to 31 March 20X5 has not yet been accounted for in the draft financial statements.

(iv)   The investments are in quoted companies that are carried at their stock market values and are classified as at fair value through profit or loss. The value shown in the statement of financial position is that at 31 March 20X4 and during the year to 31 March 20X5 the investments have risen in value by an average of 10%. Harrington has not reflected this increase in its financial statements.

(v)   On 1 October 20X4 there had been a fully subscribed rights issue of 1 for 4 at 60c. This has been recorded in the above statement of financial position.

(vi)   Income tax on the profits for the year to 31 March 20X5 is estimated at $260,000. The figure in the statement of comprehensive income is the underprovision for income tax for the year to 31 March 20X4. The carrying value of Harrington's net assets is $1.4 million more than their tax base at 31 March 20X5. The income tax rate is 25%.

Required:

(a)   Prepare a restated statement of comprehensive income for the year to 31 March 20X5 reflecting the information in notes (i) to (vi) above.   **(9 marks)**

(b)   Prepare a statement of changes in equity for the year to 31 March 20X5.   **(6 marks)**

(c)   Prepare a restated statement of financial position at 31 March 20X5 reflecting the information in notes (i) to (vi) above.   **(10 marks)**

(Total: 25 marks)

31   CHAMBERLAIN

The following trial balance relates to Chamberlain, a publicly listed company, at 30 September 20X4:

	$000	$000
Ordinary share capital		200,000
Retained earnings at 1 October 20X3		162,000
6% Loan note (issued in 20X2)		50,000
Deferred tax (note (iv))		17,500
Land and buildings at cost (land element $163 million (note (i)))	403,000	
Plant and equipment at cost (note (i))	180,000	
Accumulated depreciation 1 October 20X3 – buildings		60,000
Accumulated depreciation 1 October 20X3 – plant and equipment		60,000
Trade receivables	48,000	
Inventory – 1 October 20X3	35,500	
Bank	12,500	
Trade payables		45,000
Revenue		246,500
Purchases	78,500	
Construction contract balance (note (ii))	5,000	
Operating expenses	29,000	
Loan interest paid	1,500	
Interim dividend	8,000	
Research and development expenditure (note (iii))	40,000	
	841,000	841,000

The following notes are relevant:

(i)   The building had an estimated life of 40 years when it was acquired and is being depreciated on a straight-line basis. Plant and equipment is depreciated at 12.5% per annum using the reducing balance basis. Depreciation of buildings and plant and equipment is charged to cost of sales.

(ii)   The construction contract balance represents costs incurred to date of $35 million less progress billings received of $30 million on a two-year construction contract that commenced on 1 October 20X3. The total contract price has been agreed at $125 million and Chamberlain expects the total contract cost to be $75 million. The company policy is to accrue for profit on uncompleted contracts by applying the percentage of completion to the total estimated profit. The percentage of completion is determined by the proportion of the contract costs to date compared to the total estimated contract costs. At 30 September 20X4, $5 million of the $35 million costs incurred to date related to unused inventory of materials on site.

Other inventory at 30 September 20X4 amounted to $38.5 million at cost.

(iii) The research and development expenditure is made up of $25 million of research, the remainder being development expenditure. The directors are confident of the success of this project which is likely to be completed in March 20X5.

(iv) The directors have estimated the provision for income tax for the year to 30 September 20X4 at $22 million. The deferred tax provision at 30 September 20X4 is to be adjusted to a credit balance of $14 million.

Required:

Prepare for Chamberlain:

(a) a statement of comprehensive income for the year to 30 September 20X4; and

(11 marks)

(b) a statement of financial position as at 30 September 20X4 in accordance with International Financial Reporting Standards as far as the information permits.

(14 marks)

Note: A statement of changes in equity is NOT required.

Disclosure notes are ONLY required for the leased plant in item (ii) above.

(Total: 25 marks)

32 PETRA

The following trial balance relates to Petra, a public listed company, at 30 September 20X5:

	$000	$000
Revenue (note (i))		197,800
Cost of sales (note (i))	114,000	
Distribution costs	17,000	
Administration costs	18,000	
Loan interest paid	1,500	
Ordinary shares of 25 cents each fully paid		40,000
Share premium		12,000
Retained earnings 1 October 20X4		34,000
6% Redeemable loan note (issued in 20X3)		50,000
Land and buildings at cost ((land element $40 million) note (ii))	100,000	
Plant and equipment at cost (note (iii))	66,000	
Deferred development expenditure (note (iv))	40,000	
Accumulated depreciation 1 October 20X4 – buildings		16,000
– plant and equipment		26,000
Accumulated amortization of development expenditure at 1 October 20X4		8,000
Income tax (note (v))	1,000	
Deferred tax (note (v))		15,000
Trade receivables	24,000	
Inventories – 30 September 20X5	21,300	
Bank	11,000	
Trade payables		15,000
	413,800	413,800

The following notes are relevant:

(i) Included in revenue is $12 million for receipts that the company's auditors have advised are commission sales. The costs of these sales, paid for by Petra, were $8 million. $3 million of the profit of $4 million was attributable to and remitted to Sharma (the auditors have advised that Sharma is the principal for these transactions). Both the $8 million cost of sales and the $3 million paid to Sharma have been included in cost of sales.

(ii) The buildings had an estimated life of 30 years when they were acquired and are being depreciated on the straight-line basis.

(iii) Included in the trial balance figures for plant and equipment is plant that had cost $16 million and had accumulated depreciation of $6 million. Following a review of the company's operations this plant was made available for sale during the year. Negotiations with a broker have concluded that a realistic selling price of this plant will be $7.5 million and the broker will charge a commission of 8% of the selling price. The plant had not been sold by the year end. Plant is depreciated at 20% per annum using the reducing balance method. Depreciation of buildings and plant is charged to cost of sales.

(iv) The development expenditure relates to the capitalized cost of developing a product called the Topaz. It had an original estimated life of five years. Production and sales of the Topaz started in October 20X3. A review of the sales of the Topaz in late September 20X5, showed them to be below forecast and an impairment test concluded that the fair value of the development costs at 30 September 20X5 was only $18 million and the expected period of future sales (from this date) was only a further two years.

(v) The balance on the income tax account in the trial balance is the under-provision in respect of the income tax liability for the year ended 30 September 20X4. The directors have estimated the provision for income tax for the year ended 30 September 20X5 to be $4 million and the required statement of financial position provision for deferred tax at 30 September 20X5 is $17.6 million.

Required:

Prepare for Petra:

(a) A statement of comprehensive income for the year ended 30 September 20X5; and

(10 marks)

(b) A statement of financial position as at 30 September 20X5.   **(10 marks)**

Note: A statement of changes in equity is NOT required. Disclosure notes are NOT required.

(c) The directors hold options to purchase 24 million shares for a total of $7.2 million. The options were granted two years ago and have been correctly accounted for. The options do not affect your answer to (a) and (b) above. The average stock market value of Petra's shares for the year ended 30 September 20X5 can be taken as 90 cents per share.

Required:

A calculation of the basic and diluted earnings per share for the year ended 30 September 20X5 (comparatives are not required).   **(5 marks)**

(Total: 25 marks)

33   TINTAGEL

Reproduced below is the draft statement of financial position of Tintagel as at 31 March 20X4.

	$000	$000
Non-current assets (note (i))		
Freehold property		126,000
Plant		110,000
Investment property at 1 April 20X3 (note (ii))		15,000
		251,000
Current assets		
Inventory (note (iii))	60,400	
Trade receivables and prepayments	31,200	
Bank	13,800	105,400
Total assets		356,400
Equity and liabilities		
Ordinary shares of 25c each		150,000
Reserves:		
Share premium	10,000	
Retained earnings – 1 April 20X3	52,500	
Retained earnings – Year to 31 March 20X4	47,500	110,000
		260,000
Non-current liabilities		
Deferred tax – at 1 April 20X3 (note (v))		18,700
Current liabilities		
Trade payables (note (iii))	47,400	
Provision for plant overhaul (note (iv))	12,000	
Taxation	4,200	
		63,600
Suspense account (note (vi))		14,100
Total equity and liabilities		356,400

Notes:

(i)   The statement of comprehensive income has been charged with $3.2 million being the first of four equal annual rental payments for an item of excavating plant. This first payment was made on 1 April 20X3. Tintagel has been advised that this is a finance lease with an implicit interest rate of 10% per annum. The plant had a fair value of $11.2 million at the inception of the lease.

None of the non-current assets have been depreciated for the current year. The freehold property should be depreciated at 2% on its cost of $130 million, the leased plant is depreciated at 25% per annum on a straight-line basis and the non-leased plant is depreciated at 20% on the reducing balance basis.

(ii)   Tintagel adopts the fair value model for its investment property. Its value at 31 March 20X4 has been assessed by a qualified surveyor at $12.4 million.

(iii)   During an inventory count on 31 March 20X4 items that had cost $6 million were identified as being either damaged or slow moving. It is estimated that they will only realize $4 million in total, on which sales commission of 10% will be payable. An invoice for materials delivered on 12 March 20X4 for $500,000 has been discovered.

It has not been recorded in Tintagel's bookkeeping system, although the materials were included in the inventory count.

(iv) Tintagel operates some heavy excavating plant which requires a major overhaul every three years. The overhaul is estimated to cost $18 million and is due to be carried out in April 20X5. The provision of $12 million represents two annual amounts of $6 million made in the years to 31 March 20X3 and 20X4.

(v) The deferred tax provision required at 31 March 20X4 has been calculated at $22.5 million.

(vi) The suspense account contains the credit entry relating to the issue on 1 October 20X3 of a $15 million 8% loan note. It was issued at a discount of 5% and incurred direct issue costs of $150,000. It is redeemable after four years at a premium of 10%. Interest is payable six months in arrears. The first payment of interest has not been accrued and is due on 1 April 20X4. The effective interest rate on the loan note is 6% per half year.

Required:

(a) Commencing with the accumulated profit figures in the above statement of financial position ($52.5 million and $47.5 million), prepare a schedule of adjustments required to these figures taking into account any adjustments required by notes (i) to (vi) above.

(11 marks)

(b) Redraft the statement of financial position of Tintagel as at 31 March 20X4 taking into account the adjustments required in notes (i) to (vi) above. **(14 marks)**

(Total: 25 marks)

34   DARIUS

The following trial balance relates to Darius at 31 March 20X6:

	$000	$000
Revenue		213,800
Cost of sales	143,800	
Closing inventories – 31 March 20X6 (note (i))	10,500	
Operating expenses	22,400	
Rental income from investment property		1,200
Finance costs (note (ii))	5,000	
Land and building – at valuation (note (iii))	63,000	
Plant and equipment – cost (note (iii))	36,000	
Investment property valuation 1 April 20X5 (note (iii))	16,000	
Accumulated depreciation 1 April 20X5 – plant and equipment		16,800
Plant held for sale	8,000	
Trade receivables	13,500	
Bank		900
Trade payables		11,800
Ordinary shares of 25 cents each		20,000
10% Redeemable preference shares of $1 each		10,000
Deferred tax (note (v))		5,200
Revaluation reserve (note (iii))		21,000
Retained earnings 1 April 20X5		17,500
	———	———
	318,200	318,200

The following notes are relevant:

(i)   An inventory count at 31 March 20X6 listed goods with a cost of $10.5 million. This includes some damaged goods that had cost $800,000. These would require remedial work costing $450,000 before they could be sold for an estimated $950,000.

(ii)   Finance costs include overdraft charges, the full year's preference dividend and an ordinary dividend of 4c per share that was paid in September 20X5.

(iii) **Non-current assets:**

       Land and building

       The land and building were revalued at $15 million and $48 million respectively on 1 April 20X5 creating a $21 million revaluation reserve. At this date the building had a remaining life of 15 years.

       Depreciation is on a straight-line basis. Darius does not make a transfer to realized profits in respect of excess depreciation.

       Plant

       All plant is depreciated at 12.5% on the reducing balance basis.

       Depreciation on both the building and the plant should be charged to cost of sales.

       Investment property

       On 31 March 20X6 a qualified surveyor valued the investment property at $13.5 million. Darius uses the fair value model in IAS 40 *Investment property* to value its investment property.

(iv)   The plant held for sale is valued in the trial balance at its carrying value in the statement of financial position. A broker has found a buyer for the plant for $6 million and will charge a fee of 5% of the sales proceeds. The sale should take place during April 20X6.

(v)   The directors have estimated the provision for income tax for the year ended 31 March 20X6 at $8 million. The deferred tax provision at 31 March 20X6 is to be adjusted (through the statement of comprehensive income) to reflect that the tax base of the company's net assets is $12 million less than their carrying amounts. The rate of income tax is 30%.

Required:

(a)   Prepare the statement of comprehensive income for Darius for the year ended 31 March 20X6.   **(12 marks)**

(b)   Prepare the statement of financial position for Darius as at 31 March 20X6. **(13 marks)**

       Notes to the financial statements are NOT required.

                                                                    (Total: 25 marks)

35   TADEON

The following trial balance relates to Tadeon, a publicly listed company, at 30 September 20X6:

	$000	$000
Revenue		277,800
Cost of sales	118,000	
Operating expenses	40,000	
Loan interest paid (note (i))	1,000	
Rental of vehicles (note (ii))	6,200	
Investment income		2,000
25 year leasehold property at cost (note (iii))	225,000	
Plant and equipment at cost	181,000	
Investments at amortized cost	42,000	
Accumulated depreciation at 1 October 20X5		
– leasehold property		36,000
– plant and equipment		85,000
Equity shares of 20 cents each fully paid		150,000
Retained earnings at 1 October 20X5		18,600
2% Loan note (note (i))		50,000
Deferred tax balance 1 October 20X5 (note (iv))		12,000
Trade receivables	53,500	
Inventories at 30 September 20X6	33,300	
Bank		1,900
Trade payables		18,700
Suspense account (note (v))		48,000
	700,000	700,000

The following notes are relevant:

(i)   The loan note was issued on 1 October 20X5. It is redeemable on 30 September 2010 at a large premium (in order to compensate for the low nominal interest rate). The finance department has calculated that the effective interest rate on the loan is 5.5% per annum.

(ii)   The rental of the vehicles relates to two separate contracts. These have been scrutinized by the finance department and they have come to the conclusion that $5 million of the rentals relate to a finance lease. The finance lease was entered into on 1 October 20X5 (the date the $5 million was paid) for a four year period. The vehicles had a fair value of $20 million (straight-line depreciation should be used) at 1 October 20X5 and the lease agreement requires three further annual payments of $6 million each on the anniversary of the lease. The interest rate implicit in the lease is to be taken as 10% per annum. (*Note:* you are not required to calculate the present value of the minimum lease payments.) The other contract is an operating lease and should be charged to operating expenses.

Other plant and equipment is depreciated at $12^1/_2\%$ per annum on the reducing balance basis.

All depreciation of property, plant and equipment is charged to cost of sales.

(iii) On 30 September 20X6 the leasehold property was revalued to $200 million. The directors wish to incorporate this valuation into the financial statements.

(iv)   The directors have estimated the provision for income tax for the year ended 30 September 20X6 at $38 million. At 30 September 20X6 there were $74 million of taxable temporary differences, of which $20 million related to the revaluation of the leasehold property (see (iii) above). The income tax rate is 20%.

(v) The suspense account balance can be reconciled from the following transactions:

The payment of a dividend in October 20X5. This was calculated to give a 5% yield on the company's share price of 80 cents as at 30 September 20X5.

The net receipt in March 20X6 of a fully subscribed rights issue of one new share for every three held at a price of 32 cents each. The expenses of the share issue were $2 million and should be charged to share premium.

Note: the cash entries for these transactions have been correctly accounted for.

Required:

Prepare for Tadeon:

(a) A statement of comprehensive income for the year ended 30 September 20X6; and

(8 marks)

(b) A statement of financial position as at 30 September 20X6. **(17 marks)**

Note: A statement of changes in equity is not required. Disclosure notes are not required.

(Total: 25 marks)

36 UPDATE

Extracts of Update's consolidated statement of comprehensive income for the year to 31 March 20X3 are:

	$000
Revenue	36,000
Cost of sales	(21,000)
Gross profit	15,000
Other operating expenses	(6,200)
Finance costs	(800)
Impairment of non-current assets	(4,000)
Income from associates	1,500
Profit before tax	5,500
Taxation	(2,800)
Profit for the period	2,700
Attributable to:	
Shareholders of the parent	2,585
Minority interest	115
	2,700

The impairment of non-current assets attracted tax relief of $1 million which has been included in the tax charge.

Update paid an interim ordinary dividend of 3c per share in June 20X2 and declared a final dividend on 25 March 20X3 of 6c per share.

The issued share capital of Update on 1 April 20X2 was:

Ordinary shares of 25c each	$3 million
8% Preference shares	$1 million

The preference shares are non-redeemable.

The company also had in issue $2 million 7% convertible loan stock dated 20X5. The loan stock will be redeemed at par in 20X5 or converted to ordinary shares on the basis of 40 new shares for each $100 of loan stock at the option of the stockholders. Update's income tax rate is 30%.

There are also in existence directors' share warrants (issued in 20X1) which entitle the directors to receive 750,000 new shares in total in 20X5 at no cost to the directors.

The following share issues took place during the year to 31 March 20X3:

- 1 July 20X2; a rights issue of 1 new share at $1.50 for every 5 shares held. The market price of Update's shares the day before the rights was $2.40.

- 1 October 20X2; an issue of $1 million 6% non-redeemable preference shares at par.

Both issues were fully subscribed.

Update's basic earnings per share in the year to 31 March 20X2 was correctly disclosed as 24c.

Required:

Calculate for Update for the year to 31 March 20X3:

(i) the dividend cover and explain its significance **(3 marks)**

(ii) the basic earnings per share including the comparative **(5 marks)**

(iii) the fully diluted earnings per share (ignore comparative); and advise a prospective investor of the significance of the diluted earnings per share figure. **(7 marks)**

(Total: 15 marks)

37   A

A is a listed company. Your client, Mr B, currently owns 300 shares in A. Mr B has recently received the published financial statements of A for the year ended 30 September 20X8. Extracts from these published financial statements, and other relevant information, are given below. Mr B is confused by the statements. He is unsure how the performance of the company during the year will affect the market value of his shares, but is aware that the published earnings per share (EPS) is a statistic which is often used by analysts in assessing the performance of listed companies.

Statements of comprehensive income — year ended 30 September

	20X8 $m	20X7 $m
Revenue	10,000	8,500
Cost of sales	(6,300)	(5,100)
Gross profit	3,700	3,400
Other operating expenses	(1,900)	(1,800)
Profit from operations	1,800	1,600
Finance costs	(300)	(320)
Profit before tax	1,500	1,280
Income tax expense	(470)	(400)
Profit for the year	1,030	880

Statements of financial position at 30 September

	20X8 $m	20X8 $m	20X7 $m	20X7 $m
Non-current assets:				
Tangible assets	4,000		3,700	
Intangible assets	3,000		–	
		7,000		3,700
Current assets:				
Inventories	1,300		1,000	
Receivables	1,500		1,200	
Cash in hand and at bank	100		90	
		2,900		2,290
		9,900		5,990
Equity:				
Share capital		1,500		500
Share premium account		2,700		500
Retained earnings		900		670
		5,100		1,670
Non-current liabilities:				
Loan notes		2,000		2,000
Current liabilities:				
Trade payables	1,700		1,200	
Taxation	500		420	
Bank overdraft	600		700	
		2,800		2,320
		9,900		5,990

Information regarding share capital:

The issued share capital of the company comprises $1 equity shares only. On 1 April 20X8, the company made a rights issue to existing shareholders of two new shares for every one share held, at a price of $3.30 per share, paying issue costs of $100,000. The market price of the shares immediately before the rights issue was $3.50 per share. No changes took place in the equity capital of A in the year ended 30 September 20X7.

Required:

(a) Compute the EPS figures (current year plus comparative) that will be included in the published financial statements of A for the year ended 30 September 20X8. **(5 marks)**

(b) Using the extracts with which you have been provided, write a short report to Mr B which identifies the key factors which have led to the change in the EPS of A since the year ended 30 September 20X7. **(15 marks)**

(c) Comment on the relevance of the EPS statistic to a shareholder like Mr B who is concerned about the market value of his shares. **(5 marks)**

(Total: 25 marks)

38 EARNIT

Earnit is a listed company. The issued share capital of the company at 1 April 20X9 was as follows:

- 500 million equity shares of 50c each;

- 100 million $1 non-equity shares, redeemable at a premium on 31 March 20Y4. The effective finance cost of these shares for Earnit is 10% per annum. The carrying value of the non-equity shares in the financial statements at 31 March 20X9 was $110 million.

Extracts from the draft consolidated statement of comprehensive income of Earnit for the year ended 31 March 20Y0 showed:

	$m
Revenue	250
Cost of sales	(130)

Gross profit	120
Other operating expenses	(40)

Profit from operations	80
Exceptional gain	10
Finance costs	(36)

Profit before tax	54
Income tax expense	(20)

Profit for the year	34

The company has a share option scheme in operation. The terms of the options are that option holders are permitted to subscribe for 1 equity share for every option held at a price of $1.50 per share. At 1 April 20X9, 100 million share options were in issue. On 1 October 20X9, the holders of 50 million options exercised their option to purchase, and 70 million new options were issued on the same terms as the existing options. During the year ended 31 March 20Y0, the average market price of an equity share in Earnit was $2.00.

There were no changes to the number of shares or share options outstanding during the year ended 31 March 20Y0 other than as noted in the previous paragraph.

Required:

(a) Compute the basic and diluted earnings per share of Earnit for the year ended 31 March 20Y0. Comparative figures are NOT required. **(5 marks)**

(b) Explain to a holder of equity shares in Earnit the usefulness of both the figures you have calculated in part (a). **(5 marks)**

(Total: 10 marks)

39 JKL

JKL is a listed entity preparing financial statements to 31 August. At 1 September 20X3, JKL had 6,000,000 50¢ shares in issue. On 1 February 20X4, the entity made a rights issue of 1 for 4 at 125¢ per share; the issue was successful and all rights were taken up. The market price of one share immediately prior to the issue was 145¢ per share. Profit after tax for the year ended 31 August 20X4 were $2,763,000.

Several years ago, JKL issued a convertible loan of $2,000,000. The loan carries an effective interest rate of 7% and its terms of conversion (which are at the option of the stockholder) are as follows:

For each $100 of loan stock:

Conversion at 31 August 20X8   105 shares

Conversion at 31 August 20X9   103 shares

JKL is subject to an income tax rate of 32%.

Required:

(a)   Calculate basic earnings per share and diluted earnings per share for the year ended 31 August 20X4.   **(7 marks)**

(b)   The IASC *Framework for the Preparation and Presentation of Financial Statements* states that the objective of financial statements is to provide information that is:

'useful to a wide range of users in making economic decisions'.

Explain to a holder of ordinary shares in JKL both the usefulness and limitations of the diluted earnings per share figure.   **(3 marks)**

(Total: 10 marks)

BUSINESS COMBINATIONS

40   HALOGEN

On 1 April 20X0 Halogen acquired a controlling interest of 75% of Stimulus. At this date Halogen issued one new ordinary share valued at $5 and paid $1.40 in cash, for every **two** shares it acquired in Stimulus. The reserves of Stimulus at the time of the date of the acquisition were:

      Retained earnings $180 million

      Revaluation reserve $40 million

The statements of financial position of Halogen and Stimulus at 31 March 20X1 are:

	Halogen		Stimulus	
	$million	$million	$million	$million
Assets				
Non-current assets				
Property, plant and equipment		910		330
Development expenditure		100		nil
Investments (including that in Stimulus)		700		60
		1,710		390
Current assets				
Inventory	224		120	
Trade receivables	264		84	
Bank	nil		25	
		488		229
Total assets		2,198		619

	Halogen		Stimulus	
	$million	$million	$million	$million
Equity and liabilities				
Equity:				
Equity shares of $1 each		1,000		200
Reserves:				
Share premium	300		nil	
Retained earnings	480		240	
Revaluation reserve	60	840	40	280
		1,840		480
Non-current liabilities				
10% Debenture		nil		60
Current liabilities				
Trade payables	178		44	
Taxation	94		35	
Bank overdraft	86	358	nil	79
Total equity and liabilities		2,198		619

The following information is relevant:

(i) At the date of acquisition the statement of financial position of Stimulus included an intangible non-current asset of $8 million in respect of the development of a new medical drug. On this date an independent specialist assessed the fair value of this intangible asset at $28 million. Halogen had been developing a similar drug and shortly after the acquisition it was decided to combine the two development projects. All information and development work on Stimulus's project was transferred to Halogen in return for a payment of $36 million. The carrying value of Stimulus's development expenditure at the date of transfer was still $8 million. Stimulus has recognized the profit on this transaction in profit or loss. Approval to market the drug is expected in September 20X1.

(ii) Both companies have a policy of keeping their land (included in property, plant and equipment) at current value.The balances on the revaluation reserves represent the revaluation surpluses at 1 April 20X0. Neither company has yet recorded further increases of $10 million and $8 million for Halogen and Stimulus respectively for the year to 31 March 20X1.

(iii) During the year to 31 March 20X1 Halogen sold goods at a price of $26 million to Stimulus at a mark-up on cost of 30%. Half of these goods were still in inventory at the year-end.

(iv) On 28 March 20X1 Stimulus recorded a payment of $12 million to settle its current account balance with Halogen. Halogen had not received this by the year-end. Inter-company current account balances are included in trade payables/receivables as appropriate.

Required:

(a) Prepare the consolidated statement of financial position of Halogen as at 31 March 20X1. **(20 marks)**

(b) Included within the investments of Halogen is an investment in a wholly owned private limited company called Lockstart. Prior to the current year Halogen has consolidated the results of Lockstart. In recent years the profits of Lockstart have been declining and in the year to 31 March 20X1 it made significant losses. In January of 20X1 the management of Halogen held a Board meeting where it was decided that the investment in Lockstart would be sold as soon as possible. No buyer had been found by 31 March 20X1.

The directors of Halogen are aware that shareholders often use a company's published financial statements to predict future performance, and this is one of the reasons why IFRS 5 *Non-current Assets Held for Sale and Discontinued Operations* requires the results of discontinued operations to be separately identified. Shareholders are thus made aware of those parts of the business that will not contribute to future profits or losses.

In the spirit of the above, the management of Halogen have decided not to consolidate the results of Lockstart for the current year (to 31 March 20X1), believing that if they were consolidated, it would give a misleading basis for predicting the group's future performance.

Required:

Comment on the suitability of the Directors' treatment of Lockstart; and state how you believe Lockstart should be treated in the group financial statements of Halogen. **(5 marks)**

Note: you are not required to amend your answer to (a) in respect of this information.

(Total: 25 marks)

41 HIGHMOOR

Highmoor, a public listed company, acquired 80% of Slowmoor's ordinary shares on 1 October 20X2. Highmoor paid an immediate $2 per share in cash and agreed to pay a further $1.20 per share if Slowmoor made a profit within two years of its acquisition. Highmoor has not recorded the contingent consideration.

The statements of financial position of the two companies at 30 September 20X3 are shown below:

	Highmoor		Slowmoor	
	$ million	$ million	$ million	$ million
Tangible non-current assets		585		172
Investments (note (ii))		225		13
Software (note (iii))		nil		40
		810		225
Current assets				
Inventory	85		42	
Trade receivables	95		36	
Tax asset	nil		80	
Bank	20	200	nil	158
Total assets		1,010		383

	Highmoor		Slowmoor	
	$ million	$ million	$ million	$ million
Equity and liabilities				
Equity:				
Ordinary shares of $1 each		400		100
Retained earnings – 1 October 20X2	230		150	
– profit/loss for year	100	330	(35)	115
		730		215
Non-current liabilities				
12% loan note	nil		35	
16% Inter company loan (note (ii))	nil	nil	45	80
Current liabilities				
Trade payables	210		71	
Taxation	70		nil	
Overdraft	nil	280	17	88
Total equity and liabilities		1,010		383

The following information is relevant:

(i)   At the date of acquisition the fair values of Slowmoor's net assets approximated to their book values.

(ii) Included in Highmoor's investments is a loan of $50 million made to Slowmoor on 1 April 20X3. On 28 September 20X3, Slowmoor paid $9 million to Highmoor. This represented interest of $4 million for the year and the balance was a capital repayment. Highmoor had not received nor accounted for the payment, but it had accrued for the loan interest receivable as part of its accounts receivable figure. There are no other intra group balances.

(iii) The software was developed by Highmoor during 20X2 at a total cost of $30 million. It was sold to Slowmoor for $50 million immediately after its acquisition. The software had an estimated life of five years and is being amortized by Slowmoor on a straight-line basis.

(iv) Due to the losses of Slowmoor since its acquisition, the directors of Highmoor are not confident it will return to profitability in the short term.

Required:

(a)   Prepare the consolidated statement of financial position of Highmoor as at 30 September 20X3, explaining your treatment of the contingent consideration.

(20 marks)

(b)   Describe the circumstances in which the consideration for an acquisition may be less than the share of the assets acquired. Your answer should refer to the particular issues of the above acquisition.   **(5 marks)**

(Total: 25 marks)

42   HIGHVELDT

Highveldt, a public listed company, acquired 75% of Samson's ordinary shares on 1 April 20X4. Highveldt paid an immediate $3.50 per share in cash and agreed to pay a further amount of $108 million on 1 April 20X5. Highveldt's cost of capital is 8% per annum. Highveldt has only recorded the cash consideration of $3.50 per share.

The summarized statements of financial position of the two companies at 31 March 20X5 are shown below:

| | Highveldt | | Samson | |
	$ million	$ million	$ million	$ million
Tangible non-current assets (note (i))		420		320
Development costs (note (iv))		Nil		40
Investments (note (ii))		300		20
		720		380
Current assets		133		91
Total assets		853		471
Equity and liabilities:				
Ordinary shares of $1 each		270		80
Reserves:				
Share premium		80		40
Revaluation reserve		45		Nil
Retained earnings – 1 April 20X4	160		134	
– year to 31 March 20X5	190	350	76	210
		745		330
Non-current liabilities				
10% inter company loan (note (ii))		Nil		60
Current liabilities		108		81
Total equity and liabilities		853		471

The following information is relevant:

(i)   Highveldt has a policy of revaluing land and buildings to fair value. At the date of acquisition Samson's land and buildings had a fair value $20 million higher than their book value and at 31 March 20X5 this had increased by a further $4 million (ignore any additional depreciation).

(ii)   Included in Highveldt's investments is a loan of $60 million made to Samson at the date of acquisition. Interest is payable annually in arrears. Samson paid the interest due for the year on 31 March 20X5, but Highveldt did not receive this until after the year end. Highveldt has not accounted for the accrued interest from Samson.

(iii)   Samson had established a line of products under the brand name of Titanware. Acting on behalf of Highveldt, a firm of specialists, had valued the brand name at a value of $40 million with an estimated life of 10 years as at 1 April 20X4. The brand is not included in Samson's statement of financial position.

(iv)   Samson's development project was completed on 30 September 20X4 at a cost of $50 million. $10 million of this had been amortized by 31 March 20X5. Development costs capitalized by Samson at the date of acquisition were $18 million. Highveldt's directors are of the opinion that Samson's development costs do not meet the criteria in IAS 38 *Intangible Assets* for recognition as an asset.

(v)   Samson sold goods to Highveldt during the year at a profit of $6 million, one-third of these goods were still in the inventory of Highveldt at 31 March 20X5.

(vi)   An impairment test at 31 March 20X5 on the notional consolidated goodwill (grossed up for the minority interest's share) indicated that it should be written down by $29 million. No other assets were impaired.

Required:

(a)   Calculate the following figures as they would appear in the consolidated statement of financial position of Highveldt at 31 March 20X5:

(i)   goodwill;   **(8 marks)**

(ii)   minority interest;   **(4 marks)**

(iii)   the following consolidated reserves:

         share premium, revaluation reserve and retained earnings.   **(8 marks)**

Note: show your workings.

(b)   Explain why consolidated financial statements are useful to the users of financial statements (as opposed to just the parent company's separate (entity) financial statements).   **(5 marks)**

(Total: 25 marks)

43   HEPBURN

(a)   On 1 October 19W9 Hepburn acquired 80% of the equity share capital of Salter by way of a share exchange. Hepburn issued five of its own shares for every two shares it acquired in Salter. The market value of Hepburn's shares on 1 October 19W9 was $3 each. The share issue has not yet been recorded in Hepburn's books. The summarized financial statements of both companies are:

Statements of comprehensive income: Year to 31 March 20X0

	Hepburn		Salter	
	$000	$000	$000	$000
Revenue		1,200		1,000
Cost of sales		(650)		(660)
Gross profit		550		340
Operating expenses		(120)		(88)
Finance costs		nil		(12)
Profit before tax		430		240
Income tax expense		(100)		(40)
Profit for the year		330		200

Statements of financial position: as at 31 March 20X0

	$000	$000	$000	$000
Non-current assets				
Property, plant and equipment		620		660
Investments		20		10
		640		670
Current assets				
Inventory	240		280	
Accounts receivable	170		210	
Bank	20	430	40	530
Total assets		1,070		1,200
Equity and liabilities				
Equity shares of $1 each		400		150
Retained earnings		410		700
		810		850
Non-current liabilities				
8% Loan notes		nil		150
Current liabilities				
Trade accounts payable	210		155	
Taxation	50		45	
Total equity and liabilities		1,070		1,200

The following information is relevant:

(i)   The fair values of Salter's assets were equal to their book values with the exception of its land, which had a fair value of $125,000 in excess of its book value at the date of acquisition.

(ii)   In the post acquisition period Hepburn sold goods to Salter at a price of $100,000, this was calculated to give a mark-up on cost of 25% to Hepburn. Salter had half of these goods in inventory at the year end.

(iii)   The current accounts of the two companies disagreed due to a cash remittance of $20,000 to Hepburn on 26 March 20X0 not being received until after the year end. Before adjusting for this, Salter's debit balance in Hepburn's books was $56,000.

Required:

Prepare a consolidated statement of comprehensive income and statement of financial position for Hepburn for the year to 31 March 20X0.   **(20 marks)**

(b)   At the same date as Hepburn made the share exchange for Salter's shares, it also acquired 6,000 'A' shares in Woodbridge for a cash payment of $20,000. The share capital of Woodbridge is made up of:

Equity voting A shares   10,000

Equity non-voting B shares   14,000

All of Woodbridge's equity shares are entitled to the same dividend rights; however during the year to 31 March 20X0 Woodbridge made substantial losses and did not pay any dividends.

Hepburn has treated its investment in Woodbridge as an available-for-sale financial asset on the basis that:

- it is only entitled to 25% of any dividends that Woodbridge may pay

- it does not have any directors on the Board of Woodbridge; and

- it does not exert any influence over the operating policies or management of Woodbridge.

Required:

Comment on the accounting treatment of Woodbridge by Hepburn's directors and state how you believe the investment should be accounted for.   **(5 marks)**

Note: you are not required to amend your answer to part (a) in respect of the information in part (b).

(Total: 25 marks)

44. HILLUSION

In recent years Hillusion has acquired a reputation for buying modestly performing businesses and selling them at a substantial profit within a period of two to three years of their acquisition. On 1 July 20X2 Hillusion acquired 80% of the ordinary share capital of Skeptik at a cost of $10,280,000. On the same date it also acquired 50% of Skeptik 10% loan notes at par. The summarized draft financial statements of both companies are:

Statements of comprehensive income: Year to 31 March 20X3

	Hillusion plc		Skeptik plc	
	$000	$000	$000	$000
Revenue		60,000		24,000
Cost of sales		(42,000)		(20,000)
Gross profit		18,000		4,000
Operating expenses		(6,000)		(200)
Loan interest received (paid)		75		(200)
Profit before tax		12,075		3,600
Taxation		(3,000)		(600)
Profit for the year		9,075		3,000

Statements of financial position: as at 31 March 20X3

	Hillusion plc	Skeptik plc
Tangible non-current assets	19,320	8,000
Investments	11,280	nil
	30,600	8,000
Current assets	15,000	8,000
Total assets	45,600	16,000
Ordinary shares of $1 each	10,000	2,000
Retained earnings	25,600	8,400
	35,600	10,400
Non-current liabilities		
10% loan notes	Nil	2,000
Current liabilities	10,000	3,600
	45,600	16,000

The following information is relevant:

(i)   The fair values of Skeptik assets were equal to their book values with the exception of its plant, which had a fair value of $3.2 million in excess of its book value at the date of acquisition. The remaining life of all of Skeptik's plant at the date of its acquisition was four years and this period has not changed as a result of the acquisition. Depreciation of plant is on a straight-line basis and charged to cost of sales. Skeptik has not adjusted the value of its plant as a result of the fair value exercise.

(ii)   In the post acquisition period Hillusion sold goods to Skeptik at a price of $12 million. These goods had cost Hillusion $9 million. During the year Skeptik had sold $10 million (at cost to Skeptik) of these goods for $15 million.

(iii) Hillusion bears almost all of the administration costs incurred on behalf of the group (invoicing, credit control, etc). It does not charge Skeptik for this service as to do so would not have a material effect on the group profit.

(iv)   Revenues and profits should be deemed to accrue evenly throughout the year.

(v)   The current accounts of the two companies were reconciled at the year-end with Skeptik owing Hillusion $750,000.

Required:

(a)   Prepare a consolidated statement of comprehensive income and statement of financial position for Hillusion for the year to 31 March 20X3.   **(20 marks)**

(b)   Explain why it is necessary to eliminate unrealized profits when preparing group financial statements; and how reliance on the entity financial statements of Skeptik may mislead a potential purchaser of the company.   **(5 marks)**

(Total: 25 marks)

Note: your answer should refer to the circumstances described in the question.

45   HORSEFIELD

Horsefield, a public company, acquired 90% of Sandfly's $1 ordinary shares on 1 April 20X0 paying $3.00 per share. The balance on Sandfly's retained earnings at this date was $800,000. On 1 October 20X1, Horsefield acquired 30% of Anthill's $1 ordinary shares for $3.50 per share. The statements of financial position of the three companies at 31 March 20X2 are shown below:

	Horsefield		Sandfly		Anthill	
	$000	$000	$000	$000	$000	$000
Non-current assets						
Property, plant and equipment		8,050		3,600		1,650
Investments		4,000		910		nil
		———		———		———
		12,050		4,510		1,650
Current assets						
Inventory	830		340		250	
Trade receivables	520		290		350	
Bank	240	1,590	nil	630	100	700
		———		———		———
Total assets		13,640		5,140		2,350

	Horsefield		Sandfly		Anthill	
	$000	$000	$000	$000	$000	$000
Equity and liabilities						
Equity:						
Ordinary shares of $1 each		5,000		1,200		600
Reserves:						
Retained earnings b/f	6,000		1,400		800	
Profit year to 31 March 20X2	1,300	7,300	800	2,200	600	1,400
		12,300		3,400		2,000
Non-current liabilities						
10% Loan notes		500		240		nil
Current liabilities						
Trade payables	620		1,060		200	
Taxation	220		250		150	
Overdraft	nil	840	190	1,500	nil	350
Total equity and liabilities		13,640		5,140		2,350

The following information is relevant:

(i) Fair value adjustments:

On 1 April 20X0 Sandfly owned an investment property that had a fair value of $120,000 in excess of its book value. The value of this property has not changed since acquisition. This property is included within investments in the statement of financial position.

Just prior to its acquisition, Sandfly was successful in applying for a six-year licence to dispose of hazardous waste. The licence was granted by the government at no cost, however Horsefield estimated that the licence was worth $180,000 at the date of acquisition.

(ii) In January 20X2 Horsefield sold goods to Anthill for $65,000. These were transferred at a mark up of 30% on cost. Two thirds of these goods were still in the inventory of Anthill at 31 March 20X2.

(iii) To facilitate the consolidation procedures the group insists that all inter company current account balances are settled prior to the year-end. However a cheque for $40,000 from Sandfly to Horsefield was not received until early April 20X2. Inter company balances are included in trade receivables and payables as appropriate.

(iv) Anthill is to be treated as an associated company of Horsefield.

Required:

(a) Prepare the consolidated statement of financial position of Horsefield as at 31 March 20X2. **(20 marks)**

(b) Discuss the matters to consider in determining whether an investment in another company constitutes associated company status. **(5 marks)**

(Total: 25 marks)

46   HAPSBURG

(a)   Hapsburg, a public listed company, acquired the following investments:

   –   On 1 April 20X3, 24 million shares in Sundial. This was by way of an immediate share exchange of two shares in Hapsburg for every three shares in Sundial plus a cash payment of $1 per Sundial share payable on 1 April 20X6. The market price of Hapsburg's shares on 1 April 20X3 was $2 each.

   –   On 1 October 20X3, 6 million shares in Aspen paying an immediate $2.50 in cash for each share.

Based on Hapsburg's cost of capital (taken as 10% per annum), $1 receivable in three years' time can be taken to have a present value of $0.75.

Hapsburg has not yet recorded the acquisition of Sundial but it has recorded the investment in Aspen. The summarized statements of financial position at 31 March 20X4 are:

	Hapsburg $000	Hapsburg $000	Sundial $000	Sundial $000	Aspen $000	Aspen $000
Non-current assets						
Property, plant and equipment		41,000		34,800		37,700
Investments		15,000		3,000		nil
		56,000		37,800		37,700
Current assets						
Inventory	9,900		4,800		7,900	
Trade and other receivables	13,600		8,600		14,400	
Cash	1,200	24,700	3,800	17,200	nil	22,300
Total assets		80,700		55,000		60,000
Equity and liabilities						
Capital and reserves						
Ordinary shares $1 each		20,000		30,000		20,000
Reserves:						
Share premium	8,000		2,000		nil	
Retained earnings	10,600	18,600	8,500	10,500	8,000	8,000
		38,600		40,500		28,000
Non-current liabilities						
10% loan note		16,000		4,200		12,000
Current liabilities						
Trade and other payables	16,500		6,900		13,600	
Bank overdraft	nil		nil		4,500	
Taxation	9,600	26,100	3,400	10,300	1,900	20,000
Total equity and liabilities		80,700		55,000		60,000

The following information is relevant:

(i)   Below is a summary of the results of a fair value exercise for Sundial carried out at the date of acquisition:

Asset	Carrying value at acquisition $000	Fair value at acquisition $000	Notes
Plant	10,000	15,000	remaining life at acquisition four years
Investments	3,000	4,500	no change in value since acquisition

The book values of the net assets of Aspen at the date of acquisition approximated to their fair values.

(ii)   The profits of Sundial and Aspen for the year to 31 March 20X4, as reported in their entity financial statements, were $4·5 million and $6 million respectively. No dividends have been paid by any of the companies during the year. All profits are deemed to accrue evenly throughout the year.

(iii)   In January 20X4 Aspen sold goods to Hapsburg at a selling price of $4 million. These goods had cost Aspen $2·4 million. Hapsburg had $2.5 million (at cost to Hapsburg) of these goods still in inventory at 31 March 20X4.

(iv)   All depreciation is charged on a straight-line basis.

Required:

Prepare the consolidated statement of financial position of Hapsburg as at 31 March 20X4.   **(20 marks)**

(b)   Some commentators have criticized the use of equity accounting on the basis that it can be used as a form of off statement of financial position financing.

Required:

Explain the reasoning behind the use of equity accounting and discuss the above comment.   **(5 marks)**

(Total: 25 marks)

47   HEDRA

Hedra, a public listed company, acquired the following investments:

(i)   On 1 October 20X4, 72 million shares in Salvador for an immediate cash payment of $195 million. Hedra agreed to pay further consideration on 30 September 20X5 of $49 million if the post acquisition profits of Salvador exceeded an agreed figure at that date. Hedra has not accounted for this deferred payment as it did not believe it would be payable, however Salvador's profits have now exceeded the agreed amount (ignore discounting).

Salvador also received a $50 million 8% loan from Hedra at the date of its acquisition.

(ii)   On 1 April 20X5, 40 million shares in Aragon by way of a share exchange of two shares in Hedra for each acquired share in Aragon. The stock market value of Hedra's shares at the date of this share exchange was $2.50. Hedra has not yet recorded the acquisition of the investment in Aragon.

The summarized statements of financial position of the three companies as at 30 September 20X5 are:

	Hedra		Salvador		Aragon	
Non-current assets	$m	$m	$m	$m	$m	$m
Property, plant and equipment		358		240		270
Investments – in Salvador		245		nil		nil
– other		45		nil		nil
		648		240		270
Current assets						
Inventories	130		80		110	
Trade receivables	142		97		70	
Cash and bank	nil	272	4	181	20	200
		920		421		470
Equity and liabilities						
Ordinary share capital ($1 each)		400		120		100
Reserves:						
Share premium	40		50		nil	
Revaluation	15		nil		nil	
Retained earnings	240	295	60	110	300	300
		695		230		400
Non-current liabilities						
8% loan note	Nil		50		Nil	
Deferred tax	45	45	Nil	50	Nil	Nil
Current liabilities						
Trade payables	118		141		40	
Bank overdraft	12		nil		nil	
Current tax payable	50	180	nil	141	30	70
		920		421		470

The following information is relevant:

(a) Fair value adjustments and revaluations:

(i) Hedra's accounting policy for land and buildings is that they should be carried at their fair values. The fair value of Salvador's land at the date of acquisition was $20 million in excess of its carrying value. By 30 September 20X5 this excess had increased by a further $5 million. Salvador's buildings did not require any fair value adjustments. The fair value of Hedra's own land and buildings at 30 September 20X5 was $12 million in excess of its carrying value in the above statement of financial position.

(ii) The fair value of some of Salvador's plant at the date of acquisition was $20 million in excess of its carrying value and had a remaining life of four years (straight-line depreciation is used).

(iii) At the date of acquisition Salvador had unrelieved tax losses of $40 million from previous years. Salvador had not accounted for these as a deferred tax asset as its directors did not believe the company would be sufficiently profitable in the near future. However, the directors of Hedra were confident that these losses would be utilized and accordingly they should be recognized as a deferred tax asset. By 30 September 20X5 the group had not yet utilized any of these losses. The income tax rate is 25%.

(b)   The retained earnings of Salvador and Aragon at 1 October 20X4, as reported in their separate financial statements, were $20 million and $200 million respectively. All profits are deemed to accrue evenly throughout the year.

(c)   An impairment test on 30 September 20X5 showed that the recoverable amount of the notional goodwill in respect of Salvador was $133 million.

(d)   The investment in Aragon has not suffered any impairment.

Required:

Prepare the consolidated statement of financial position of Hedra as at 30 September 20X5.

(25 marks)

48   HOLDRITE, STAYBRITE AND ALLBRITE

Holdrite purchased 75% of the issued share capital of Staybrite and 40% of the issued share capital of Allbrite on 1 April 20X4.

Details of the purchase consideration given at the date of purchase are:

Staybrite: a share exchange of 2 shares in Holdrite for every 3 shares in Staybrite plus an issue to the shareholders of Staybrite of 8% loan notes redeemable at par on 30 June 20X6 on the basis of $100 loan note for every 250 shares held in Staybrite.

Allbrite: a share exchange of 3 shares in Holdrite for every 4 shares in Allbrite plus $1 per share acquired in cash.

The market price of Holdrite's shares at 1 April 20X4 was $6 per share.

The summarized income statements for the three companies for the year to 30 September 20X4 are:

	Holdrite	Staybrite	Allbrite
	$000	$000	$000
Revenue	75,000	40,700	31,000
Cost of sales	(47,400)	(19,700)	(15,300)
Gross profit	27,600	21,000	15,700
Operating expenses	(10,480)	(9,000)	(9,700)
Operating profit	17,120	12,000	6,000
Finance cost	(170)	–	–
Profit before tax	16,950	12,000	6,000
Income tax expense	(4,800)	(3,000)	(2,000)
Profit for period	12,150	9,000	4,000

The following information is relevant:

(i)   A fair value exercise was carried out for Staybrite at the date of its acquisition with the following results:

(ii)

	Book value	Fair value
	$000	$000
Land	20,000	23,000
Plant	25,000	30,000

The fair values have not been reflected in Staybrite's financial statements. The increase in the fair value of the plant would create additional depreciation of $500,000 in the post acquisition period in the consolidated financial statements to 30 September 20X4.

Depreciation of plant is charged to cost of sales.

(ii)   The details of each company's share capital and reserves at 1 October 20X3 are:

	Holdrite	Staybrite	Allbrite
	$000	$000	$000
Equity shares of $1 each	20,000	10,000	5,000
Share premium	5,000	4,000	2,000
Retained earnings	18,000	7,500	6,000

(iii)   In the post acquisition period Holdrite sold goods to Staybrite for $10 million. Holdrite made a profit of $4 million on these sales. One-quarter of these goods were still in the inventory of Staybrite at 30 September 20X4.

(iv)   An impairment test on the notional goodwill of Staybrite (grossed up for the minority interest's share) at 30 September 20X4 indicated it was overstated by $1 million. The investment in Allbrite was not impaired.

(v)   Holdrite paid a dividend of $5 million on 20 September 20X4.

Required:

(a)   Calculate the goodwill arising on the purchase of the shares in both Staybrite and Allbrite at 1 April 20X4.   **(8 marks)**

(b)   Prepare a consolidated statement of comprehensive income for the Holdrite Group for the year to 30 September 20X4.   **(15 marks)**

(c)   Show the movement on the consolidated retained earnings attributable to Holdrite for the year to 30 September 20X4.   **(2 marks)**

(Total: 25 marks)

Note: The additional disclosures in IFRS *3 Business Combinations* relating to a newly acquired subsidiary are not required.

49   HYDAN

On 1 October 20X5 Hydan, a publicly listed company, acquired a 60% controlling interest in Systan paying $9 per share in cash. Prior to the acquisition Hydan had been experiencing difficulties with the supply of components that it used in its manufacturing process. Systan is one of Hydan's main suppliers and the acquisition was motivated by the need to secure supplies. In order to finance an increase in the production capacity of Systan, Hydan made a non-dated loan at the date of acquisition of $4 million to Systan that carried an actual and effective interest rate of 10% per annum. The interest to 31 March 20X6 on this loan has been paid by Systan and accounted for by both companies. The summarized draft financial statements of the companies are:

Statements of comprehensive income for the year ended 31 March 20X6

	Hydan	Systan Pre-acquisition	Systan Post-acquisition
	$000	$000	$000
Revenue	98,000	24,000	35,200
Cost of sales	(76,000)	(18,000)	(31,000)
Gross profit	22,000	6,000	4,200
Operating expenses	(11,800)	(1,200)	(8,000)
Interest income	350	nil	nil
Finance costs	(420)	nil	(200)
Profit/(loss) before tax	10,130	4,800	(4,000)
Income tax (expense)/relief	(4,200)	(1,200)	1,000
Profit/(loss) for the period	5,930	3,600	(3,000)

Statements of financial position as at 31 March 20X6

	Hydan	Systan
	$000	$000
Non-current assets		
Property, plant and equipment	18,400	9,500
Investments (including loan to Systan)	16,000	nil
	34,400	9,500
Current assets	18,000	7,200
Total assets	52,400	16,700
Equity and liabilities		
Ordinary share capital of $1 each	10,000	2,000
Share premium	5,000	500
Retained earnings	20,000	6,300
	35,000	8,800
Non-current liabilities		
7% bank loan	6,000	nil
10% loan from Hydan	nil	4,000
Current liabilities	11,400	3,900
Total equity and liabilities	52,400	16,700

The following information is relevant:

(i) At the date of acquisition, the fair values of Systan's property, plant and equipment were $1.2 million in excess of their carrying amounts. This will have the effect of creating an additional depreciation charge (to cost of sales) of $300,000 in the consolidated financial statements for the year ended 31 March 20X6. Systan has not adjusted its assets to fair value.

(ii)   In the post acquisition period Systan's sales to Hydan were $30 million on which Systan had made a consistent profit of 5% of the selling price. Of these goods, $4 million (at selling price to Hydan) were still in the inventory of Hydan at 31 March 20X6. Prior to its acquisition Systan made all its sales at a uniform gross profit margin.

(iii) Included in Hydan's current liabilities is $1 million owing to Systan. This agreed with Systan's receivables ledger balance for Hydan at the year end.

(iv)   An impairment review of the consolidated goodwill at 31 March 20X6 revealed that its current value was 12.5% less than its carrying amount.

(v)   Neither company paid a dividend in the year to 31 March 20X6.

Required:

(a)   Prepare the consolidated statement of comprehensive income for the year ended 31 March 20X6 and the consolidated statement of financial position at that date.

(20 marks)

(b)   Discuss the effects that the acquisition of Systan appears to have had on Systan's operating performance   **(5 marks)**

(Total: 25 marks)

50   HOSTERLING

Hosterling purchased the following equity investments:

On 1 October 20X5: 80% of the issued share capital of Sunlee. The acquisition was through a share exchange of three shares in Hosterling for every five shares in Sunlee. The market price of Hosterling's shares at 1 October 20X5 was $5 per share.

On 1 July 20X6: 6 million shares in Amber paying $3 per share in cash and issuing to Amber's shareholders 6% (actual and effective rate) loan notes on the basis of $100 loan note for every 100 shares acquired.

The summarized statements of comprehensive income for the three companies for the year ended 30 September 20X6 are:

	Hosterling $000	Sunlee $000	Amber $000
Revenue	105,000	62,000	50,000
Cost of sales	(68,000)	(36,500)	(61,000)
Gross profit/(loss)	37,000	25,500	(11,000)
Other income (note (i))	400	nil	nil
Distribution costs	(4,000)	(2,000)	(4,500)
Administrative expenses	(7,500)	(7,000)	(8,500)
Finance costs	(1,200)	(900)	nil
Profit/(loss) before tax	24,700	15,600	(24,000)
Income tax (expense)/credit	(8,700)	(2,600)	4,000
Profit/(loss) for the period	16,000	13,000	(20,000)

The following information is relevant:

(i)   The other income is a dividend received from Sunlee on 31 March 20X6.

(ii)   The details of Sunlee's and Amber's share capital and reserves at 1 October 20X5 were:

	Sunlee	Amber
	$000	$000
Equity shares of $1 each	20,000	15,000
Retained earnings	18,000	35,000

(iii)   A fair value exercise was carried out at the date of acquisition of Sunlee with the following results:

	Carrying amount	Fair value	Remaining life (straight line)
	$000	$000	
Intellectual property	18,000	22,000	still in development
Land	17,000	20,000	not applicable
Plant	30,000	35,000	five years

The fair values have not been reflected in Sunlee's financial statements.

Plant depreciation is included in cost of sales.

No fair value adjustments were required on the acquisition of the shares in Amber.

(iv)   In the year ended 30 September 20X6 Hosterling sold goods to Sunlee at a selling price of $18 million. Hosterling made a profit of cost plus 25% on these sales. $7.5 million (at cost to Sunlee) of these goods were still in the inventories of Sunlee at 30 September 20X6.

(v)   Impairment tests for both Sunlee and Amber were conducted on 30 September 20X6. They concluded that the goodwill of Sunlee should be written down by $1.6 million and, due to its losses since acquisition, the investment in Amber was worth $21.5 million.

(vi)   All trading profits and losses are deemed to accrue evenly throughout the year.

Required:

(a)   Calculate the goodwill arising on the acquisition of Sunlee at 1 October 20X5.

(5 marks)

(b)   Calculate the carrying amount of the investment in Amber at 30 September 20X6 under the equity method prior to the impairment test.   **(4 marks)**

(c)   Prepare the consolidated statement of comprehensive income for the Hosterling Group for the year ended 30 September 20X6.   **(16 marks)**

(Total: 25 marks)

51 AJ

AJ is a law stationery business. In 2002, the majority of its board of directors was replaced. The new board decided to adopt a policy of expansion through acquisition. The statements of financial position at 31 March 20X5 of AJ and of two entities in which it holds substantial investments are shown below:

	AJ $000	AJ $000	BK $000	BK $000	CL $000	CL $000
Non-current assets:						
Property, plant and equipment	12,500		4,700		4,500	
Investments	18,000		–		1,300	
		30,500		4,700		5,800
Current assets:						
Inventories	7,200		8,000		–	
Trade receivables	6,300		4,300		3,100	
Financial assets	–		–		2,000	
Cash	800		–		900	
		14,300		12,300		6,000
		44,800		17,000		11,800
Equity:						
Called up share capital ($1 shares)		10,000		5,000		2,500
Reserves		14,000		1,000		4,300
		24,000		6,000		6,800
Non-current liabilities:						
Loan notes		10,000		3,000		–
Current liabilities:						
Trade payables	8,900		6,700		4,000	
Income tax	1,300		100		600	
Short-term borrowings	600		1,200		400	
		10,800		8,000		5,000
		44,800		17,000		11,800

Notes to the statements of financial position:

Note 1 – Investment by AJ in BK

On 1 April 2002, AJ purchased $2 million loan notes in BK at par.

On 1 April 20X3, AJ purchased 4 million of the ordinary shares in BK for $7.5 million in cash, when BK's reserves were $1.5 million.

At the date of acquisition of the shares, BK's property, plant and equipment included land recorded at a cost of $920,000. At the date of acquisition, the fair value of the land was $1,115,000. No other adjustments in respect of fair value were required to BK's assets and liabilities upon acquisition. BK has not recorded the fair value in its own accounting records.

Note 2 – Investment by AJ in CL

On 1 October 20X4, AJ acquired 1 million shares in CL, a book distributor, when the reserves of CL were $3.9 million. The purchase consideration was $4.4 million. Since the acquisition, AJ has had the right to appoint one of the five directors of CL. The remaining shares in CL are owned principally by three other investors.

No fair value adjustments were required in respect of CL's assets or liabilities upon acquisition.

Note 3 – Goodwill

During March 20X5, AJ conducted an impairment review of goodwill. As a result, the value of goodwill acquired by AJ on the acquisition of BK is now $1.7 million.

Note 4 – Intra-group trading

BK supplies legal books to AJ. On 31 March 20X5, AJ's inventories included books purchased at a total cost of $1 million from BK. BK's mark-up on books is 25%.

Required:

(a)   Explain, with reasons, how the investments in BK and CL will be treated in the consolidated financial statements of the AJ group.   **(5 marks)**

(b)   Prepare the consolidated statement of financial position for the AJ group at 31 March 20X5.
       Full workings should be shown.   **(20 marks)**

                                                    (Total: 25 marks)

ANALYSING AND INTERPRETING FINANCIAL STATEMENTS

52   COMPARATOR

Comparator assembles computer equipment from bought in components and distributes them to various wholesalers and retailers. It has recently subscribed to an interfirm comparison service. Members submit accounting ratios as specified by the operator of the service, and in return, members receive the average figures for each of the specified ratios taken from all of the companies in the same sector that subscribe to the service. The specified ratios and the average figures for Comparator's sector are shown below.

Ratios of companies reporting a full year's results for periods ending between 1 July 20X3 and 30 September 20X3

Return on capital employed	22.1%
Net asset turnover	1.8 times
Gross profit margin	30%
Net profit (before tax) margin	12.5%
Current ratio	1.6:1
Quick ratio	0.9:1
Inventory holding period	46 days
Accounts receivable collection period	45 days
Accounts payable payment period	55 days
Debt to equity	40%
Dividend yield	6%
Dividend cover	3 times

Comparator's financial statements for the year to 30 September 20X3 are set out below:

Statement of comprehensive income

	$000
Revenue	2,425
Cost of sales	(1,870)
Gross profit	555
Other operating expenses	(215)
Operating profit	340
Finance costs	(34)
Exceptional item (note (ii))	(120)
Profit before taxation	186
Income tax	(90)
Profit for the period	96

	$000
Extracts of changes in equity:	
Retained earnings – 1 October 20X2	179
Net profit for the period	96
Dividends paid	(90)
(interim $60,000; final $30,000)	
Retained earnings – 30 September 20X3	185

Statement of financial position

	$000	$000
Non-current assets (note (i))		540
Current assets		
Inventory	275	
Accounts receivable	320	
Bank	nil	595
		1,135
Equity		
Ordinary shares (25 cents each)		150
Retained earnings		185
		335
Non-current liabilities		
8% loan notes		300
Current liabilities		
Bank overdraft	65	
Trade accounts payable	350	
Taxation	85	500
		1,135

Notes

(i) The details of the non-current assets are:

	Cost	Accumulated depreciation	Net book value
	$000	*$000*	*$000*
At 30 September 20X3	3,600	3,060	540

(ii) The exceptional item relates to losses on the sale of a batch of computers that had become worthless due to improvements in microchip design.

(iii) The market price of Comparator's shares throughout the year averaged $6.00 each.

Required:

(a) Explain the problems that are inherent when ratios are used to assess a company's financial performance.

Your answer should consider any additional problems that may be encountered when using interfirm comparison services such as that used by Comparator. **(7 marks)**

(b) Calculate the ratios for Comparator equivalent to those provided by the interfirm comparison service. **(6 marks)**

(c) Write a report analysing the financial performance of Comparator based on a comparison with the sector averages. **(12 marks)**

(Total: 25 marks)

53   RYTETREND

Rytetrend is a retailer of electrical goods. Extracts from the company's financial statements are set out below:

Statement of comprehensive income for the year ended 31 March:	20X3 $000	20X3 $000	20X2 $000	20X2 $000
Revenue		31,800		23,500
Cost of sales		(22,500)		(16,000)
Gross profit		9,300		7,500
Other operating expenses		(5,440)		(4,600)
Operating profit		3,860		2,900
Interest payable – loan notes	(260)		(500)	
overdraft	(200)	(460)	nil	(500)
Profit before taxation		3,400		2,400
Taxation		(1,000)		(800)
Profit for the year		2,400		1,600
Extract from statement of changes in equity				
Retained earnings – brought forward		5,880		4,680
Profit for the year		2,400		1,600
Dividends		(600)		(400)
Retained earnings – carried forward		7,680		5,880

Statements of financial position as at 31 March:

	20X3		20X2	
	$000	$000	$000	$000
Non-current assets (note (i))		24,500		17,300
Current assets				
Inventory	2,650		3,270	
Receivables	1,100		1,950	
Bank	nil		400	
		3,750		5,620
Total assets		28,250		22,920
Equity and liabilities				
Ordinary capital ($1 shares)		11,500		10,000
Share premium		1,500		nil
Retained earnings		7,680		5,880
		20,680		15,880
Non-current liabilities				
10% loan notes		nil		4,000
6% loan notes		2,000		nil
Current liabilities				
Bank overdraft	1,050		nil	
Trade payables	3,300		2,260	
Taxation	720		630	
Warranty provision (note (ii))	500	5,570	150	3,040
Total equity and liabilities		28,250		22,920

Notes

(i) The details of the non-current assets are:

	Cost $000	Accumulated depreciation $000	Net book value $000
At 31 March 20X2	27,500	10,200	17,300
At 31 March 20X3	37,250	12,750	24,500

During the year there was a major refurbishment of display equipment. Old equipment that had cost $6 million in September 19W8 was replaced with new equipment at a gross cost of $8 million. The equipment manufacturer had allowed Rytetrend a trade in allowance of $500,000 on the old display equipment. In addition to this Rytetrend used its own staff to install the new equipment. The value of staff time spent on the installation has been costed at $300,000, but this has not been included in the cost of the asset. All staff costs have been included in operating expenses. All display equipment held at the end of the financial year is depreciated at 20% on its cost. No equipment is more than five years old.

(ii) Operating expenses contain a charge of $580,000 for the cost of warranties on the goods sold by Rytetrend. The company makes a warranty provision when it sells its products and cash payments for warranty claims are deducted from the provision as they are settled.

Required:

(a)   Prepare a statement of cash flows for Rytetrend for the year ended 31 March 20X3.

(12 marks)

(b)   Write a report briefly analysing the operating performance and financial position of Rytetrend for the years ended 31 March 20X2 and 20X3.   **(13 marks)**

Your report should be supported by appropriate ratios.   **(Total: 25 marks)**

54   BIGWOOD

Bigwood, a public company, is a high street retailer that sells clothing and food. The managing director is very disappointed with the current year's results. The company expanded its operations and commissioned a famous designer to restyle its clothing products. This has led to increased sales in both retail lines, yet overall profits are down.

Details of the financial statements for the two years to 30 September 20X4 are shown below.

Statements of comprehensive income:	Year to 30 September 20X4		Year to 30 September 20X3	
	$000	$000	$000	$000
Revenue – clothing	16,000		15,600	
– food	7,000	23,000	4,000	19,600
Cost of sales – clothing	14,500		12,700	
– food	4,750	(19,250)	3,000	(15,700)
Gross profit		3,750		3,900
Other operating expenses		(2,750)		(1,900)
Operating profit		1,000		2,000
Interest expense		(300)		(80)
Profit before tax		700		1,920
Income tax expense		(250)		(520)
Profit for period		450		1,400

Movement on retained earnings:	Year to 30 September 20X4	Year to 30 September 20X3
	$000	$000
Retained earnings b/f	1,900	1,100
Profit for the period	450	1,400
Dividends paid	(600)	(600)
Retained earnings c/f	1,750	1,900

Statements of financial position as at:	Year to 30 September 20X4		Year to 30 September 20X3	
	$000	$000	$000	$000
Property, plant and equipment at cost		17,000		9,500
Accumulated depreciation		(5,000)		(3,000)
		12,000		6,500
Current Assets				
Inventory – clothing	2,700		1,360	
– food	200		140	
Trade receivables	100		50	
Bank	Nil	3,000	450	2,000
Total assets		15,000		8,500
Equity and liabilities				
Issued ordinary capital ($1 shares)		5,000		3,000
Share premium		1,000		Nil
Retained earnings		1,750		1,900
		7,750		4,900
Non-current liabilities				
Long-term loans		3,000		1,000
Current liabilities				
Bank overdraft	930		Nil	
Trade payables	3,100		2,150	
Current tax payable	220	4,250	450	2,600
		15,000		8,500

Note: the directors have signalled their intention to maintain annual dividends at $600,000 for the foreseeable future.

The following information is relevant:

(i)   The increase in property, plant and equipment was due to the acquisition of five new stores and the refurbishment of some existing stores during the year. The carrying value of fixtures scrapped at the refurbished stores was $1.2 million; they had originally cost $3 million. Bigwood received no scrap proceeds from the fixtures, but did incur costs of $50,000 to remove and dispose of them. The losses on the refurbishment have been charged to operating expenses. Depreciation is charged to cost of sales apportioned in relation to floor area (see below).

(ii)   The floor sales areas (in square metres) were:

	30 September 20X4	30 September 20X3
Clothing	48,000	35,000
Food	6,000	5,000
	54,000	40,000

(iii)   The share price of Bigwood averaged $6.00 during the year to 30 September 20X3, but was only $3.00 at 30 September 20X4.

(iv)	The following ratios have been calculated:	*20X4*	*20X3*
	Return on capital employed	9.3%	33.9%
	Net asset turnover	2.1 times	3.3 times
	Gross profit margin		
	– clothing	9.4%	18.6%
	– food	32.1%	25%
	Net profit (after tax) margin	2.0%	7.1%
	Current ratio	0.71:1	0.77:1
	Inventory holding period		
	– clothing	68 days	39 days
	– food	15 days	17 days
	Accounts payable period	59 days	50 days
	Gearing	28%	17%
	Interest cover	3.3 times	25 times

Required:

(a) Prepare, using the indirect method, a statement of cash flows for Bigwood for the year to 30 September 20X4. **(12 marks)**

(b) Write a report analysing the financial performance and financial position of Bigwood for the two years ended 30 September 20X4. **(13 marks)**

Your report should utilize the above ratios and the information in your statement of cash flows. It should refer to the relative performance of the clothing and food sales and be supported by any further ratios you consider appropriate.

(Total: 25 marks)

55 MINSTER

Minster is a publicly listed company. Details of its financial statements for the year ended 30 September 20X6, together with a comparative statement of financial position, are:

Statement of financial position at	*30 September 20X6*		*30 September 20X5*	
	$000	$000	$000	$000
Non-current assets (note (i))				
Property, plant and equipment		1,280		940
Software		135		Nil
Investments at fair value through profit and loss		150		125
		1,565		1,065
Current assets				
Inventories	480		510	
Trade receivables	270		380	
Amounts due from construction contracts	80		55	
Bank	Nil	830	35	980
Total assets		2,395		2,045

	30 September 20X6		30 September 20X5	
	$000	$000	$000	$000
Equity and liabilities				
Equity shares of 25 cents each		500		300
Reserves				
Share premium (note (ii))	150		85	
Revaluation reserve	60		25	
Retained earnings	950	1,160	965	1,075
		1,660		1,375
Non-current liabilities				
9% loan note	120		Nil	
Environmental provision	162		Nil	
Deferred tax	18	30	25	25
Current liabilities				
Trade payables	350		555	
Bank overdraft	25		40	
Current tax payable	60	435	50	645
Total equity and liabilities		2,395		2,045

Statement of comprehensive income for the year ended 30 September 20X6

Revenue	1,397
Cost of sales	(1,110)
Gross profit	287
Operating expenses	(125)
	162
Finance costs (note (i))	(40)
Investment income and gain on investments	20
Profit before tax	142
Income tax expense	(57)
Profit for the year	85

The following supporting information is available:

(i)   Included in property, plant and equipment is a coal mine and related plant that Minster purchased on 1 October 20X5. Legislation requires that in ten years' time (the estimated life of the mine) Minster will have to landscape the area affected by the mining. The future cost of this has been estimated and discounted at a rate of 8% to a present value of $150,000. This cost has been included in the carrying amount of the mine and, together with the unwinding of the discount, has also been treated as a provision. The unwinding of the discount is included within finance costs in the statement of comprehensive income.

Other land was revalued (upward) by $35,000 during the year.

Depreciation of property, plant and equipment for the year was $255,000.

There were no disposals of property, plant and equipment during the year.

The software was purchased on 1 April 20X6 for $180,000.

The market value of the investments had increased during the year by $15,000. There have been no sales of these investments during the year.

(ii)   On 1 April 20X6 there was a bonus (scrip) issue of equity shares of one for every four held utilising the share premium reserve. A further cash share issue was made on 1 June 20X6. No shares were redeemed during the year.

(iii)   A dividend of 5 cents per share was paid on 1 July 20X6.

Required:

(a)   Prepare a statement of cash flows for Minster for the year to 30 September 20X6 in accordance with IAS 7 *Statements of cash flows*.   **(15 marks)**

(b)   Comment on the financial performance and position of Minster as revealed by the above financial statements and your statement of cash flows.   **(10 marks)**

(Total: 25 marks)

56   PENDANT

Pendant is a small family owned business. A client of yours has been asked to provide credit for Pendant. The client has provided you with the statements of financial position and some supporting information for Pendant for the years to 31 March 20X0 and 20X1. The client wants an opinion on Pendant's financial position.

Pendant – Statement of financial position

	31 March 20X1		31 March 20X0	
	$000	$000	$000	$000
Non-current assets				
Property, plant and equipment		1,290		1,120
Software (in development)		300		100
		1,590		1,220
Current assets				
Inventory	490		540	
Trade receivables	787		584	
Investments – Government securities	30		180	
Bank	nil	1,307	125	1,429
Total assets		2,897		2,649
Equity and liabilities				
Equity shares of $1 each		500		400
Reserves				
Share premium	150		80	
Retained earnings	1,084	1,234	1,092	1,172
Equity		1,734		1,572
Non-current liabilities				
Finance lease obligations	290		60	
Deferred tax	12	302	172	232
Current liabilities				
Trade payables	663		602	
Bank overdraft	45		nil	
Taxation	83		213	
Finance lease obligations	70	861	30	845
Total equity and liabilities		2,897		2,649

The following supporting information is available:

(i)   Details relating to the non-current assets are (in $000s):

	31 March 20X1			31 March 20X0		
	Cost	Depreciation	NBV	Cost	Depreciation	NBV
Freehold land and buildings	nil	nil	nil	700	120	580
Leasehold land and buildings	500	20	480	nil	nil	nil
Purchased plant	550	250	300	620	200	420
Plant on finance lease	650	140	510	150	30	120
			1,290			1,120

On 1 April 20X0 Pendant sold its freehold property for $800,000. Pendant then acquired another property on a 25-year lease at a capital cost of $500,000.

The total amount of payments made in the year to 31 March 20X1 in respect of finance leases was $265,000, of which $35,000 was for interest. Interest costs of the bank overdraft were $10,000.

During the same period 'purchased' plant which had originally cost $200,000 was sold for $75,000 giving a profit of $18,000.

(ii)   The total tax charge (including deferred tax) in the statement of comprehensive income for the year to 31 March 20X1 was $31,000.

(iii) During the year some Government securities, which are shown at cost in the statement of financial position, were sold at a profit of $27,000. This profit was credited to the statement of comprehensive income, as was $15,000 of income received from the securities. No other Government securities were traded during the year.

(iv)   Pendant paid an interim dividend during the year to 31 March 20X1 of $150,000.

Required:

(a)   As far as the information permits, prepare a statement of cash flows for Pendant for the year to 31 March 20X1 in accordance with IAS 7 *Statements of cash flows*.

(20 marks)

(b)   Identify the important areas that you would draw your client's attention to based on the information in the question and the statement of cash flows prepared in (a). You are not required to calculate ratios.   **(5 marks)**

(Total: 25 marks)

57   CHARMER

The summarized financial statements of Charmer for the year to 30 September 20X1, together with a comparative statement of financial position, are:

Statement of comprehensive income	$000
Revenue	7,482
Cost of sales	(4,284)
Gross profit	3,198
Operating expenses	(1,479)
Interest payable	(260)
Investment income	120
Profit before tax	1,579
Income tax	(520)
Profit for the period	1,059

Statement of financial position as at:	30 September 20X1			30 September 20X0		
	$000 Cost/valuation	$000 Depreciation	$000 NBV	$000 Cost/valuation	$000 Depreciation	$000 NBV
Assets						
Non-current assets						
Property, plant and equipment	3,568	1,224	2,344	3,020	1,112	1,908
Investment			690			nil
			3,034			1,908
Current assets						
Inventory		1,046			785	
Accounts receivable		935			824	
Short term treasury bills		120			50	
Bank		nil	2,101		122	1,781
Total assets			5,135			3,689
Total equity and liabilities						
Equity:						
Ordinary shares of $1 each			1,400			1,000
Reserves:						
Share premium		460			160	
Revaluation		190			40	
Retained earnings						
b/f	92			47		
Net profit for period	1,059			65		
Dividends	(180)			(20)		
Retained earnings c/f		971	1,621		92	292
			3,021			1,292
Non-current liabilities						
Deferred tax		439			400	
Government grants		275			200	
10% Convertible loan stock		nil	714		400	1,000
Current liabilities						
Trade accounts payable		644			760	
Accrued interest		40			25	
Provision for negligence claim		nil			120	
Provision for income tax		480			367	
Government grants		100			125	
Overdraft		136	1,400		Nil	1,397
Total equity and liabilities			5,135			3,689

The following information is relevant:

(i) *Non-current assets*

Property, plant and equipment is analysed as follows:

	30 September 20X1			30 September 20X0		
	Cost/ valuation	Depreciation	NBV	Cost/ valuation	Depreciation	NBV
	$000	$000	$000	$000	$000	$000
Land and Buildings	2,000	760	1,240	1,800	680	1,120
Plant	1,568	464	1,104	1,220	432	788
	3,568	1,224	2,344	3,020	1,112	1,908

On 1 October 20X0 Charmer recorded an increase in the value of its land of $150,000.

During the year an item of plant that had cost $500,000 and had accumulated depreciation of $244,000 was sold at a loss (included in cost of sales) of $86,000 on its carrying value.

(ii) *Government grant*

A credit of $125,000 for the current year's amortization of government grants has been included in cost of sales.

(iii) *Share capital and loan stocks*

The increase in the share capital during the year was due to the following events:

(1) On 1 January 20X1 there was a bonus issue (out of the share premium account) of one bonus share for every 10 shares held.

(2) On 1 April 20X1 the 10% convertible loan stock holders exercised their right to convert to ordinary shares. The terms of conversion were 25 ordinary shares of $1 each for each $100 of 10% convertible loan stock.

and

(3) The remaining increase in the ordinary shares was due to a stock market placement of shares for cash on 12 August 20X1.

(iv) *Provision for negligence claim*

In June 20X1 Charmer made an out of court settlement of a negligence claim brought about by a former employee. The dispute had been in progress for two years and Charmer had made provisions for the potential liability in each of the two previous years. The unprovided amount of the claim at the time of settlement was $30,000 and this was charged to operating expenses.

Required:

Prepare a statement of cash flows for Charmer for the year to 30 September 20X1 in accordance with IAS 7 *Statements of cash flows*. **(25 marks)**

58 PLANTER

The following information relates to Planter, a small private company. It consists of an opening statement of financial position as at 1 April 20X3 and a listing of the company's ledger accounts at 31 March 20X4 after the draft operating profit (of $15,600) had been calculated.

Planter – Statement of financial position as at 1 April 20X3

	$	$
Non-current assets		
Land and buildings (at valuation $49,200 less accumulated depreciation of $5,000)		44,200
Plant (at cost of $70,000 less accumulated depreciation of $22,500)		47,500
Investments at cost		16,900
		108,600
Current assets		
Inventory	57,400	
Trade receivables	28,600	
Bank	1,200	87,200
Total assets		195,800
Equity and liabilities		
Capital and Reserves:		
Ordinary shares of $1 each		25,000
Reserves:		
Share premium	5,000	
Revaluation reserve	12,000	
Retained earnings	70,300	87,300
		112,300
Non-current liabilities		
8% Loan notes		43,200
Current liabilities		
Trade payables	31,400	
Taxation	8,900	40,300
Total equity and liabilities		195,800

Ledger account listings at 31 March 20X4

	Dr $	Cr $
Ordinary shares of $1 each		50,000
Share premium		8,000
Retained earnings – 1 April 20X3		70,300
Operating profit – year to 31 March 20X4		15,600
Revaluation reserve		18,000
8% Loan notes		39,800
Trade payables		26,700
Accrued loan interest		300
Taxation	1,100	
Land and buildings at valuation	62,300	
Plant at cost	84,600	
Buildings – accumulated depreciation 31 March 20X4		6,800
Plant – accumulated depreciation 31 March 20X4		37,600
Investments at cost	8,200	
Trade receivables	50,400	
Inventory – 31 March 20X4	43,300	
Bank		1,900
Investment income		400
Profit on sale of investments		2,300
Loan interest	1,700	
Ordinary dividend	26,100	
	277,700	277,700

Notes

(i)   There were no disposals of land and buildings during the year. The increase in the revaluation reserve was entirely due to the revaluation of the company's land.

(ii) Plant with a net book value of $12,000 (cost $23,500) was sold during the year for $7,800. The loss on sale has been included in the profit before interest and tax.

(iii) Investments with a cost of $8,700 were sold during the year for $11,000. There were no further purchases of investments. These investments are all in unquoted companies and therefore their fair value cannot be reliably estimated.

(iv) On 10 October 20X3 a bonus issue of 1 for 10 ordinary shares was made utilising the share premium account. The remainder of the increase in ordinary shares was due to an issue for cash on 30 October 20X3.

(v)   The balance on the taxation account is after settlement of the provision made for the year to 31 March 20X3. A provision for the current year has not yet been made.

Required:

From the above information, prepare a statement of cash flows using the indirect method for Planter in accordance with IAS 7 *Statements of cash flows* for the year to 31 March 20X4.

(25 marks)

59   CASINO

(a)   Casino is a publicly listed company. Details of its statements of financial position as at 31 March 20X5 and 20X4 are shown below together with other relevant information:

Statement of financial position as at	31 March 20X5		31 March 20X4	
Non-current assets (note (i))	$m	$m	$m	$m
Property, plant and equipment		880		760
Intangible assets		400		510
		1,280		1,270
Current assets				
Inventory	350		420	
Trade receivables	808		372	
Interest receivable	5		3	
Short term deposits	32		120	
Bank	15	1,210	75	990
Total assets		2,490		2,260
Share capital and reserves				
Ordinary shares of $1 each		300		200
Reserves				
Share premium	60		nil	
Revaluation reserve	112		45	
Retained earnings	1,098	1,270	1,165	1,210
		1,570		1,410
Non-current liabilities				
12% loan note	nil		150	
8% variable rate loan note	160		nil	
Deferred tax	90	250	75	225
Current liabilities				
Trade payables	530		515	
Bank overdraft	125		nil	
Taxation	15		110	
		670		625
Total equity and liabilities		2,490		2,260

The following supporting information is available:

(i) Details relating to the non-current assets are:

Property, plant and equipment at:

	31 March 20X5			31 March 20X4		
	Cost/ Valuation	Depreciation	Carrying value	Cost/ Valuation	Depreciation	Carrying value
	$m	$m	$m	$m	$m	$m
Land and buildings	600	12	588	500	80	420
Plant	440	148	292	445	105	340
			----			----
			880			760

Casino revalued the carrying value of its land and buildings by an increase of $70 million on 1 April 20X4. On 31 March 20X5 Casino transferred $3 million from the revaluation reserve to retained earnings representing the realization of the revaluation reserve due to the depreciation of buildings.

During the year Casino acquired new plant at a cost of $60 million and sold some old plant for $15 million at a loss of $12 million.

There were no acquisitions or disposals of intangible assets.

(ii) The following extract is from the draft statement of comprehensive income for the year to 31 March 20X5:

	$m	$m
Operating loss		(32)
Interest receivable		12
Finance costs		(24)

Loss before tax		(44)
Income tax repayment claim	14	
Deferred tax charge	(15)	(1)
	----	----
Loss for the period		(45)

The finance costs are made up of:		
Interest expenses		(18)
Penalty cost for early redemption of fixed rate loan		(6)
		----
		(24)

(iii) The short-term deposits meet the definition of cash equivalents.

(iv) Dividends of $25 million were paid during the year.

Required:

As far as the information permits, prepare a statement of cash flows for Casino for the year to 31 March 20X5 in accordance with IAS 7 *Statements of cash flows.* **(20 marks)**

(b)   In recent years many analysts have commented on a growing disillusionment with the usefulness and reliability of the information contained in some companies' statements of comprehensive income.

Required:

Discuss the extent to which a company's statement of cash flows may be more useful and reliable than its statement of comprehensive income.   **(5 marks)**

(Total: 25 marks)

60   TABBA

The following draft financial statements relate to Tabba, a private company.

Statements of financial position as at:	*30 September 20X5*		*30 September 20X4*	
	$000	$000	$000	$000
Tangible non-current assets (note (ii))		10,600		15,800
Current assets				
Inventories	2,550		1,850	
Trade receivables	3,100		2,600	
Insurance claim (note (iii))	1,500		1,200	
Cash and bank	850	8,000	nil	5,650
Total assets		18,600		21,450
Equity and liabilities				
Share capital ($1 each)		6,000		6,000
Reserves:				
Revaluation (note (ii))	nil		1,600	
Retained earnings	2,550	2,550	850	2,450
		8,550		8,450
Non-current liabilities				
Finance lease obligations (note (ii))	2,000		1,700	
6% loan notes	800		nil	
10% loan notes	nil		4,000	
Deferred tax	200		500	
Government grants (note (ii))	1,400	4,400	900	7,100
Current liabilities				
Bank overdraft	nil		550	
Trade payables	4,050		2,950	
Government grants (note (ii))	600		400	
Finance lease obligations (note (ii))	900		800	
Current tax payable	100	5,650	1,200	5,900
Total equity and liabilities		18,600		21,450

The following information is relevant:

(i)   Statement of comprehensive income extract for the year ended 30 September 20X5:

	$000
Operating profit before interest and tax	270
Interest expense	(260)
Interest receivable	40
Profit before tax	50
Net tax credit	50
Profit for the period	100

Note: the interest expense includes finance lease interest.

(ii)   The details of the tangible non-current assets are:

	Cost	Accumulated depreciation	Carrying value
	$000	$000	$000
At 30 September 20X4	20,200	4,400	15,800
At 30 September 20X5	16,000	5,400	10,600

During the year Tabba sold its factory for its fair value $12 million and agreed to rent it back, under an operating lease, for a period of five years at $1 million per annum. At the date of sale it had a carrying value of $7.4 million based on a previous revaluation of $8.6 million less depreciation of $1.2 million since the revaluation. The profit on the sale of the factory has been included in operating profit. The surplus on the revaluation reserve related entirely to the factory. No other disposals of non-current assets were made during the year.

Plant acquired under finance leases during the year was $1.5 million. Other purchases of plant during the year qualified for government grants of $950,000 received in the year.

Amortization of government grants has been credited to cost of sales.

(iii) The insurance claim relates to flood damage to the company's inventories which occurred in September 20X4. The original estimate has been revised during the year after negotiations with the insurance company. The claim is expected to be settled in the near future.

Required:

(a)   Prepare a statement of cash flows using the indirect method for Tabba in accordance with IAS 7 *Statements of cash flows* for the year ended 30 September 20X5.

(17 marks)

(b)   Using the information in the question and your statement of cash flows, comment on the change in the financial position of Tabba during the year ended 30 September 20X5.

(8 marks)

Note: you are not required to calculate any ratios.   (Total: 25 marks)

61   PJ GAMEWRITERS

You are assistant to the Finance Director (FD) of OPQ, a well-known retailer of music, video and games products. OPQ's profit margins are under increasing pressure because of the entry of online retailers into the market. As part of their response to this challenge, OPQ's directors have decided to invest in entities in the supply chain of their most popular products. They are currently considering the acquisition of the business that supplies some of its best-selling computer games, PJ Gamewriters (PJ). The FD has asked you, as a preliminary step, to examine the most recent financial statements of the entity.

PJ was established in 19W9 by twin brothers, Paul and James, who had recently graduated in computing. Their first business success was a simulated empire building game; this has continued to bring in a large proportion of PJ's revenue. However, they have also been successful in a range of other games types such as combat simulations, golf and football management games. The business has grown rapidly from year to year, and by 20X5 it employed ten full-time games writers. Manufacture and distribution of the software in various formats is outsourced, and the business operates from office premises in a city centre. PJ bought the freehold of the office premises in 2002, and its estimated market value is now $900,000, nearly $350,000 in excess of the price paid in 2002. Apart from the freehold building, the business owns few non-current assets.

The equity shares in PJ are owned principally by Paul, James and their parents, who provided the initial start-up capital. Paul and James are the sole directors of the business. A small proportion of the shares (around 8%) is owned by five of the senior software writers. PJ is now up for sale as the principal shareholders wish to realize the bulk of their investment in order to pursue other business interests. It is likely that about 90% of the shares will be for sale. The copyrights of the games are owned by PJ, but no value is attributed to them in the financial statements.

PJ's statement of comprehensive income and summarized statement of changes in equity for the year ended 31 July 20X5, and statement of financial position at that date (all with comparatives) are as follows:

PJ: Statement of comprehensive income for the year ended 31 July 20X5

	20X5	20X4
	$000	$000
Revenue	2,793	2,208
Cost of sales (see note below)	(1,270)	(1,040)
Gross profit	1,523	1,168
Operating expenses	(415)	(310)
Profit from operations	1,108	858
Interest receivable	7	2
Profit before tax	1,115	860
Income tax expense	(331)	(290)
Profit for the period	784	570

Note: Cost of sales comprises the following:

	20X5 $000	20X4 $000
Games writers' employment costs	700	550
Production costs	215	160
Directors' remuneration	200	200
Other costs	155	130
	1,270	1,040

PJ: Summarized statement of changes in equity for the year ended 31 July 20X5

	20X5 $000	20X4 $000
Opening balance	703	483
Profit for the period	784	570
Dividends	(500)	(350)
Closing balance	987	703

PJ: Statement of financial position at 31 July 20X5

	20X5 $000	20X5 $000	20X4 $000	20X4 $000
Non-current assets:				
Property, plant and equipment		610		620
Current assets:				
Inventories	68		59	
Trade receivables	460		324	
Cash	216		20	
		744		403
		1,354		1,023
Equity:				
Share capital	60		60	
Retained earnings	927		643	
		987		703
Current liabilities:				
Trade and other payables	36		30	
Income tax	331		290	
		367		320
		1,354		1,023

Required:

(a) Prepare a report on the financial performance and position of PJ Gamewriters, calculating and interpreting any relevant accounting ratios. **(17 marks)**

(b) Explain the limitations of your analysis, identifying any supplementary items of information that would be useful. **(8 marks)**

(Total: 25 marks)

62 DM

DM, a listed entity, has just published its financial statements for the year ended 31 December 20X4. DM operates a chain of 42 supermarkets in one of the six major provinces of its country of operation. During 20X4, there has been speculation in the financial press that the entity was likely to be a takeover target for one of the larger national chains of supermarkets that is currently under-represented in DM's province. A recent newspaper report has suggested that DM's directors are unlikely to resist a takeover. The six board members are all nearing retirement, and all own significant minority shareholdings in the business.

You have been approached by a private shareholder in DM. She is concerned that the directors have a conflict of interests and that the financial statements for 20X4 may have been manipulated.

The statement of comprehensive income and summarized statement of changes in equity of DM, with comparatives, for the year ended 31 December 20X4, and a statement of financial position, with comparatives, at that date are as follows:

DM: Statement of comprehensive income for the year ended 31 December 20X4

	20X4	20X3
	$m	$m
Revenue, net of sales tax	1,255	1,220
Cost of sales	(1,177)	(1,145)
Gross profit	78	75
Operating expenses	(21)	(29)
Profit from operations	57	46
Finance cost	(10)	(10)
Profit before tax	47	36
Income tax expense	(14)	(13)
Profit for the period	33	23

DM: Summarized statement of changes in equity for the year ended 31 December 20X4

	20X4	20X3
	$m	$m
Opening balance	276	261
Profit for the period	33	23
Dividends	(8)	(8)
Closing balance	301	276

DM: Statement of financial position at 31 December 20X4

	20X4		20X3	
	$m	$m	$m	$m
Non-current assets:				
Plant, property and equipment		680		675
Current assets:				
Inventories	47		46	
Trade receivables	12		13	
Cash	46		12	
	____		____	
		105		71
		____		____
		785		746
		____		____
Equity:				
Share capital	150		150	
Retained earnings	151		126	
	____		____	
		301		276
Non-current liabilities:				
Interest-bearing borrowings	142		140	
Deferred tax	25		21	
	____		____	
		167		161
Current liabilities:				
Trade and other payables	297		273	
Short-term borrowings	20		36	
	____		____	
		317		309
		____		____
		785		746
		____		____

Notes:

1   DM's directors have undertaken a reassessment of the useful lives of non-current tangible assets during the year. In most cases, they estimate that the useful lives have increased and the depreciation charges in 20X4 have been adjusted accordingly.

2   Six new stores have been opened during 20X4, bringing the total to 42.

3   Four key ratios for the supermarket sector (based on the latest available financial statements of 12 listed entities in the sector) are as follows:

   (i)   Annual sales per store: $27.6m

   (ii)   Gross profit margin: 5.9%

   (iii)   Net profit margin: 3.9%

   (iv)   Non-current asset turnover: 1.93.

Required:

(a) Prepare a report, addressed to the investor, analysing the performance and position of DM based on the financial statements and supplementary information provided above. The report should also include comparisons with the key sector ratios, and it should address the investor's concerns about the possible manipulation of the 20X4 financial statements. **(20 marks)**

(b) Explain the limitations of the use of sector comparatives in financial analysis.

(5 marks)

(Total: 25 marks)

63 EFG

You are a management accountant at EFG, an entity that has recently embarked upon an aggressive programme of acquisitions in order to grow its market share as rapidly as possible. EFG has targeted J, a well-established entity operating in the same sector, but with a significant level of export sales.

In order to be able to respond to opportunities quickly, EFG has established a basic set of four key financial ratios to assess the performance and position of target businesses. If a business's ratios fall within the set criteria, more detailed analysis will follow, prior to the launch of a formal bid.

The four key ratios and the criteria are as follows:

Gross profit margin	Should exceed 25%
Operating profit margin	Should exceed 13%
Return on total capital employed	Should exceed 25%
Gearing (long-term liabilities/shareholders' funds)	Should not exceed 25%

J's most recent financial statements are as follows:

J: Statement of comprehensive income for the year ended 31 January 20X4

	$000
Revenue	1,810
Cost of sales	(1,381)
Gross profit	429
Operating expenses	(236)
Profit from operations	
Finance cost	193
	(9)
Profit before tax	184
Income tax expense	(50)
Profit for the year	134

J: Statement of changes in equity for the year ended 31 January 20X4

	Share capital $000	Revaluation reserve $000	Retained earnings $000	Total $000
Balance at 1 February 20X3	350	210	96	656
Transfer to realized profits		(10)	10	–
Net profit for period			134	134
Dividends			(21)	(21)
Balance at 31 January 20X4	350	200	219	769

J: Statement of financial position at 31 January 20X4

	$000	$000
Non-current assets:		
Property, plant and equipment		707
Current assets:		
Inventories	201	
Trade receivables	247	
Cash	18	
		466
		1,173
Equity and liabilities:		
Share capital	350	
Revaluation reserve	200	
Retained earnings	219	
		769
Non-current liabilities:		
Long-term borrowings		248
Current liabilities:		
Trade payables	142	
Income tax	14	
		156
		1,173

J's directors, who each hold a significant percentage of the ordinary share capital in the entity, are interested in EFG's potential bid, and they have co-operated fully in providing information. On a recent visit to the entity, EFG's finance director has ascertained that, in many respects, the financial and operating policies of the two businesses are very similar.

However, there are some differences, summarized as follows.

1   J has a policy of revaluation of property, but EFG's key ratios are set on the assumption of valuation at depreciated historical cost. J owns one property, a warehouse building that was revalued five years ago. At that time, the revaluation surplus was $250,000, and the estimated useful life of the property was 25 years, assuming a residual value of nil. J depreciates property on the straight-line basis and recognizes the charge within cost of sales.

2   J employs a highly skilled team of sales representatives who are paid a substantial profit-related bonus at the end of each year. For the year ended 31 January 20X4, the total bonus paid was $96,000, included in operating expenses. EFG's operating policy

does not include the payment of bonuses to staff; the directors prefer to reward staff by a fixed salary. The financial controller estimates that EFG's operating policy would involve payment of additional fixed salaries of $50,000 instead of the bonus.

3   The issued share capital of J includes $50,000 of 4% preferred stock. The directors of EFG believe that this should be classified as a long-term liability.

4   J values inventories using an average cost basis, whereas EFG's valuation policy is first in, first out (FIFO). J's accountants have estimated that the valuation of their opening and closing inventories on a FIFO basis would be:

At 1 February 20X3 $208,000

At 31 January 20X4 $218,000

J's opening inventories at average cost were $197,000.

Required:

(a)   Calculate the four key financial ratios for J *before* making any adjustments in respect of changes required by EFG's financial and operating policies.   **(2 marks)**

(b)   Calculate the four key financial ratios for J *after* making adjustments in respect of changes required by EFG's financial and operating policies. (For this purpose assume that the alteration in respect of the remuneration of sales representatives would take effect from 1 February 20X3.) Using EFG's criteria, advize the directors on whether or not they should pursue the potential acquisition of J.   **(16 marks)**

(c)   Discuss the principal advantages and limitations of EFG's approach to the initial appraisal of acquisition opportunities, identifying any specific weaknesses in the appraisal of J.   **(7 marks)**

(Total: 25 marks)

Note: Ignore any deferred tax implications.

64   BZJ GROUP

You advise a private investor who holds a portfolio of investments in smaller listed companies.Recently, she has received the annual report of the BZJ Group for the financial year ended 31 December 20X5. In accordance with her usual practice, the investor has read the Chairman's statement, but has not looked in detail at the figures.Relevant extracts from the Chairman's statement are as follows:

'Following the replacement of many of the directors, which took place in early March 20X5, your new board has worked to expand the group's manufacturing facilities and to replace non-current assets that have reached the end of their useful lives. A new line of storage solutions was designed during the second quarter and was put into production at the beginning of September. Sales efforts have been concentrated on increasing our market share in respect of storage products, and in leading the expansion into Middle Eastern markets.

The growth in the business has been financed by a combination of loan capital and the issue of additional shares. The issue of 300,000 new $1 shares was fully taken up on 1 November 20X5, reflecting, we believe, market confidence in the group's new management. Dividends have been reduced in 20X5 in order to increase profit retention to fund the further growth planned for 20X6. The directors believe that the implementation of their medium- to long-term strategies will result in increased returns to investors within the next two to three years.'

The group's principal activity is the manufacture and sale of domestic and office furniture. Approximately 40% of the product range is bought in from manufacturers in other countries.

Extracts from the annual report of the BZJ Group are as follows:

BZJ Group: Consolidated statement of comprehensive income for the year ended 31 December 20X5

	20X5 $000	20X4 $000
Revenue	120,366	121,351
Cost of sales	(103,024)	(102,286)
Gross profit	17,342	19,065
Operating expenses	(11,965)	(12,448)
Profit from operations	5,377	6,617
Interest payable	(1,469)	(906)
Profit before tax	3,908	5,711
Income tax expense	(1,125)	(1,594)
Profit for the period	2,783	4,117
Other comprehensive income		
Gain on property revaluation	2,000	Nil
Total comprehensive income for the period	4,783	4,117
Profit attributable to:		
Owners of the parent	2,460	3,676
Minority interest	323	441
	2,783	4,117
Total comprehensive income attributable to:		
Owners of the parent	4,460	3,676
Minority interest	323	441
	4,783	4,117

BZJ Group: Summarized consolidated statement of changes in equity for the year ended 31 December 20X5 (attributable to owners of the parent)

	Share capital $000	Share premium $000	Reval. reserve $000	Retained earnings $000	Total 20X5 $000	Total 20X4 $000
Opening balance	2,800	3,000		18,823	24,623	21,311
Total comprehensive income for the period			2,000	2,460	4,460	3,676
Issue of share capital	300	1,200			1,500	–
Dividends paid 31/12				(155)	(155)	(364)
Closing balance	3,100	4,200	2,000	21,128	30,428	24,623

BZJ Group: Consolidated statement of financial position at 31 December 20X5

	20X5		*20X4*	
	$000	$000	$000	$000
Non-current assets:				
Property, plant and equipment	40,643		21,322	
Goodwill	1,928		1,928	
Trademarks and patents	1,004		1,070	
		43,575		24,320
Current assets:				
Inventories	37,108		27,260	
Trade receivables	14,922		17,521	
Cash	–		170	
		52,030		44,951
		95,605		69,271
Equity:				
Share capital ($1 shares)	3,100		2,800	
Share premium	4,200		3,000	
Revaluation reserve	2,000		–	
Retained earnings	21,128		18,823	
		30,428		24,623
Minority interest		2,270		1,947
		32,698		26,570
Non-current liabilities				
Interest-bearing borrowings		26,700		16,700
Current liabilities:				
Trade and other payables	31,420		24,407	
Income tax	1,125		1,594	
Short-term borrowings	3,662		–	
		36,207		26,001
		95,605		69,271

Required:

(a) Calculate the earnings per share figure for the BZJ Group for the years ended 31 December 20X5 and 20X4, assuming that there was no change in the number of ordinary shares in issue during 20X4. **(3 marks)**

(b) Produce a report for the investor that:

(i) analyses and interprets the financial statements of the BZJ Group, commenting upon the group's performance and position; and **(17 marks)**

(ii) discusses the extent to which the Chairman's comments about the potential for improved future performance are supported by the financial statement information for the year ended 31 December 20X5. **(5 marks)**

(Total: 25 marks)

65   ACQUIRER AND TARGET

You are the accountant of Acquirer. Your company has the strategy of growth by acquisition and your directors have identified an entity, Target, which they wish to investigate with a view to launching a takeover bid. Your directors consider that the directors of Target will contest any bid and will not be very co-operative in providing background information on the entity. Therefore, relevant financial information is likely to be restricted to the publicly available financial statements.

Your directors have asked you to compute key financial ratios from the latest financial statements of Target (for the year ended 30 November 2002) and compare the ratios with those for other entities in a similar sector. Accordingly, you have selected ten broadly similar entities and have presented the directors with the following calculations:

Ratio	Basis of calculation	Ratio for Target	Spread of ratios for comparative entities		
			Highest	Average	Lowest
Gross profit margin	$\dfrac{\text{Gross profit}}{\text{Revenue}}$	42%	44%	38%	33%
Operating profit margin	$\dfrac{\text{Profit from operations}}{\text{Revenue}}$	29%	37%	30%	26%
Return on total capital	$\dfrac{\text{Profit from operations}}{\text{Total capital}}$	73%	92.5%	69%	52%
Interest cover	$\dfrac{\text{Profit from operations}}{\text{Finance cost}}$	1.8 times	3.2 times	2.5 times	1.6 times
Gearing	$\dfrac{\text{Debt capital}}{\text{Total capital}}$	52%	56%	40%	28%
Dividend cover	$\dfrac{\text{Profit after tax}}{\text{Dividend}}$	5.2 times	5 times	4 times	3 times
Inventory turnover	$\dfrac{\text{Cost of sales}}{\text{Closing inventory}}$	4.4 times	4.5 times	4 times	3.2 times
Receivables days	$\dfrac{\text{Trade receivables}}{\text{1 day's sales revenue}}$	51 days	81 days	62 days	49 days

Assume that it is now November 20X3.

Required:

(a)   Using the ratios provided, write a report that compares the financial performance and position of Target to the other entities in the survey. Where an issue arises that reflects particularly favourably or unfavourably on Target, you should assess its relevance to a potential acquirer.   **(16 marks)**

(b)   Identify any reservations you have regarding the extent to which the ratios provided can contribute to an acquisition decision by the directors of Acquirer. You should highlight the extent to which the financial statements themselves might help you to overcome the reservations you have identified.   **(9 marks)**

(Total: 25 marks)

66 INVESTOR

Investor is an entity that seeks to grow by acquisition. The entity is cash rich and is therefore more concerned about the profitability of potential investments than their cash-generating ability. Earnings per share is regarded as a key corporate performance indicator.

The directors have identified two possible targets for takeover – Alpha and Beta. Alpha is a subsidiary of another entity, while the shares in Beta are held by its directors. The most recent audited accounts of Alpha and Beta have been obtained. Both entities disclose earnings per share on a voluntary basis. The directors of Investor have noted that the earnings per share of Alpha is higher than that of Beta and have concluded that the performance of Alpha must therefore be superior.

Statements of comprehensive income of the two entities – year ended 31 March 20X4

	Alpha	Beta
	$000	$000
Revenue	42,000	44,000
Cost of sales	(20,000)	(24,500)
Gross profit	22,000	19,500
Other operating expenses	(15,000)	(14,000)
Profit from operations	7,000	5,500
Finance cost	(290)	(980)
Profit before tax	6,710	4,520
Income tax expense	(2,000)	(1,300)
Net profit for the year	4,710	3,220
Earnings per share	157 cents	107 cents

Other relevant information concerning the two entities:

1 – Alpha's terms of trade

- Alpha has loan capital of $7 million provided by an entity that is part of the same group. Alpha pays interest at 3% per annum on these loans whereas the current market rate is 6% per annum.

- Included in the revenue of Alpha is $15 million representing sales to a fellow subsidiary, Gamma. Alpha earns of profit margin of 60% on these intra-group sales. The profit margin that Alpha earns on sales of similar products outside the group is 50%.

- Alpha receives administrative services from its parent, but no charge is made for the services. The directors of Alpha estimate that the market value of such services in the year ended 31 March 20X4 was $1.5 million. Similar charges borne by Beta are presented in other operating expenses.

2 – Rates of tax

Both entities pay tax at a rate of 30% on profits. All adjustments made to profit (see requirement (b)) are subject to tax at this rate.

3 – Issued capital

Both entities have an issued share capital of $3 million in $1 shares. This issued capital has not changed during the year ended 31 March 20X4.

Required:

(a) Identify the factors that should be considered when comparing the financial statements of two entities for the purposes of decision making. **(6 marks)**

(b) Explain and compute any adjustments you consider should be made to the earnings per share of Alpha, so that the directors of Investor can validly compare this figure with that of Beta.

You should re-compute the earnings per share of Alpha, but you do not need to write out the adjusted statement of comprehensive income of Alpha. **(8 marks)**

(c) Write a report to the directors of Investor identifying the underlying differences between the earnings per share of Alpha and Beta. You should clearly indicate any limitations in your conclusions based on the information available to you. **(11 marks)**

(Total: 25 marks)

67 PHOENIX

Phoenix has carried on business for a number of years as a retailer of a wide variety of consumer products. The company operates from a number of stores around the United Kingdom. In recent years the company has found it necessary to provide credit facilities to its customers in order to maintain growth in sales. As a result of this decision the liability to the company's bankers has increased substantially. The statutory financial statements of the company for the year ended 30 June 20X9 have recently been published and extracts are provided below, together with comparative figures for the previous two years.

Statements of comprehensive income for the years ended 30 June

	20X7	20X8	20X9
	$m	$m	$m
Revenue	1,850	2,200	2,500
Cost of sales	(1,250)	(1,500)	(1,750)
Gross profit	600	700	750
Other operating costs	(550)	(640)	(700)
Operating profit	50	60	50
Interest from credit sales	45	60	90
Interest payable	(25)	(60)	(110)
Profit before taxation	70	60	30
Tax payable	(23)	(20)	(10)
Profit for the period	47	40	20
Dividends paid	30	30	20

Statements of financial position at 30 June

	20X7 $m	20X8 $m	20X9 $m
Tangible non-current assets	278	290	322
Inventories	400	540	620
Trade receivables	492	550	633
Cash	12	12	15
Trade and other payables	(300)	(300)	(300)
Tax payable	(20)	(20)	(8)
Bank loans	(320)	(520)	(610)
Other interest-bearing borrowings	(200)	(200)	(320)
	342	352	352
Share capital	90	90	90
Reserves	252	262	262
	342	352	352

Other information

- Depreciation charged for the three years in question was as follows:

Year ended 30 June:	20X7 $m	20X8 $m	20X9 $m
	55	60	70

- The other interest bearing borrowings are secured by a floating charge over the assets of Phoenix. Their repayment is due on 30 June 20Y9.

- The bank loans are unsecured. The maximum lending facility the bank will provide is $630m.

- Over the past three years the level of credit sales has been:

Year ended 30 June:	20X7 $m	20X8 $m	20X9 $m
	300	400	600

The company offers extended credit terms for certain products to maintain market share in a highly competitive environment.

Given the steady increase in the level of bank loans which has taken place in recent years, the company has recently written to its bankers to request an increase in the lending facility. The request was received by the bank on 15 October 20X9, two weeks after the 20X9 statutory accounts were published. The bank is concerned at the steep escalation in the level of the loans and has asked for a report on the financial performance of Phoenix for the last three years.

Required:

As a consultant management accountant employed by the bankers of Phoenix, prepare a report to the bank which analyses the financial performance of Phoenix for the period covered by the financial statements. Your report may take any form you wish, but you are aware of the particular concern of the bank regarding the rapidly increasing level of lending. Therefore it may be appropriate to include aspects of performance that could have contributed to the increase in the level of bank lending. **(25 marks)**

68 EXPAND AGAIN

You are the management accountant of Expand – a large group that seeks to grow by acquisition. The directors of Expand have identified two potential target entities (A and B) and obtained copies of their financial statements. Extracts from these financial statements, together with notes providing additional information, are given below:

Statements of comprehensive income – year ended 31 December 20X1

	A	B
	$000	$000
Revenue	68,000	66,000
Cost of sales	(42,000)	(45,950)
Gross profit	26,000	20,050
Other operating expenses	(18,000)	(14,000)
Profit from operations	8,000	6,050
Finance cost	(3,000)	(4,000)
Profit before tax	5,000	2,050
Income tax expense	(1,500)	(1,000)
Profit for the period	3,500	1,050
Other comprehensive income		
Gain on property revaluation	Nil	6,000
Total comprehensive income for the period	3,500	7,050

Statements of changes in equity – year ended 31 December 20X1

	A	B
	$000	$000
Balance at 1 January 20X1	22,000	16,000
Total comprehensive income for the period	3,500	7,050
Dividends paid	(2,000)	(1,000)
Balance at 31 December 20X1	23,500	22,050

Statements of financial position at 31 December 20X1

	A		B	
	$000	$000	$000	$000
Non-current assets:				
Property, plant and equipment	32,000		35,050	
		32,000		35,050
Current assets:				
Inventories	6,000		7,000	
Trade receivables	12,000		10,000	
		18,000		17,000
		50,000		52,050
Equity:				
Share capital ($1 shares)		16,000		12,000
Revaluation reserve		Nil		5,000
Retained earnings		7,500		5,050
		23,500		22,050
Non-current liabilities				
Long-term borrowings		16,000		18,000
Current liabilities				
Trade payables	5,000		5,000	
Income tax	1,500		1,000	
Short-term borrowings	4,000		6,000	
		10,500		12,000
		50,000		52,050

Notes to the financial statements

(1)   Sale by A to X

On 31 December 20X1, A supplied goods, at the normal selling price of $2.4 million, to another company, X. A's normal selling price is at a mark up of 60% on cost. X paid for the goods in cash on the same day. The terms of the selling agreement were that A would repurchase these goods on 30 June 2002 for $2.5 million. A has accounted for the transaction as a sale.

(2)   Revaluation of non-current assets by B

B revalued its non-current assets for the first time on 1 January 20X1. The non-current assets of A are very similar in age and type to the non-current assets of B. However, A has a policy of maintaining all its non-current assets at depreciated historical cost. Both companies charge depreciation of non-current assets to cost of sales. A has transferred the excess depreciation for the year of $1 million on the revalued assets from the revaluation reserve to retained earnings.

Expand uses ratio analysis to appraise potential investment opportunities. It is normal practice to base the appraisal on four key ratios:

- return on capital employed
- gross profit margin
- turnover of capital employed
- gearing.

For the purposes of the ratio analysis, Expand computes:

(i)   capital employed as capital and reserves plus borrowings;

(ii)   borrowings as long-term borrowings plus short-term borrowings.

Your assistant has computed the four key ratios for the two enterprises from the financial statements provided and the results are summarized below:

Ratio	A	B
Return on capital employed	18.4%	13.1%
Gross profit margin	38.2%	30.4%
Turnover of capital employed	1.6	1.4
Gearing	46.0%	52.1%

Your assistant has informed you that, on the basis of the ratios calculated, the performance of A is superior to that of B in all respects. Therefore, Expand should carry out a more detailed review of A with a view to making a bid to acquire it. However, you are unsure whether this is necessarily the correct conclusion given the information provided in Notes 1 and 2.

Required:

(a)   Explain and compute the adjustments that would be appropriate in respect of Notes 1 and 2 so as to make the financial statements of A and B comparable for analysis.

(12 marks)

(b)   Recalculate the four key ratios mentioned in the question for both A and B AFTER making the adjustments you have recommended in your answer to part (a). You should provide appropriate workings to support your calculations.   **(6 marks)**

(c)   In the light of the work that you have carried out in answer to parts (a) and (b), evaluate your assistant's conclusion that a more detailed review of A should be carried out, with a view to making a bid to acquire it.   **(7 marks)**

(Total: 25 marks)

Section 2

ANSWERS TO PRACTICE QUESTIONS

A CONCEPTUAL FRAMEWORK FOR FINANCIAL REPORTING

1   IASB FRAMEWORK

Key answer tips

Parts (a) and (b) are very straightforward if you have done your work properly. The three adjustments required in part (c) focus on controversial areas. Remember that with compound financial instruments such as a convertible loan, the liability amount is calculated by discounting the cash flows at the rate applicable to a non-convertible loan; this rate will be higher than the rate on the convertible, because it does not include the 'equity sweetener'.

(a)   The purpose of the Framework is to assist the various bodies and users that may be interested in the financial statements of an entity. It is there to assist the IASB itself, other standard setters, preparers, auditors and users of financial statements and any other party interested in the work of the IASB. More specifically:

  –   to assist the Board in the development of new and the review of existing standards.It is also believed that the Framework will assist in promoting harmonization of the preparation of financial statements and also reduce the number of alternative accounting treatments permitted by IFRSs

  –   national standard setters that have expressed a desire for local standards to be compliant with IFRS will be assisted by the Framework

  –   the Framework will help preparers to apply IFRS more effectively if they understand the concepts underlying the Standards; additionally the Framework should help in dealing with new or emerging issues which are, as yet, not covered by an IFRS

  –   the above is also true of the work of the auditor; in particular the Framework can assist the auditor in determining whether the financial statements conform to IFRS

  –   users should be assisted by the Framework in interpreting the performance of entities that have complied with IFRS.

It is important to realize that the Framework is not itself an accounting standard and thus cannot override a requirement of a specific standard. Indeed, the Board recognizes that there may be (rare) occasions where a particular IFRS is in conflict with the Framework; in these cases the requirements of the standard should prevail. The Board believes that such conflicts will diminish over time as the development of new and (revised) existing standards will be guided by the Framework and the Framework itself is being revised based on the experience of working with it.

(b) **Definition of assets:**

The IASB's Framework defines assets as 'a resource controlled by an entity as a result of past events and from which future economic benefits are expected to flow to the entity'. The first part of the definition puts the emphasis on control rather than ownership. This is done so that the statement of financial position reflects the substance of transactions rather than their legal form. This means that assets that are not legally owned by an entity, but over which the entity has the rights that are normally conveyed by ownership, are recognized as assets of the entity. Common examples of this would be finance leased assets and other contractual rights such as aircraft landing rights. An important aspect of control of assets is that it allows the entity to restrict the access of others to them. The reference to past events prevents assets that may arise in future from being recognized early.

Definition of liabilities:

The IASB's Framework defines liabilities as 'a present obligation of the entity arising from past events, the settlement of which is expected to result in an outflow from the entity of resources embodying economic benefits'. Many aspects of this definition are complementary (as a mirror image) to the definition of assets, however the IASB stresses that the essential characteristic of a liability is that the entity has a present obligation. Such obligations are usually legally enforceable (by a binding contract or by statute), but obligations also arise where there is an expectation (by a third party) of an entity assuming responsibility for costs where there is no legal requirement to do so. Such obligations are referred to as constructive (by IAS 37 *Provisions, contingent liabilities and contingent assets*). An example of this would be repairing or replacing faulty goods (beyond any warranty period) or incurring environmental costs (e.g. landscaping the site of a previous quarry) where there is no legal obligation to do so. Where entities do incur constructive obligations it is usually to maintain the goodwill and reputation of the entity. One area of difficulty is where entities cannot be sure whether an obligation exists or not; it may depend upon a future uncertain event. These are more generally known as contingent liabilities.

Importance of the definitions of assets and liabilities:

The definitions of assets and liabilities are fundamental to the Framework. Apart from forming the obvious basis for the preparation of a statement of financial position, they are also the two elements of financial statements that are used to derive the equity interest (ownership) which is the residue of assets less liabilities. Assets and liabilities also have a part to play in determining when income (which includes gains) and expenses (which include losses) should be recognized. Income is recognized (in the statement of comprehensive income) when there is an increase in future economic benefits relating to increases in assets or decreases in liabilities, provided they can be measured reliably. Expenses are the opposite of this. Changes in assets and liabilities arising from contributions from, and distributions to, the owners are excluded from the definitions of income and expenses.

Currently there is a great deal of concern over 'off balance sheet finance'. This is an aspect of what is commonly referred to as creative accounting. Many recent company failure scandals have been in part due to companies having often massive liabilities that have not been included on the statement of financial position. Robust definitions, based on substance, of assets and liabilities in particular should ensure that only real assets are included on the statement of financial position and all liabilities are also included. In contradiction to the above point, there have also been occasions where companies have included liabilities on their statements of financial position where they do not meet the definition of liabilities in the Framework. Common examples of this are general provisions and accounting for future costs and losses (usually as part of the acquisition of a subsidiary). Companies have used these general provisions to smooth profits, i.e. creating a provision when the company has a good year (in terms of profit) and releasing them to boost profits in a bad year. Providing for future costs and losses during an acquisition may effectively allow them to bypass the statement of comprehensive income as they would become part of the goodwill figure.

(c) (i) Whilst it is acceptable to value the goodwill of $2.5 million of Trantor (the subsidiary) on the basis described in the question and include it in the consolidated statement of financial position, the same treatment cannot be afforded to Peterlee's own goodwill. The calculation may indeed give a realistic value of $4 million for Peterlee's goodwill, and there may be no difference in nature between the goodwill of the two companies, but it must be realized that the goodwill of Peterlee is internal goodwill and IFRSs prohibit such goodwill appearing in the financial statements. The main basis of this conclusion is one of reliable measurement. The value of acquired (purchased) goodwill can be evidenced by the method described in the question (there are also other acceptable methods), but this method of valuation is not acceptable as a basis for recognising internal goodwill.

(ii) Accruing for future costs such as this landscaping on an annual basis may seem appropriate and was common practice until recently. However, it is no longer possible to account for this type of future cost in this manner, so the directors' suggestion is unacceptable. IAS 37 *Provisions, contingent liabilities and contingent assets* requires such costs to be accounted for in full as soon as they become unavoidable. The Standard says that the estimate of the future cost should be discounted to a present value (as in this example at $2 million). The accounting treatment is rather controversial; the cost should be included in the statement of financial position as a provision (a credit entry/balance), but the debit is to the cost of the asset to give an initial carrying amount of $8 million. This has the effect of 'grossing up' the statement of financial position by including the landscaping costs as both an asset and a liability. As the asset is depreciated on a systematic basis ($800,000 per annum assuming straight-line depreciation), the landscaping costs are charged to the statement of comprehensive income over the life of the asset. As the discount is 'unwound' (and charged as a finance cost) this is added to the statement of financial position provision such that, at the date when the liability is due to be settled, the provision is equal to the amount due (assuming estimates prove to be accurate).

(iii) The directors' suggestion that the convertible loan should be recorded as a liability of the full $5 million is incorrect. The reason why a similar loan without the option to convert to equity shares (such that it must be redeemed by cash only) carries a higher interest rate is because of the value of the equity option that is contained within the issue proceeds of the $5 million. If the company performs well over the period of the loan, the value of its equity shares should rise and thus it would (probably) be beneficial for the loan note holders to opt for the equity share alternative. IAS 32 and 39 dealing with financial instruments require the value of the option is to be treated as equity rather than debt. The calculation of value of the equity is as follows:

	$000
Year 1 400 × 0.91	364
Year 2 400 × 0.83	332
Year 3 (5,000 + 400) × 0.75	4,050
Present value of the cash flows at 10% = initial liability	4,746
Proceeds of issue	5,000
Equity (β)	254
The 20X6 finance charge in the statement of comprehensive income is 10% × 4,746	475
The end-20X6 liability is 4,746 + 475 – interest paid (8% × 5,000)	4,821

2   ANGELINO

Key answer tips

Part (a) is a fairly standard discussion but in part (b) you must apply your knowledge to receivables factoring, sale and leaseback and consignment inventory. These are likely to be popular areas of the syllabus with the examiner.

(a)   Most forms of off balance sheet financing have the effect of what is, in substance, debt finance either not appearing on the statement of financial position at all or being netted off against related assets such that it is not classified as debt. Common examples would be structuring a lease such that it fell to be treated as an operating lease when it has the characteristics of a finance lease, complex financial instruments classified as equity when they may have, at least in part, the substance of debt and 'controlled' entities having large borrowings (used to benefit the group as a whole), that are not consolidated because the financial structure avoids the entities meeting the definition of a subsidiary.

The main problem of off balance sheet finance is that it results in financial statements that do not faithfully represent the transactions and events that have taken place. Faithful representation is an important qualitative characteristic of useful information (as described in the *Framework for the preparation and presentation of financial statements*). Financial statements that do not faithfully represent that which they purport to lack reliability. A lack of reliability may mean that any decisions made on the basis of the information contained in financial statements are likely to be incorrect or, at best, suboptimal.

The level of debt on a statement of financial position is a direct contributor to the calculation of an entity's statement of financial position gearing, which is considered as one of the most important financial ratios. It should be understood that, to a point, the use of debt financing is perfectly acceptable. Where statement of financial position gearing is considered low, borrowing is relatively inexpensive, often tax efficient and can lead to higher returns to shareholders. However, when the level of borrowings becomes high, it increases risk in many ways. Off balance sheet financing may lead to a breach of loan covenants (a serious situation) if such debt were to be recognized on the statement of financial position in accordance with its substance.

High gearing is a particular issue to equity investors. Equity (ordinary shares) is sometimes described as residual return capital. This description identifies the dangers (to owners) when an entity has high gearing. The dividend that the equity shareholders might expect is often based on the level of reported profits. The finance cost of debt acts as a reduction of the profits available for dividends. As the level of debt increases, higher interest rates are also usually payable to reflect the additional risk borne by the lender, thus the higher the debt the greater the finance charges and the lower the profit. Many off balance sheet finance schemes also disguise or hide the true finance cost which makes it difficult for equity investors to assess the amount of profits that will be needed to finance the debt and consequently how much profit will be available to equity investors. Furthermore, if the market believes or suspects an entity is involved in 'creative accounting' (and off balance sheet finance is a common example of this) it may adversely affect the entity's share price.

An entity's level of gearing will also influence any decision to provide further debt finance (loans) to the entity. Lenders will consider the nature and value of the assets that an entity owns which may be provided as security for the borrowings. The presence of existing debt will generally increase the risk of default of interest and capital repayments (on further borrowings) and existing lenders may have a prior charge on assets available as security. In simple terms if an entity has high borrowings, additional borrowing is more risky and consequently more expensive. A prospective lender to an entity that already has high borrowings, but which do not appear on the statement of financial position is likely to make the wrong decision. If the correct level of borrowings were apparent, either the lender would not make the loan at all (too high a lending risk) or, if it did make the loan, it would be on substantially different terms (e.g. charge a higher interest rate) so as to reflect the real risk of the loan.

Some forms of off balance sheet financing may specifically mislead suppliers that offer credit. It is a natural precaution that a prospective supplier will consider the statement of financial position strength and liquidity ratios of the prospective customer. The existence of consignment inventories may be particularly relevant to trade suppliers. Sometimes consignment inventories and their related current liabilities are not recorded on the statement of financial position as the wording of the purchase agreement may be such that the legal ownership of the goods remains with the supplier until specified events occur (often the onward sale of the goods). This means that other suppliers cannot accurately assess an entity's true level of trade payables and consequently the average payment period to suppliers, both of which are important determinants in deciding whether to grant credit.

(b) (i) Factoring is a common method of entities releasing the liquidity of their trade receivables. The accounting issue that needs to be decided is whether the trade receivables have been sold, or whether the income from the finance house for their 'sale' should be treated as a short term loan. The main substance issue with this type of transaction is to identify which party bears the risks (i.e. of slow and non-payment by the customer) relating to the asset. If the risk lies with the finance house (Omar), the trade receivables should be removed from the statement of financial position (derecognized in accordance with IAS 39). In this case it is clear that Angelino still bears the risk relating to slow and non-payment. The residual payment by Omar depends on how quickly the receivables are collected; the longer it takes, the less the residual payment (this imputes a finance cost). Any balance uncollected by Omar after six months will be refunded by Angelino which reflects the non-payment risk.

Thus the correct accounting treatment for this transaction is that the cash received from Omar (80% of the selected receivables) should be treated as a current liability (a short term loan) and the difference between the gross trade receivables and the amount ultimately received from Omar (plus any amounts directly from the credit customers themselves) should be recognized in profit or loss. The classification of the amount recognized is likely to be a mixture of administrative expenses (for Omar collecting receivables), finance expenses (reflecting the time taken to collect the receivables) and the impairment of trade receivables (bad debts).

(ii)   This is an example of a sale and leaseback of a property. Such transactions are part of normal commercial activity, often being used as a way to improve cash flow and liquidity. However, if an asset is sold at an amount that is different to its fair value there is likely to be an underlying reason for this. In this case it appears (based on the opinion of the auditor) that Finaid has paid Angelino $2 million more than the building is worth. No (unconnected) company would do this knowingly without there being some form of 'compensating' transaction. This sale is 'linked' to the five year rental agreement. The question indicates the rent too is not at a fair value, being $500,000 per annum ($1,300,000 – $800,000) above what a commercial rent for a similar building would be.

It now becomes clear that the excess purchase consideration of $2 million is an 'in substance' loan (rather than sales proceeds – the legal form) which is being repaid through the excess ($500,000 per annum) of the rentals. Although this is a sale and leaseback transaction, as the building is freehold and has an estimated remaining life (20 years) that is much longer than the five year leaseback period, the lease is not a finance lease and the building should be treated as sold and thus derecognized.

The correct treatment for this item is that the sale of the building should be recorded at its fair value of $10 million, thus the profit on disposal would be $2.5 million ($10 million – $7.5 million). The 'excess' of $2 million ($12 million – $10 million) should be treated as a loan (non-current liability). The rental payment of $1.3 million should be split into three elements; $800,000 building rental cost, $200,000 finance cost (10% of $2 million) and the remaining $300,000 is a capital repayment of the loan.

(iii) The treatment of consignment inventory depends on the substance of the arrangements between the manufacturer and the dealer (Angelino). The main issue is to determine if and at what point in time the cars are 'sold'. The substance is determined by analysing which parties bear the risks (e.g. slow moving/obsolete inventories, finance costs) and receive the benefits (e.g. use of inventories, potential for higher sales, protection from price increases) associated with the transaction.

Supplies from Monza

Angelino has, and has actually exercised, the right to return the cars without penalty (or been required by Monza to transfer them to another dealer), which would indicate that it has not 'bought' the cars. There are no finance costs incurred by Angelino, however Angelino would suffer from any price increases that occurred during the three month holding/display period. These factors seem to indicate that the substance of this arrangement is the same as its legal form i.e. Monza should include the cars in its statement of financial position as inventory and therefore Angelino will not record a purchase transaction until it becomes obliged to pay for the cars (three months after delivery or until sold to customers if sooner).

Supplies from Capri

Although this arrangement seems similar to the above, there are several important differences. Angelino is bearing the finance costs of 1% per month (calling it a display charge is a distraction). The option to return the cars should be ignored because it is not likely to be exercised due to commercial penalties (payment of transport costs and loss of deposit). Finally the purchase price is fixed at the date of delivery rather than at the end of six months. These factors strongly indicate that Angelino bears the risks and rewards associated with ownership and should recognize the inventory and the associated liability in its financial statements at the date of delivery.

3   REVENUE RECOGNITION

Key answer tips

The introductory paragraph is there to set the scene and to lead you in the general direction that the Examiner intends you to go. Therefore in part (a) it is not enough to discuss general examples of the differences between substance and form without relating this to revenue recognition issues.

Be prepared to consider other issues in the rest of your answer, for example part (c) tests your knowledge of IASs 20 and 37 and part (d) also tests your knowledge of IAS 8.

(a)   The *Framework* advocates that revenue recognition issues are resolved within the definition of assets (gains) and liabilities (losses). Gains include all forms of income and revenue as well as gains on non-revenue items. Gains and losses are defined as increases or decreases in net assets other than those resulting from transactions with owners. Thus in its *Framework*, the IASB takes a statement of financial position approach to defining revenue. In effect a recognisable increase in an asset results in a gain. The more traditional view, which is largely the basis used in IAS 18 *Revenue*, is that (net) revenue recognition is part of a transactions based accruals or matching process with the statement of financial position recording any residual assets or liabilities such as receivables and payables. The issue of revenue recognition arises out of the need to report company performance for specific periods. The *Framework* identifies three stages in the recognition of assets (and liabilities):

- initial recognition, when an item first meets the definition of an asset;

- subsequent remeasurement, which may involve changing the value (with a corresponding effect on income) of a recognized item; and

- possible derecognition, where an item no longer meets the definition of an asset.

For many simple transactions both the *Framework's* approach and the traditional approach (IAS 18) will result in the same profit (net income). If an item of inventory is bought for $100 and sold for $150, net assets have increased by $50 and the increase would be reported as a profit. The same figure would be reported under the traditional transactions based reporting (sales of $150 less cost of sales of $100). However, in more complex areas the two approaches can produce different results.

An example of this would be deferred income. If a company received a fee for a 12 month tuition course in advance, IAS 18 would treat this as deferred income (on the statement of financial position) and release it to income as the tuition is provided and matched with the cost of providing the tuition. Thus the profit would be spread (accrued) over the period of the course. If an asset/liability approach were taken, then the only liability the company would have after the receipt of the fee would be for the cost of providing the course. If only this liability is recognized in the statement of financial position, the whole of the profit on the course would be recognized on receipt of the income. This is not a prudent approach and has led to criticism of the *Framework* for this very reason. Arguably the treatment of government grants under IAS 20 (as deferred income) does not comply with the Framework as deferred income does not meet the definition of a liability.

Other standards that may be in conflict with the Framework are the use of the accretion approach in IAS 11 *Construction Contracts* and a deferred tax liability in IAS 12 *Income Taxes* may not fully meet the *Framework's* definition of a liability.

The principle of substance over form should also be applied to revenue recognition. An example of where this can impact on reporting practice is on sale and repurchase agreements. Companies sometimes 'sell' assets to another company with the right to buy them back on predetermined terms that will almost certainly mean that they will be repurchased in the future. In substance this type of arrangement is a secured loan and the 'sale' should not be treated as revenue. A less controversial area of the application of substance in relation to revenue recognition is with agency sales. IAS 18 says, where a company sells goods acting as an agent, those sales should not be treated as sales of the agent, instead only the commission from the sales is income of the agent. Recently several internet companies have been accused of boosting their revenue figures by treating agency sales as their own.

(b)   Sales made by Derringdo of goods from Gungho must be treated under two separate categories. Sales of the A grade goods are made by Derringdo acting as an agent of Gungho. For these sales Derringdo must only record in revenue the amount of commission (12.5%) it is entitled to under the sales agreement. There may also be a receivable or payable for Gungho in the statement of financial position. Sales of the B grade goods are made by Derringdo acting as a principal, not an agent. Thus they will be included in revenue with their cost included in cost of sales.

	$000
Revenue (4,600 (W1) + 11,400 (W2))	16,000
Cost of sales (W2)	(8,550)
Gross profit	7,450

Workings: (all figures in $000)	*A grade*
(W1) **Opening inventory**	2,400
Transfers/purchases	18,000
	20,400
Closing inventory	(2,000)
Cost of sales	18,400
Selling price (to give 50% gross profit)	36,800
Gross profit	18,400
Commission (12.5% × 36,800)	4,600

	B grade
(W2) **Opening inventory**	1,000
Transfers/purchases	8,800
	9,800
Closing inventory	(1,250)
Cost of sales	8,550
Selling price (8,550 × 4 /3 see below)	11,400

A gross profit margin of 25% is equivalent to a mark up on cost of $^1/_3$. Thus if cost of sales is multiplied by $^4/_3$ this will give the relevant selling price.

(c)   (i)   The IASB's *Framework* defines liabilities as obligations to transfer economic benefits as a result of past transactions. Such transfers of economic benefits are to third parties and normally as cash payments. Traditionally and in compliance with IAS 20, capital based government grants are treated as deferred credits and spread over the life of the related assets. This is the application of the matching concept. A strict interpretation of the *Framework* would not normally allow deferred credits to be treated as liabilities as there is usually no obligation to transfer economic benefits. In this particular example the only liability that may occur in respect of the grant would be if Derringdo were to sell the related asset within four years of its purchase. A possible argument would be that the grant should be treated as a reducing liability (in relation to a potential repayment) over the four-year claw back period. On closer consideration this would not be appropriate. The repayment would only occur if the asset were sold, thus it is potentially a contingent liability. As Derringdo has no intention to sell the asset there is no reason to believe that the repayment will occur, thus it is not a reportable contingent liability. The implication of this is that the company's policy for the government grant does not comply with the definition of a liability in the *Framework*. Applying the guidance in the *Framework* would require the whole of the grant to be included in income as it is 'earned' i.e. in the year of receipt.

(ii)   **Treatment under the company's policy**

Statement of comprehensive income extract year to 31 March 20X3

	$
Depreciation – plant ((800,000 – 120,000 estimated residual value)/10 years $\times$ $^6/_{12}$)	Dr 34,000
Government grant ((800,000 $\times$ 30%)/10 years $\times$ $^6/_{12}$)	Cr 12,000
Statement of financial position extracts as at 31 March 20X3	$
Non-current assets:	
Plant at cost	800,000
Accumulated depreciation	(34,000)
	766,000
Current liabilities:	
Government grant (240,000/10 years)	24,000
Non-current liabilities:	
Government grant (240,000 – 12,000 – 24,000)	204,000

Treatment under the *Framework*

Statement of comprehensive income extract year to 31 March 20X3	$
Depreciation – plant ((800,000 – 120,000 estimated residual value) /10 years $\times$ $^6/_{12}$)	Dr 34,000
Government grant (whole amount)	Cr 240,000
Statement of financial position extracts as at 31 March 20X3	$
Non-current assets:	
Plant at cost	800,000
Accumulated depreciation	(34,000)
	766,000

(d)   On first impression, it appears that the company has changed its accounting policy from recognising carpet sales at the point of fitting to recognising them at the point when they are ordered and paid for. If this were the case then the new accounting policy should be applied as if it had always been in place and the revenue recognized in the year to 31 March 20X3 would be $23 million. Without the change in policy, sales would have been $22.6 million (23m + 1.2m – 1.6m). Sales made from the retail premises during the current year, but not yet fitted ($1.6 million) will not be recognized until the following period. A corresponding adjustment is made recognising the equivalent figure ($1.2 million) from the previous year. The difference between the $23 million and $22.6 million would be a prior period adjustment (less the cost of sales relating to this amount). This analysis assumes that the figures are material.

Despite first impressions, the above is not a change of accounting policy. This is because a change of accounting policy only occurs where the same circumstances are treated differently. In this case there are different circumstances. Derringdo has changed its method of trading; it is no longer responsible for any errors that may occur during the fitting of the carpets. An accounting policy that is applied to circumstances that differ from previous circumstances is not a change of accounting policy. Thus the amount to be recognized in revenue for the year to 31 March 20X3 would be $24.2 million (23m + 1.2m). Whilst this appears to boost the current year's income it would be mitigated by the payments to the sub-contractors for the carpet fitting.

4   HISTORIC COST

Key answer tips

(a)   Describe the effect of price inflation on the statement of financial position and the statement of comprehensive income. Move on to describe the limitations of the use of HCA as a means of assessing a business's performance. Do not forget to describe how three different users may be misled by such information.

(b)   GPP   •   *advantages:* transaction based, objective, verifiable, adjusted by government inflation index.

        •   understood by shareholders.

        •   *disadvantages:* statistical; relevance of government index depends on company's activities; misleading for highly geared companies.

        CCA   •   *advantages:* corrects most limitations of HCA; reflects current values; more relevant to calculations of dividends, wage claims.

        •   *disadvantages:* difficulty in setting values; methods of determining values; effect on share prices.

(a)   The main drawback of the use of historic cost accounts for assessing the performance of a business is that they do not take into account the current values of assets and, to a lesser extent, liabilities. This can become a serious problem and give misleading information when either specific or general price inflation rates are considered to be high. The effect is that many of the values of the assets in the statement of financial position are understated, and, partly because of related depreciation, profits tend to be overstated. More detailed criticisms of historic cost accounts during a period of rising prices are:

Effects on the statement of financial position

(i)   Most non-current assets can be considerably understated in terms of their current worth. The most affected assets tend to be land and buildings, investments and some plant.

(ii)   In general net current assets tend not to be affected by inflation mainly because they are monetary in nature. The possible exception is trading inventories.

(iii)   Liabilities tend to be ignored when current values are discussed. This may be an error because, for example, a long term loan carrying a fixed rate of interest, may have a current value that is considerably different to when it was taken out (ignoring the possibility of any repayments). This is because current interest rates may have changed (often as a reaction to levels of inflation) since the loan was originally taken out.

(iv)   The statement of financial position equation dictates that if the net assets are understated, then so too are equity.

Effects on the statement of comprehensive income

Many costs tend to be understated in terms of their current value. Where this occurs it means the profit is overstated in as much as the use of lower costs leads to a higher profit. Many commentators argue that pure historical cost profits are made up of a current operating profit (see below) plus inflationary gains relating to the:

- costs of goods sold (both purchased and manufactured). This can be mitigated, but not completely removed, by the use of LIFO, however this is not common practice in many countries and is now prohibited by IAS 2 *Inventories*

- depreciation charges for non-current assets. In historic cost accounts these are based on historical values rather than current values, and therefore understate the values of the assets that have been used (consumed) during the period

- some methods of accounting for inflation include monetary working capital and/or 'gearing' adjustments to historical cost profits. These are intended to reflect the inflation effects of holding net monetary working capital and debt.

The above combined effects lead to the following criticisms and limitations of the use of historic cost accounts to assess a business's performance:

Lack of comparability

It may be invalid to compare the results of two companies. One company may have assets that are relatively old (and of lower cost) whereas another company may have similar, but more recently purchased (and of higher cost) assets. In effect such companies would have a similar operating capacity, but it would be recorded at different values. This situation can also be found within a single company that has operating divisions with similar characteristics to the above scenario. Management may assess their relative performance using historical costs (which would be an invalid basis) to make decisions relating to future investment or even closure.

There is also a lack of comparability between a company's current year's results and those of previous years i.e. trend analysis may be distorted.

Conceptual inconsistency

Accounting theorists sometimes argue that historic cost accounts are not internally consistent because they are in fact 'mixed value' accounts. This means that some historical costs are at current values, whereas other historical costs are at out-of-date values. Thus current values, of say revenue, are being matched with out-of-date values such as depreciation relating to older assets.

Many important ratios which are calculated as a basis for interpreting and assessing company performance can be distorted by inflation. Important examples are: return on capital employed, profit margins, many asset turnover ratios, gearing levels and earnings per share.

The misleading effects of the above on different users

Investors may find it difficult to compare the results of different companies as a basis for investment decisions. A shareholder may be tempted to accept a low bid for his/her shares if weight is given to the asset backing, based on book values, of the shares. Dividends may seem low in relation to reported profits, this may be because management is recommending dividends based on a current operating profit.

Employees may make high wage demands based on reported profit rather than current operating profits.

Governments generally tax reported profits which means companies pay tax on higher, inflation boosted, profits.

(b) The advantages and criticisms of General (Current) Purchasing Power and Current Cost Accounting are set out below:

General (Current) Purchasing Power Accounts

It is claimed that GPP accounts retain many of the advantages of historic cost accounts and overcome some of their deficiencies. Like historic cost accounts GPP accounts are transaction based, and are therefore objective and verifiable. This is because they are a restatement of historic cost accounts (which possess the above qualities) adjusted for the movement in an inflation index, usually published by the government.

Because the statement of comprehensive income and the statement of financial position are adjusted for price movements over time, GPP accounts are said to be comparable between companies and over time. This overcomes many of the difficulties of historic cost accounts.

If the index used to adjust the historic cost accounts is a consumer based index (as it usually is), then they are more appropriate to shareholders because this index is well understood by them and more appropriate to their spending patterns. The figure for equity is said to be a measure of the spending power (or consumption) that is being forgone in making (or holding) the investment in the company, and can be judged in those terms.

Opponents or critics of GPP accounting argue that many of the claimed advantages may not be true. GPP accounts suffer from some practical as well as theoretical problems:

(i) GPP values are not real values, current or otherwise; they are the result of statistical calculations. For many companies the GPP values of their non-current assets will only be similar to their real (current) values if the movement of the specific price indexes relating to those assets is similar to that of the General Price Index. An extreme case of this problem would occur where there was general (retail) price inflation, but the company trades in an activity where the prices of the goods they manufacture and supply are falling. Hi-fi, video and computer equipment may be examples of this. Average measures of inflation, particularly if they are measures of consumer inflation, are not usually appropriate to account for specific price inflation experienced by companies, which differs from company to company.

(ii) Most items in the statement of comprehensive income are adjusted by the average inflation factor for the period. During periods of inflation this is greater than one and can give the general effect of increased profits. Although this effect is mitigated by higher depreciation charges, GPP profits for profitable companies can be higher than their historic cost profits. A major criticism of historic cost accounts is that they overstate operating profits, GPP accounts can worsen this problem rather than solve it. Highly geared companies tend to show even greater GPP profits (due to gains on net monetary liabilities), and such companies are more vulnerable when inflation is high. This is because interest rates are often increased by Governments in an attempt to control inflation. This has a detrimental effect on companies with high variable rate borrowings.

Current Cost Accounting

Current cost accounting principles, from a conceptual point of view, are more soundly based and therefore more difficult to criticize than GPP accounts. They correct most of the limitations of historic cost accounts that are due to increased price levels. They reflect the current values of a company's specific assets although this is not necessarily the current cost of those assets. The reported current operating profit is considered to be more relevant to many decisions such as dividend distribution, employee wage claims and even as a basis for taxation.

The problems of CCA lie in their preparation and understanding. In practical terms it can be very difficult to determine the current value of assets, and many alternative forms of current value exist e.g. replacement cost, realisable value and value in use. Methods of determining current costs include the use of manufacturers' price lists for plant and inventory, professional revaluation of assets e.g. land and buildings and the use of specific price indexes published by government agencies. Whatever method is used it is often subjective and sometimes complex. This makes the cost of the preparation and audit of current cost accounts expensive.

An interesting point arising from the past use of CCA in some countries is that when current cost results of companies were published there was no significant differential change in share prices relating to the current cost information. The Efficient Market Hypothesis would suggest that if CCA provided 'new' information then market prices would react. An interpretation of the above observation is that the information revealed by CCA was already 'known' by the market makers and imputed into share prices. Thus many feel that the expense of producing CCA gives no benefit to users. This perhaps explains why historic cost accounts are still dominant in financial reporting.

5   CREATIVE ACCOUNTING

Key answer tips

In part (i) you must illustrate your answer with relevant examples.

(i)   Creative accounting is a term in general use to describe the practice of applying inappropriate accounting policies or entering into complex or 'special purpose' transactions with the objective of making a company's financial statements appear to disclose a more favourable position, particularly in relation to the calculation of certain 'key' ratios, than would otherwise be the case. Most commentators believe creative accounting stops short of deliberate fraud, but is nonetheless undesirable as it is intended to mislead users of financial statements.

Probably the most criticized area of creative accounting relates to off balance sheet financing. This occurs where a company has financial obligations that are not recorded on its statement of financial position. There have been several examples of this in the past:

- finance leases treated as operating leases

- borrowings (usually convertible loan stock) being classified as equity

- secured loans being treated as 'revenue' (sale and repurchase agreements)

- the non-consolidation of 'special purpose vehicles' that have been used to raise finance

- offsetting liabilities against assets (certain types of accounts receivable factoring)

The other main area of creative accounting is that of increasing or smoothing profits. Examples of this are:

- the use of inappropriate provisions (this reduces profit in good years and increases them in poor years)

- not providing for liabilities, either at all or not in full, as they arise. This is often related to environmental provisions, decommissioning costs and constructive obligations

- restructuring costs not being recognized in profit or loss (often related to a newly acquired subsidiary – the costs are effectively added to goodwill).

It should be noted that recent International Accounting Standards have now prevented many of the above past abuses, however more recent examples of creative accounting are in use by some of the new Internet/Dot.com companies. Most of these companies do not (yet) make any profit so other performance criteria such as site 'hits', conversion rates (browsers turning into buyers), burn periods (the length of time cash resources are expected to last) and even revenue are massaged to give a more favourable impression.

(ii) One of the primary characteristics of financial statements is reliability i.e. they must faithfully represent the transactions and other events that have occurred. It can be possible for the economic substance of a transaction (effectively its commercial intention) to be different from its strict legal position or 'form'. Thus financial statements can only give a faithful representation of a company's performance if the substance of its transactions is reported. It is worth stressing that there will be very few transactions where their substance is different from their legal form, but for those where it is, they are usually very important. This is because they are material in terms of their size or incidence, or because they may be intended to mislead.

Common features which may indicate that the substance of a transaction (or series of connected transactions) is different from its legal form are:

- Where the ownership of an asset does not rest with the party that is expected to experience the risks and rewards relating to it (i.e. equivalent to control of the asset).

- Where a transaction is linked with other related transactions. It is necessary to assess the substance of the series of connected transactions as a whole.

- The use of options within contracts. It may be that options are either almost certain to be (or not to be) exercised. In such cases these are not really options at all and should be ignored in determining commercial substance.

- Where assets are sold at values that differ from their fair values (either above or below fair values).

Many complex transactions often contain several of the above features. Determining the true substance of transactions can be a difficult and sometimes subjective procedure.

6   S

Key answer tips

Notice the way in which the answer approaches the problem.

Identify the benefits and risks associated with the asset in the question (in this case, trade receivables) and then analyse the transaction to see which of the parties actually has the benefits and risks in practice.

MEMORANDUM

To: The Board of Directors

From: The Management Accountant

Subject: How the receivables factoring arrangement will be reported in the financial statements

Date: 25 April 20X8

The legal form of the transaction is that S has transferred the title to the receivables to the factor, F. However, the key issue is whether S has actually assigned its receivables to F in practice or whether S has merely raised a secured loan from F. In order to determine the substance of the arrangement it is necessary to establish which party bears the risks and enjoys the benefits associated with the receivables.

The main benefit of holding trade receivables is normally an eventual cash inflow, while the main risks are slow payment and non-recovery (i.e. bad debts).

The terms of the agreement can be analysed as follows:

- F only accepts receivables subject to credit approval, so that S bears the risk of slow payment and irrecoverable receivables.

- S receives only 70% of the receivables at the time of assignment. The remaining sums, less interest charged by F, are only paid to S after the receivables have been collected by F. Again, S bears slow payment risk.

- Although F administers the scheme and collects the receivables, S must pay a fee for this service. Additionally, all amounts not paid within 90 days are re-assigned to S and S must repay any monies advanced in respect of those receivables. S is bearing the risk of irrecoverable receivables.

- F charges further interest based on the balance on the factoring account, the size of which depends on the speed with which receivables are collected. S is bearing slow payment risk.

From this analysis it is clear that S is bearing all the risks associated with the receivables and that the commercial substance of the relationship is that F has provided a loan secured on the receivables. The risks to S are mitigated to some extent, because F can only obtain reimbursement for irrecoverable receivables out of the proceeds of other receivables assigned to it.

S should recognize the receivables as an asset until they have been collected by F. The sum advanced from F should be treated as a loan. S should record expenses for interest, administration charges and bad debts in its statement of comprehensive income.

7   FLOW

Journal entries

Sale of the property to River on 1 April 20X7

	$	$
Dr Bank	850,000	
Cr Deferred income (statement of financial position)		300,000
Cr Property disposal		550,000
Dr Property disposal	500,000	
Cr Property: Cost		500,000
Dr Property: Accumulated depreciation	60,000	
Cr Property disposal		60,000
Dr Property disposal	110,000	
Cr Statement of comprehensive income		110,000

Being the sale and leaseback of property

Comments:

S has entered into a sale and leaseback agreement with River which must be accounted for in accordance with the requirements of IAS 17 *Leases*. Because the leaseback is an operating lease, rather than a finance lease, the substance of the agreement is that S has sold the property to River and no longer has the risks and rewards of ownership. Therefore the property is removed from the statement of financial position.

IAS 17 requires that the profit on disposal of the property should be calculated as the difference between the fair value of the property and its net book value at the date of sale (550,000 – 440,000).

Payment of the first rental to River on 31 March 20X8

	$	$
Dr Operating lease rental	100,000	
Cr Bank		100,000

Being the first rental payment to River

	$	$
Dr Deferred income	30,000	
Cr Operating lease rental		30,000

Being the amortization of the excess of the sale proceeds of the property over its fair value (300,000 ÷ 10).

Comments:

The property was sold for an amount in excess of its fair value and so IAS 17 requires that the difference of $300,000 between the sale proceeds and the fair value of the property (850,000 – 550,000) is deferred and credited to income over the period for which the asset is expected to be used, in this case ten years. This has the effect of reducing the annual rental to $70,000.

Tutorial note: It would be possible to argue that the lease should be treated in accordance with its commercial substance, which is that of an operating lease for the continued use of the property, plus an interest bearing loan. The journal entries for the sale of the property would be as before, except that the $300,000 excess of the sales proceeds over fair value would be credited to a loan account, rather than to deferred income. The loan repayment would be divided into three parts:

- Normal annual operating lease rental of $50,000. This is accounted for on a straight line basis over the term of the lease.

- Interest on the loan of $300,000, charged at the rate which River normally applies to similar fixed rate loans.

- Repayment of the capital portion of the loan.

The journal entry would be as follows:

	$	$
Dr Operating lease rental	50,000	
Dr Interest charge (balancing figure)	20,000	
Dr Loan (300,000 ÷ 10)	30,000	
Cr Bank		100,000

8   BLFB

Key answer tips

The examiner has been kind to you in asking for journal entries to show how the transactions should have been shown. Working these out actually makes the situation much clearer. Even at this stage of your studies, you will often find that sketching out journals is a useful tool.

(a)   **MEMORANDUM**

To: Assistant

From: Management Accountant

Subject: Reporting the substance of transactions

Date: 22 November 20Y0

(i)   **Determining the substance of a transaction**

The substance of a transaction is its true commercial effect, which may be different from its legal form. Financial statements do not provide a fair presentation (or true and fair view) of an entity's performance and position unless they report the economic substance of transactions.

For most transactions there is no difference between economic substance and legal form. However, some transactions are very complex and the effect of these is not always apparent. For example, a transaction may be linked with others so that the effect can only be understood when all the transactions are considered together. In determining the substance of a transaction, all aspects of it should be considered, including any future transactions that are likely to arise as a result.

In order to determine the substance of a transaction, it is necessary to decide whether the transaction has given rise to new assets or liabilities or changed existing assets or liabilities. An entity has an asset if it experiences the benefits and risks associated with ownership of an asset, regardless of whether it legally owns the asset. An entity has a liability if it cannot avoid an outflow of economic benefits (money or services) as a result of a past transaction or event. Assets and liabilities (and changes in them) are recognized if it is probable that any future economic benefit associated with them will flow to or from the entity and they are capable of being measured reliably at a monetary amount.

(ii) **Why transactions should be accounted for according to their substance**

Some transactions used to be deliberately structured so that their commercial substance was different from their strict legal form. For example, an entity might sell an asset to another party. Under the terms of the sale agreement, it would be able to repurchase the asset at a specified future date and in the meantime the entity would continue to use it. This transaction is legally a sale, but has the commercial effect of a secured loan.

By recording the strict legal form of this type of transaction, entities could avoid recognising assets and liabilities in their financial statements. This distorted performance measures such as return on capital employed and gearing so that users of the financial statements were given misleading information.

Users of the financial statements need information that is relevant and reliable. Financial statements cannot provide relevant or reliable information unless they report the true effect of transactions. The comparability and understandability of financial statements is also enhanced by reporting economic substance rather than legal form.

(b) (i) **Journal entries to record the correct treatment of the timber**

	$m	$m
1 July 20X9		
Dr Revenue	45.0	
Cr Payables (Southland Bank)		45.0
Dr Inventories	40.0	
Cr Cost of sales		40.0

Being the reversal of the sale of the timber and recognition of the profit, the reinstatement of the timber and the recognition of a secured loan from Southland Bank.

30 June 20Y0

Dr Interest payable (statement of comprehensive income)	3.6	
Cr Payables (Southland Bank)		3.6

Being the accrual of interest payable on the secured loan from Southland Bank for the year (45 × 8% (W)).

(ii) **Explanation of journal entries**

Although this transaction appears to be a sale, it is actually a means of raising finance. BLFB continues to hold the timber during the five year period, and therefore it experiences the risks associated with holding this type of inventory; it must keep the timber secure and maintain controlled conditions. It will also eventually be able to repurchase the timber and use it to generate income (economic benefits).

The commercial substance of the transaction is that Southland Bank has made a loan to the company, using the timber as security. Therefore the transaction cannot be treated as a sale and the journal entries recording the revenue for $45 million and the profit of $5 million must be reversed. The loan of $45 million must also be recognized.

The difference between the 'selling price' of $45 million and the 'repurchase price' of $66.12 million represents loan interest and this should be accrued over the term of the loan at a constant rate on the carrying amount. The interest is charged as an expense in profit or loss and added to the carrying value of the loan. The rate of interest implicit in the loan is 8% (W) and therefore interest payable for the year ended 30 June 20Y0 is $3.6 million and the carrying value of the loan at 30 June 20Y0 is $48.6 million.

Working

The interest rate implicit in the loan is calculated as:

$$\frac{\text{Amount borrowed}}{\text{Amount repayable}} = \frac{45}{66.12} = 0.681.$$

From discount tables this is 8% over five years.

9   LMN

(a)   (i)   Recognition is the depiction of an element of the financial statements in words and by a monetary amount and the inclusion of that amount in the financial statement totals.

The general recognition criteria in the *Framework* are that an item should be recognized in the financial statements if:

. It meets one of the definitions of an element of the financial statements

. There is sufficient evidence that the change in assets or liabilities inherent in the item has occurred (including, where appropriate, evidence that a future inflow or outflow of benefit will occur).

For example, a contract is an enforceable, but as yet unperformed, promise given to or by an external party to transfer assets and/or liabilities in the future.

These only provide sufficient evidence where there is a 'firm commitment', i.e. the contract can be enforced (either commercially or legally and practically) by an external party (usually another party to the contract).

The item can be measured at a monetary amount with sufficient reliability.

For many items an estimate will be necessary. The use of reasonable estimates is a normal part of the preparation of financial statements. Provided the estimate is reasonably reliable and prudent it should be recognized.

A good example of the above is in the recognition of attributable profit on construction contracts. Provided a reasonable estimate can be made of the degree of completion and the gain, and the gain is prudently estimated, then profit is recognized.

Recognition is triggered where a past event indicates that there has been a measurable change in the assets or liabilities of the entity.

Derecognition is appropriate where a past event has eliminated a previously recognized asset or liability or where evidence is no longer sufficiently strong to support continued recognition.

An asset will only be recognized if it gives rights or other access to future economic benefits controlled by an entity as a result of past transactions or events, and it can be measured with sufficient reliability

A liability will only be recognized if there is an obligation to transfer economic benefits as a result of past transactions or events, and it can be measured with sufficient reliability.

Income is recognized in the statement of comprehensive income when an increase in future economic benefits arises from an increase in an asset (or a reduction in a liability), and it can be measured reliably.

Evidence is needed to ascertain whether the gain has been 'earned', i.e. an increase in equity interest/net assets had occurred before the end of the reporting period. Income reflected in the statement of comprehensive income is seen as particularly important since the statement of comprehensive income is used as a primary measure of performance. Hence a gain included here must be earned and realized.

Realization is concerned with restricting recognition to those items whose existence and amount is particularly well evidenced. This will usually mean that conversion into cash or cash equivalents has occurred or is reasonably assured.

If a gain fails to meet the tests of being earned and realized, it may still meet the general recognition criteria. In this case, such a gain should be recognized in other comprehensive income, e.g. unrealized holding gain on the revaluation of a property held for consumption in the business (rather than for its investment potential).

Expenses are recognized in the statement of comprehensive income when a decrease in future economic benefits arises from a decrease in an asset or an increase in a liability, and it can be measured reliably.

Evidence is needed to ascertain whether a decrease in equity /net assets had occurred before the end of the reporting period. Where a loss is not to be recognized, i.e. the expenditure is carried forward to the next period as an asset under the matching concept, sufficient evidence must exist.

(b)   The key issue here is whether the motor vehicles are actually assets of LMN in substance, or whether IJK continues to hold them. The fact that IJK continues to have legal title to the vehicles may be irrelevant.

Revenue from the sale of goods should be recognized when the seller transfers the significant risks and rewards of ownership to the buyer. The vehicles have been sold to LMN if the significant risks and rewards of ownership have also been transferred.

LMN appears to bear some of the risks of ownership:

- It is required to incur the costs of insuring the vehicles against loss or damage.

- Because the price of the vehicles is fixed at the time of their delivery, it bears the risk of loss if the price is reduced between the date of delivery and the date of sale.

However, LMN does not appear to bear the risk of loss due to obsolescence, because it can return the vehicles to IJK without incurring a penalty. In addition, LMN does not have to pay for the vehicles until they are sold to a third party.

LMN has some of the benefits of ownership:

- It can hold whichever ranges and models it wishes, subject to an upper limit of 80 vehicles.

- The price of the vehicles is fixed at the time of delivery, so LMN is protected from price rises between the date of delivery and the date of sale to a third party.

- It can use any of the vehicles for demonstration purposes or road testing.

However, LMN does have to pay a rental charge to IJK if it drives the vehicles for more than a specified number of kilometres. This suggests that LMN does not have all the benefits of ownership.

From the analysis above it is not clear which of the parties has the significant risks and rewards of ownership. It may be necessary to look at what actually happens in practice. For example, how often are vehicles actually returned to IJK? If the answer is 'never', this suggests that the vehicles are assets of LMN. However, on the basis of the information above, IJK appears to have the more significant risks and rewards, including the risk of obsolescence and the risk of slow payment, as it does not receive payment until the vehicles are sold to a third party.

This suggests that IJK should recognize the unsold vehicles as inventory and should not recognize revenue until the goods are sold to a third party.

10   DCB

Key answer tips

Part (a) is relatively easy; part (b) is slightly trickier. As well as briefly explaining what each of the three adjustments are you must explain the reason for including each of them in the current cost statement of comprehensive income.

(a)   **Defects of historical cost accounting**

There are many problems associated with traditional historical cost accounting.

- The amounts at which non-monetary assets (such as property, plant and equipment and inventories) are stated bears no relation to their current value and therefore provides a poor guide to the resources available to the business. Holding gains are not shown in the financial statements until assets are sold, even though many believe that these make an important contribution to an entity's overall financial performance.

- In a company's statement of comprehensive income, out of date costs are matched against current revenues. This produces an overstated and misleading profit figure.

- The statement of comprehensive income fails to show gains or losses made by owing money or holding monetary assets such as trade receivables and trade payables. When prices are rising, holding a cash balance results in a loss of purchasing power, while borrowing money may result in a gain in purchasing power.

- Because profits are overstated and assets are understated, return on capital employed and similar measures may be extremely misleading.

- Trend information, such as that provided by comparative figures or in a five-year summary, is distorted because it fails to take into account the changing value of money over time.

As a result of the above, users of financial statements find it extremely difficult to assess a company's progress from year to year or to compare the results of different operations.

(b) **How current cost accounting adjustments contribute to the maintenance of capital**

Under the traditional approach to capital maintenance associated with historical cost accounting, a company has made a profit for an accounting period if its capital (its net assets) at the end of the period is greater than its capital at the beginning of the period. Under current cost accounting, a company only makes a profit if its operating capital at the end of the period is greater than its operating capital at the beginning of the period. A company's operating capital is its ability to produce a certain volume of goods and services.

- The cost of sales adjustment is the difference between the current cost of sales and the historical cost of sales. It uplifts the cost of the inventory sold to its value to the business at the date that it is sold. The company only records a profit if the proceeds of sale are greater than the current cost of the inventory at the date of sale (representing the value to the business of inventory consumed). This ensures that enough earnings are retained to purchase the same amount of goods that were sold in the previous period.

- The depreciation adjustment is the difference between depreciation based on the historical cost of property, plant and equipment and depreciation based on current cost (value to the business or deprival value). The company only makes a profit if sale proceeds are sufficient to cover current cost depreciation and therefore sufficient earnings are retained to replace all its operating assets and to continue production at the same level as before.

- The loss on net monetary position (sometimes called the monetary working capital adjustment) is the increase in the real value of monetary working capital (trade receivables and trade payables) that has occurred during the year. When trade receivables are realized in cash the company makes a loss because the cash is based on the historical amount of the debt rather than the current amount. The adjustment recognizes this loss in the statement of comprehensive income and ensures that enough earnings are retained in the business to maintain the current level of monetary working capital.

A REGULATORY FRAMEWORK FOR FINANCIAL REPORTING

11 IASCF

Key answer tips

Parts (a) and (b) are standard bookwork. Make sure that you answer all of the requirements that are listed. Part (c) invites you to give your opinion. Don't be dogmatic, but state both successes and failures in the move towards convergence.

Note: The International Accounting Standards Board (IASB) has decided that its standards will be called International Financial Reporting Standards (IFRSs), and that this term should be taken to encompass both Standards and Interpretations issued by the IASB (IFRS and IFRIC), and the International Accounting Standards (IASs) and Standing Interpretations Committee Interpretations (SICs) issued by its predecessor standard setter, the IASC Board. References in this answer to IFRS should be taken to have the same meaning as that used by the IASB.

(a)   In recognition of the increasing importance of international accounting standards, in 1999 the Board of the IASB recommended and subsequently adopted a new constitution and structure. A new supervisory body, The International Accounting Standards Committee Foundation, was incorporated in the USA in February 2001 as an independent not-for-profit organization. Its constitution was further revised in 2005. It is governed by 19 IASC Foundation Trustees who must have an understanding of international issues relevant to accounting standards for use in the world's capital markets. The main objectives of the IASC Foundation are:

- to develop a single set of global accounting standards that require high quality, transparent and comparable information in financial statements to help users in making economic decisions;

- to promote the use and application of these standards; and

- to bring about convergence of national accounting standards and international accounting standards.

The subsidiary bodies of the IASC Foundation are the International Accounting Standards Board (IASB) (based in London, UK), the Standards Advisory Council (SAC) and the International Financial Reporting Interpretations Committee (IFRIC).

The International Accounting Standards Board. The result of a restructuring process saw the IASB assume the responsibility for setting accounting standards from its predecessor body, the International Accounting Standards Committee. The Trustees of the IASCF appoint the members of all of the above bodies. They also set the agenda of, and raise finance for, the IASB; however the IASB has sole responsibility for setting accounting standards, International Financial Reporting Standards (IFRSs), following rigorous and open due process.

The Standards Advisory Council provides a forum for experts from different countries and different business sectors with an interest in international financial reporting to offer advice when drawing up new standards. Its main objectives are to give advice to the Trustees and IASB on agenda decisions and work priorities and on the major standard-setting projects.

The **International Financial Reporting Interpretations Committee** has taken over the work of the previous Standing Interpretations Committee. It is really a compliance body whose role is to provide rapid guidance on the application and interpretation of international accounting standards where contentious or divergent interpretations have arisen. It operates an open due process in accordance with its approved procedures. Its pronouncements (interpretations – SICs and IFRICs) are important because financial statements cannot be described as complying with IFRSs unless they also comply with the interpretations.

Other bodies

The prominence of the IASB has been enhanced even further by its relationship with the **International Organization of Securities Commissions (IOSCO)**. IOSCO is an influential organization of the world's security commissions (stock exchanges). In 1995 the IASC agreed to develop a core set of standards which, when endorsed by IOSCO, would be used as an acceptable basis for cross-border listings. In May 2000 this was achieved. Thus it can be said that international accounting standards may be the first tentative steps towards global accounting harmonization. As part of its harmonization process the European Union requires listed companies in all member states to prepare their consolidated financial statements using IFRSs from 2005.

National standard setters such as the UK's Accounting Standards Board and the USA's Financial Accounting Standards Board have a role to play in the formulation of international accounting standards. Seven of the leading national standard setters work closely with the IASB. The IASB see this as a 'partnership' between IASB and these national bodies as they work together to achieve the convergence of accounting standards world wide. Often the IASB will ask members of national standard setting bodies to work on particular projects in which those countries have greater experience or expertise. Many countries that are committed to closer integration with IFRSs will publish domestic standards equivalent (sometimes identical) to IFRSs on a concurrent timetable.

(b)   **The International Accounting Standard Setting Process**

As referred to above the IASB is ultimately responsible for setting international accounting standards. The Board (advised by the SAC) identifies a subject and appoints an Advisory Committee to advise on the issues relevant to the given topic. Depending on the complexity and importance of the subject matter the IASB may develop and publish Discussion Documents for public comment. Following the receipt and review of comments the IASB then develops and publishes an Exposure Draft for public comment. The usual comment period for both of these is ninety days. Finally, and again after a review of any further comments, an International Financial Reporting Standard (IFRS) is issued. The IASB also publishes a Basis for Conclusions which explains how it reached its conclusions and gives information to help users to apply the Standard in practice. In addition to the above the IASB will sometimes conduct public hearings where proposed standards are openly discussed and occasionally field tests are conducted to ensure that proposals are practical and workable around the world.

The authority of international accounting standards is a rather difficult area. The IASB has no power to enforce international accounting standards within those countries/ enterprises that choose to adopt them. This means that the enforcement of international accounting standards is in the hands of the regulatory systems of the individual adopting countries. There is no doubt the regulatory systems in different parts of the world differ from each other considerably in their effectiveness. For example in the UK the Financial Reporting Review Panel (FRRP) is a body that investigates departures from the UK's regulatory system (which now includes the use of international accounting standards for listed companies). The FRRP has wide and effective powers of enforcement, but not all countries have equivalent bodies, thus it can be argued that international accounting standards are not enforced in a consistent manner throughout the world.

Complementary to international accounting standards, there also exist international auditing standards and part of the rigour and transparency that the use of international accounting standards brings is due to the fact that those companies adopting international accounting standards should also be audited in accordance with international auditing standards. This auditing aspect is part of IOSCO's requirements for financial statements to be used for cross-border listing purposes.

Where it becomes apparent (often through press reports) that there is widespread inconsistency in the interpretation of an international accounting standard, or where it is perceived that a standard is not clear enough in a particular area, the IFRIC may act to remedy/clarify the position thus supplementing the body of international standards. However where it becomes apparent (perhaps through a modified audit report) that a company has departed from IFRSs there is little that the IASB can do directly to enforce them.

(c)   **The success of the process**

Any measure of success is really a matter of opinion. There is no doubt that the growing acceptance of IFRSs through IOSCO's endorsement, the European Union requirement for their use by listed companies and the ever increasing number of countries that are either adopting international accounting standards outright or basing their domestic standards very closely on IFRSs is a measure of the success of the IASB. Equally there is widespread recognition that in recent years the quality of international accounting standards has improved enormously due to the improvements project and subsequent continuing improvements.

However the IASB is not without criticism. Some countries that have developed sophisticated regulatory systems feel that IFRSs are not as rigorous as the local standards and this may give cross-border listing companies an advantage over domestic companies. Some requirements of international accounting standards are regarded as quite controversial, e.g. deferred tax (part of IAS 12), financial instruments and derivatives (IAS 32 and 39) and accounting for retirement benefits (IAS 19). Many IFRSs are complex and the benefits of applying them to smaller enterprises may outweigh the costs. Also some securities exchanges that are part of IOSCO require non-domestic companies that are listing by filing financial statements prepared under IFRSs to produce a reconciliation to local GAAP. This involves reconciling the IFRS statement of comprehensive income and statement of financial position assets, liabilities and equity, to what they would be if local GAAP had been used. The USA is an important example of this requirement. Critics argue that this requirement of the Securities Exchange Commission (SEC) negates many of the benefits of being able to use a single set of financial statements to list on different security exchanges. This is because to produce reconciliation to local GAAP is almost as much work and expense as preparing financial statements in the local GAAP which was usually the previous requirement.

However in recent years the IASB and the FASB in the US have formed an agreement known as the Memorandum of Understanding whereby they will jointly progress the process of harmonization of IFRS and US GAAP. This has led to a number of joint projects in process such as the development of a new conceptual framework, a project on business combinations and one of fair values in financial statements. The aim is that by 20X9 the requirement to produce a reconciliation from IFRS financial statements to US GAAP will be lifted by the SEC.

Despite these criticisms there is no doubt that the work of IASB has already led, and in the future will lead, to further improvement in financial reporting throughout the world.

12   CONCEPTUAL FRAMEWORK

Key answer tips

Parts a), b) and c) are standard bookwork from the Framework but it is essential background knowledge. Part d) introduces not-for-profit entities which are a new element of the F7 syllabus.

(a)   A conceptual framework could be defined as a coherent system of interrelated objectives and fundamental principles. It is a framework which prescribes the nature, function and limits of financial accounting and financial statements. In the US there is a more specific definition which is that it is 'a constitution, a coherent system of interrelated objectives and fundamentals that can lead to consistent standards and that prescribes the nature, function and limits of financial accounting and financial statements'.

(b)   There are a variety of arguments for having a conceptual framework. Firstly it enables accounting standards and GAAP to be developed in accordance with agreed principles and underlying assumptions and concepts. It therefore avoids 'fire fighting', whereby accounting standards are developed in a piecemeal way in response to specific problems or abuses. Such an approach can lead to inconsistencies between different accounting standards and also between accounting standards and relevant local legislation.

The lack of a conceptual framework may mean that certain critical issues are not addressed.

For example, until the *Framework for preparation and presentation of financial statements* was published there was no definition of basic terms such as 'asset' or 'liability' in any accounting standard which is obviously fundamental to a consistent treatment of accounting transactions and events.

In a world where transactions have become more complex and businesses more sophisticated an overall conceptual framework can help preparers of financial statement and their auditors deal with complex transactions and particularly those which are not the subject of an accounting standard.

The alternative to a principles based conceptual framework as we have under the IASB is a rules based framework which some would argue is what is seen in the US. However it can be argued that a principles based framework means that accounting standards based upon such principles are harder to circumvent. It also means that the standard setting process is less likely to be influenced by those with vested interests such as large companies or particular business sectors.

(c) The *Framework for the Preparation and Presentation of Financial Statements* was originally developed by the IASC in 1989. It sets out concepts underlying the preparation and presentation of financial statements. However it is not an accounting standard and nothing in the Framework overrides a specific accounting standard.

The stated purpose of the *Framework* is to:

- assist the IASB in the development of future accounting standards and in its review of existing International Accounting Standards

- assist the IASB by providing a basis for reducing the number of alternative accounting treatments permitted by International Accounting Standards

- assist national standard-setting bodies in developing national standards

- assist preparers of financial statements in applying International Accounting Standards

- and in dealing with topics that do not form the subject of an International Accounting Standard

- assist auditors in forming an opinion about whether financial statements conform with International Accounting Standards

- assist users of financial statements in interpreting the information contained in financial statements prepared in conformity with International Accounting Standards

- provide those who are interested in the work of the IASB with information about its approach to the formulation of International Accounting Standards.

(d) The main aim of not-for-profit entities is to provide value for money rather than making a profit. Value for money is achieved by a combination of effectiveness, efficiency and economy.

Effectiveness means achieving the objectives (usually non-monetary) of the organization. The objectives of not-for-profit and public sector entities will differ depending upon the type of entity. For example a school may have the objectives of teaching a certain number of children and achieving certain academic standards. A hospital may have the objectives of treating out-patients within a particular time scale or minimising the number of empty beds. Effectiveness is therefore measured by identifiable measures of achievement in reaching those goals or objectives.

Efficiency means using the resources available well. It is effectively the quantity of output obtained for a given measure of input. Efficiency means getting more out of fewer inputs and thereby reducing the cost of output. In a school it might be measured by the pupil to teacher ratio and in a hospital by the number of patients seen by a consultant during a surgery.

Economy means keeping the cost of input resources as low as possible. This is achieved by paying less for the inputs that are required to meet the objectives or provide the service. In a school giving more teaching time to classroom assistants rather than higher paid teachers would be a form of economy or in a hospital scheduling duties to a nurse rather than a doctor.

In general accounting standards are designed to measure financial performance accurately and consistently, to report the financial position accurately and consistently and to account for the stewardship of the directors of the resources and assets.

Not-for-profit and public sector organizations do not aim to achieve a profit but will have to account for their income and costs. Such entities will have to account for their effectiveness, economy and efficiency even if they do not have to produce financial statements for the public (although in many cases may do so).

Therefore some measurement accounting standards will be relevant such as those relating to inventory, non-current assets, leasing etc. However others relating purely to reporting such as earnings per share will not be so relevant.

13 USERS AND QUALITIES

Key answer tips

All of the topics covered in this question are essential background knowledge which you may have to use or apply in other questions.

(a)   The objective of financial statements is to provide information about the financial position, performance and changes in financial position of an enterprise that is useful to a wide range of users in making economic decisions. Financial statements also show the results of the stewardship of management, that is the accountability of management for the resources entrusted to it.

(b)   Financial statements meet the common needs of most users. However, financial statements do not provide all the information that users may need to make economic decisions, since they largely portray the financial effects of past events and do not necessarily provide non-financial information.

Arguably the most important group of users are investors or shareholders who are the providers of risk capital.

They are interested in information that is useful in taking decisions about their investment or potential investment in the entity. As a result, they are concerned with the risk inherent in, and return provided by, their investments. They need information on the entity's financial performance and financial position that helps them to assess its cash generation abilities and its financial adaptability.

Other users of financial statements, and their information needs, include the following:

- Lenders who will be interested in information that enables them to determine whether their loans will be repaid, and whether the interest attaching to them will be paid, when due. Potential lenders are interested in information that helps them to decide whether to lend to the entity and on what terms.

- Suppliers and other trade payables who will be interested in information that enables them to decide whether to sell to the entity and to assess the likelihood that amounts owing to them will be paid when due.

- Employees who will be interested in information about the stability and profitability of their employer and their long-term employment prospects. They will also be interested in information that helps them to assess the ability of their employer to provide remuneration, employment opportunities and retirement benefits.

- Customers will be interested in information about the entity's continued existence. This is especially so when they are dependent on the entity for example if product warranties are involved or if specialized replacement parts may be needed.

- Governments and their agencies will be interested in the allocation of resources and, therefore, the activities of entities. They also require information in order to regulate the activities of entities, assess taxation and provide a basis for national statistics.

- The public will be interested in information about the trends and recent developments in the entity's prosperity and the range of its activities. For example, an entity may make a substantial contribution to a local economy by providing employment and using local suppliers.

(c) Qualitative characteristics are the attributes that make information provided in financial statements useful to others. The *Framework* identifies four qualitative characteristics – relevance, reliability, comparability and understandability – which are subject to a threshold quality of materiality

Information has the quality of **relevance** when it influences the economic decisions of users by helping them evaluate past, present or future events or by confirming, or correcting, their past evaluations. Information about financial position and past performance is frequently used as the basis for predicting future financial position and performance and other matters in which users are directly interested, such as dividend and wage payments. To have predictive value, information need not be in the form of an explicit forecast.

The ability to make predictions from financial statements is enhanced, however, by the manner in which information concerning past transactions and events is displayed. For example, the predictive value of the statement of comprehensive income is enhanced if unusual, abnormal and infrequent items of income or expense are separately disclosed.

The predictive and confirmatory roles of information are interrelated. For example, information about the current level and structure of asset holdings has value to users when they endeavour to predict the ability of the enterprise to take advantage of opportunities and its ability to react to adverse situations.

There are several monetary attributes that could be used in financial statements, e.g. historical cost, current cost or net realisable value. The choice of attribute to be reported should be based on its relevance to the economic decisions of users.

Reliable information can be depended upon to present a faithful representation and is neutral, error free, complete and prudent.

If information is to represent faithfully the transactions and other events that it purports to represent, they must be accounted for and presented in accordance with their substance and economic reality and not merely their legal form. Information must also be neutral to be reliable, that is, free from bias. Financial statements are not neutral if, by the selection or presentation of information, they influence the making of a decision or judgement in order to achieve a predetermined result or outcome.

Information must be complete and free from error within the bounds of materiality. A material error or an omission can cause the financial statements to be false or misleading and thus unreliable and deficient in terms of their relevance.

Uncertainty surrounds many of the events and circumstances that are reported on in financial statements. It is dealt with in those statements by disclosing the nature and extent of the uncertainty involved and by exercising prudence. Prudence means exercising a degree of caution in making judgements about estimates required under conditions of uncertainty, such that gains and assets are not overstated and losses and liabilities are not understated. The existence of assets and gains requires more confirmatory evidence and greater reliability of measurement than are required for liabilities and losses.

It is not necessary to exercise prudence where there is no uncertainty. Nor is it appropriate to use prudence as a reason for, for example, creating hidden reserves or excessive provisions, deliberately understating assets or gains, or deliberately overstating liabilities or losses. That would mean that the financial statements are not neutral and, therefore, are not reliable.

Comparability is also a required attribute of financial information. Users must be able to compare the financial statements of an entity over time to identify trends in its financial position and performance and also be able to compare the financial statements of different entities to evaluate their relative financial performance and financial position.

For this to be the case there must be consistency of accounting treatment and adequate disclosure. An important implication of comparability is that users are informed of the accounting policies employed in preparation of the financial statements, any changes in those policies and the effects of such changes. Compliance with accounting standards, including the disclosure of the accounting policies used by the enterprise, helps to achieve comparability.

Because users wish to compare the financial position, performance and changes in financial position of an enterprise over time, it is important that the financial statements show corresponding information for the preceding periods.

Finally information must be understandable.**Understandability** depends on the way in which information is presented and the capabilities of users. It is assumed that users have a reasonable knowledge of business and economic activities and are willing to study the information provided with reasonable diligence.

For information to be understandable users need to be able to perceive its significance however information that is relevant and reliable should not be excluded from the financial statements simply because it is difficult for some users to understand.

(d)   In practice, a balancing, or trade-off, between qualitative characteristics is often necessary. Generally the aim is to achieve an appropriate balance among the characteristics in order to meet the objective of financial statements.

Relevance and reliability

Where there is a conflict between qualitative characteristics, the aim is to achieve an appropriate balance among them in order to meet the objectives of financial statements. The relative importance of different characteristics is a matter of professional judgement.

Conflicts may arise over timeliness. A delay in providing information can make it out of date and less relevant, but reporting on transactions and other events before all the uncertainties are resolved may make information less reliable. Financial information should not be provided until it is sufficiently reliable.

Neutrality and prudence

Neutrality involves freedom from bias. Prudence is potentially biased because it seeks to ensure that gains or assets are not overstated and losses or liabilities are not understated in conditions of uncertainty. It is necessary to find a balance that ensures that deliberate understatement of assets or gains and overstatement of liabilities or losses does not occur.

Cost and benefit

It is also important to balance the benefit and the cost of providing information and this is a pervasive constraint rather than a qualitative characteristic. The benefits derived from information should exceed the cost of providing it.

FINANCIAL STATEMENTS

14 BROADOAK

Key answer tips

Parts (a) and (b) represent relatively easy marks, but notice that the requirement is to write about specific parts of IAS 16 only. The Examiner commented that many candidates explained the rules for determining when an asset is impaired, or digressed onto other asset related topics, which was not required.

(a) (i) Although the broad principles of accounting for non-current assets were well understood by the accounting profession, applying these principles to practical situations resulted in complications and inconsistency. For the most part, IAS 16 codified existing good practice, but it did include specific rules which were intended to achieve improved consistency and more transparency.

Cost

The cost of an item of property, plant and equipment comprises its purchase price and any other costs directly attributable to bringing the asset into a working condition for its intended use. This is expanded upon as follows:

— purchase price is after the deduction of any trade discounts or rebates (but not early settlement discounts), but it does include any transport and handling costs (delivery, packing and insurance), non-refundable taxes (e.g. sales taxes such as VAT/GST, stamp duty, import duty). If the payment is deferred beyond normal credit terms this should be taken into account either by the use of discounting or substituting a cash equivalent price;

— direct attributable costs are the incremental costs that would have been avoided had the assets not been acquired. For self-constructed assets this includes labour costs of own employees. Abnormal costs such as wastage and errors are excluded. Other directly attributable costs include:

• installation costs and site preparation costs; and

• professional fees (e.g. legal fees, architects fees).

— IAS 37 *Provisions, Contingent Liabilities and Contingent Assets* says that if the estimated costs of removing and dismantling an asset and restoring its site qualify as a liability, they should be provided for and added to the cost of the relevant asset.

In addition IAS 23 *Borrowing Costs* allows (under the allowed alternative method) directly attributable borrowing costs to be capitalized. Directly attributable borrowing costs are those that would have been avoided had there been no expenditure on the asset.

Finally, the carrying amount of an asset may be reduced by any applicable government grants under IAS 20 *Accounting for Government Grants and Disclosure of Government Assistance.*

(ii) **Subsequent expenditure**

Traditionally the appropriate accounting treatment of subsequent expenditure on non-current assets revolved around whether it represented a revenue expense, in effect maintenance or a repair, or whether it represented an improvement that should be capitalized. Under IAS 16 there are no separate criteria for recognising subsequent expenditure. All costs, initial costs and subsequent costs, are recognized as assets if, and only if, it is probable that future economic benefits associated with the item will flow to the entity and the cost of the item can be measured reliably. All other subsequent expenditure should be recognized in the statement of comprehensive income as it is incurred. Examples of circumstances where subsequent expenditure should be capitalized are where it:

–   represents a modification that enhances the economic benefits of an asset (in excess of its previously assessed standard of performance). This could be an increase in its life or production capacity;

–   upgrades an asset with the effect of improving the quality of output; or

–   is on a new production process that reduces operating costs.

In addition to the above, the Standard says it is important to take into account the circumstances of the expenditure. For example, normal servicing and overhaul of plant is a revenue cost but, if the expenditure represents a major overhaul of an asset that restores its previous life, and the consumption of the previous economic benefits has been reflected by past depreciation charges, then the expenditure should be capitalized (subject to not exceeding its recoverable amount). A further example of where subsequent expenditure should be capitalized is where a major component of an asset that has been treated separately (for depreciation purposes) is replaced or restored (e.g. new engines for an aircraft).

(b)   Revaluation (particularly of properties) has been an area of great flexibility and inconsistency, often leading to misleading financial statements and accusations of 'creative accounting'. Under IAS 16 revaluations are permitted under its revaluation model for the measurement of assets subsequent to their initial recognition. The standard brings some order and consistency to the practice of revaluations.

Where an entity chooses to revalue one item of property, plant and equipment, it must also revalue the entire class of assets to which it belongs. Further, sufficiently regular revaluations should be made such that the carrying amounts of revalued assets should not differ materially to their fair values at the reporting period end. The standard stops short of requiring annual valuations, but it does contain detailed rules on the basis and frequency of valuation. It should be noted that where an asset has been written down to its recoverable amount due to impairment, this is not classed as being a policy of revaluation. The effect of the above is that it prevents selective or favourable valuations being reported whilst ignoring adverse movements, and where a company has chosen to revalue its assets (or class thereof), the values must be kept up-to-date.

Surpluses and deficits

These are measured as the difference between the revalued amounts and the book (carrying) values at the date of the valuation.

Increases (gains) are recognized in the statement of comprehensive income within other comprehensive income under the heading of revaluation surplus unless, and to the extent that, they reverse a previous loss (on the same asset) that has been recognized in profit or loss. In which case they should be recognized in profit or loss.

Decreases in valuations (revaluation losses) should normally be charged to the statement of comprehensive income. However, where they relate to an asset that has previously been revalued upwards, then to the extent that the losses do not exceed the amount standing to the credit of the asset in the revaluation reserve, they should be charged directly to that reserve (again as part of other comprehensive income).

Any impairment loss on revalued property, plant or equipment, recognisable under IAS 36 *Impairment of Assets*, is treated as a revaluation loss under IAS 16.

Gains and losses on disposal

The gain or loss on disposal is measured as the difference between the net sale proceeds and the carrying value of the asset at the date of sale. In the past some companies reverted to historical cost values to calculate a gain on disposal thus inflating the gain (assuming assets had increased in value). All gains and losses should be recognized in profit or loss in the period of the disposal. Any revaluation surplus standing to the credit of a disposal asset should be transferred to retained earnings (as a movement in the statement of changes in equity).

(c) (i) The initial measurement of the cost at which the plant would be capitalized is calculated as follows:

	$	$
Basic list price of plant		240,000
Less trade discount of 12.5% on list price		(30,000)
		210,000
Shipping and handling costs		2,750
Estimated pre-production testing		12,500
Site preparation costs		
Electrical cable installation (14,000 – 6,000)	8,000	
Concrete reinforcement	4,500	
Own labour costs	7,500	20,000
Dismantling and restoration costs (15,000 + 3,000)		18,000
Initial cost of plant		263,250

Note: the early settlement discount is a revenue item (probably deducted from administration costs). The maintenance cost is also a revenue item, although a proportion of it would be a prepayment at the end of the year of acquisition (the amount would be dependent on the date of acquisition). The cost of the specification error must be recognized in profit or loss.

(ii) **Broadoak**	*30 September 20X0*	*30 September 20X1*
	$	$
Statement of comprehensive income extract		
In profit for the year:		
Amortization	(20,000)	(21,000)
Revaluation loss	Nil	(25,000)
In other comprehensive income		
Gain/(loss) on property revaluation	11,000	(10,000)
Statement of changes in equity extract		
Transfer of revaluation surplus:		
to retained earnings		1,000
from revaluation reserve		(1,000)
Statement of financial position extract		
Leasehold (W)	231,000	175,000
Revaluation reserve (W)	61,000	50,000

Workings:

Leasehold

Cost 1 October 19W9	240,000
Amortization to 30 September 20X0 (240,000/12 years)	(20,000)
	220,000
Revaluation gain	11,000
Carrying value 30 September 20X0	231,000
Amortization to 30 September 20X1 (231,000/ 11 years)	(21,000)
	210,000
Revaluation loss to revaluation reserve	(10,000)
Remaining loss to statement of comprehensive income	(25,000)
Carrying value 30 September 20X1	175,000

Revaluation reserve

Balance 1 October 19W9	50,000
Revaluation gain (see above)	11,000
Balance 30 September 20X0	61,000
Transfer to retained earnings (11,000 × 1/11)	(1,000)
Revaluation loss (see above)	(10,000)
Balance 30 September 20X1	50,000

15 ELITE LEISURE AND ADVENT

Key answer tips

Both parts of this question are fairly straightforward non-current asset questions.

(a) The cruise ship is an example of what can be called a complex asset. This is a single asset that should be treated as if it was a collection of separate assets, each of which may require a different depreciation method/life. In this case the question identifies three components to the cruise ship. The carrying amount of the asset at 30 September 20X3 (eight years after acquisition) would be:

Component	Cost $m	Depreciation $m		Carrying value $m
Ship's fabric	300	96	$(300/25 \times 8)$	204
Cabins and entertainment area	150	100	$(150/12 \times 8)$	50
Fittings				
Propulsion system	100	75	$(100/40,000 \times 30,000)$	25
	550	271		279

Ship's fabric

This is the most straightforward component. It is being depreciated over a 25 year life and depreciation of $12 million (300/25 years) would be required in the year ended 30 September 20X4. The repainting of the ship's fabric does not meet the recognition criteria of an asset and should be treated as repairs and maintenance.

Cabins and entertainment area and fittings

During the year these have had a limited upgrade at a cost of $60 million. This has extended the remaining useful life from four to five years. The costs of the upgrade meet the criteria for recognition as an asset. The original fittings have not been replaced thus the additional $60 million would be added to the cost of the fittings and the new carrying amount of $110 million will be depreciated over the remaining life of five years to give a charge for the year of $22 million.

Propulsion system

This has been replaced by a new system so the carrying value of the system ($25 million) must be written off and depreciation of the new system for the year ended 30 September 20X5 (based on use) would be $14 million (140 million/50,000 × 5,000).

Elite Leisure – statement of comprehensive income extract – year ended 30 September 20X4:

		$m
Depreciation	– ship's fabric	12
	– cabin and entertainment fittings	22
	– propulsion system	14
Disposal loss	– propulsion system	25
Repainting ship's fabric		20
		93

Elite Leisure – statement of financial position extract – as at 30 September 20X4

Non-current assets

Cruise ship (see working)   406

Workings (in $ million):

Component	Cost $m	Depreciation $m		Carrying value $m
Ship's fabric	300	108	(300/25 × 9)	192
Cabins and entertainment area fittings	210	122	(100 + 22)	88
Propulsion system	140	14		126
	650	244		406

(b)   (i)   **Non-current assets**

	30 September 20X4 $million	30 September 20X3 $million
Property, plant and equipment (note 1)	316	285
Intangible assets (note 2)	100	270

Note 1 Property, plant and equipment	Land and buildings $million	Plant $million	Total $million
Cost or valuation:			
At 1 October 20X3	280	150	430
Additions		50	50
Revaluation (see tutorial note)	(15)	Nil	(15)
At 30 September 20X4	265	200	465
Accumulated depreciation:			
At 1 October 20X3	40	105	145
Charge for year (see tutorial note)	9	35	44
Revaluation (see tutorial note)	(40)	Nil	(40)
At 30 September 20X4	9	140	149
Carrying value 30 September 20X4	256	60	316

The land and buildings were revalued by [   ] on an existing use basis on 1 October 20X3. They are being depreciated on a straight-line basis over a 25 year life. Plant is depreciated at 20% per annum on cost.

Tutorial note: these amounts can be calculated as:

	Land $million	Buildings $million
Cost	80	200
Depreciation (5/25)	Nil	(40)
Carrying value at 30.9.X3	80	160
Revaluation surplus	5	20
Revalued amount at 1.10.X3	85	180

The $40 million buildings depreciation accumulated at 30.9.X3 must be written back. As the total revaluation surplus is only $25 million, the $15 million difference must write down the valuation amount, to $265 million (85 + 180).

Deprecation on the buildings in 20X4 is $9 million (180/20 remaining useful life).

	$million
Plant depreciation	
Re b/f: 150 × 20%	30
Re acquisition: 50 × 20% × ½	5
	35

Note 2 Intangible assets:

	Telecomm- unication licence $million	Total $million
Cost at 1 October 20X3	300	300
And at 30 September 20X4	300	300
Accumulated amortization		
1 October 20X3	30	30
Amortization charge for year	30	30
Impairment charge for year (bal fig)	140	140
At 30 September 20X4	200	200
Carrying value 30 September 20X4	100	100

After the impairment charge the licence will be amortized over its remaining life of eight years on a straight-line basis.

(ii)   The usefulness of the above disclosures is:

– users can determine which type of non-current assets a business owns. There is a great deal of difference between owning say land and buildings compared with intangibles. The above figures give an illustration of this; the property has increased in value whereas the licence has fallen dramatically. Another factor relevant to this distinction is that it is usually easier to raise finance using property as security, whereas it can be difficult to raise finance on intangibles due to the volatility of their values.

– it is useful to know whether non-current assets are carried at historical cost or at revalued amount. If a company is using historical cost, it may be that statement of financial position values are seriously understated with a consequential effect on depreciation charges.

– information on accumulated depreciation gives a broad indication of the age of the relevant assets. In the case of Advent above, other than the plant acquired during the year, plant is almost fully depreciated. The implication of this, assuming the depreciation policy is appropriate, is that further acquisitions will be required in the near future. This in turn has future cash flow implications.

– it can also be noted that no disposals of plant have occurred, thus the acquisition of plant represents an increase in capacity. This may be an indication of growth.

– the disclosure of the impairment charge as part of the accumulated depreciation disclosures is self-evident. Users can determine that the acquisition of the licence appears to have been a financial disaster. Where a non-current asset is carried at historical cost, as in this case, the impairment is included as part of the depreciation rather than as a write down (revaluation) of the cost of the asset.

16 WILDERNESS GROUP

Key answer tips

In part (a), remember to discuss cash generating units as well as individual assets. Part (b) (i) requires application of this knowledge but part (ii) also requires you to consider IAS 38 and brands.

(a) (i) An impairment loss arises where the carrying amount of an asset is higher than its recoverable amount. The recoverable amount of an asset is defined in IAS 36 *Impairment of assets* as the higher of its fair value less costs to sell and its value in use (fair value less cost to sell was previously referred to as net selling price). Thus an impairment loss is simply the difference between the carrying amount of an asset and the higher of its fair value less costs to sell and its value in use.

Fair value:

The fair value could be based on the amount of a binding sale agreement or the market price where there is an active market. However many (used) assets do not have active markets and in these circumstances the fair value is based on a 'best estimate' approach to an arm's length transaction. It would not normally be based on the value of a forced sale. In each case the costs to sell would be the incremental costs directly attributable to the disposal of the asset.

Value in use:

The value in use of an asset is the estimated future net cash flows expected to be derived from the asset discounted to a present value. The estimates should allow for variations in the amount, timing and inherent risk of the cash flows. A major problem with this approach in practice is that most assets do not produce independent cash flows i.e. they usually produce cash flows in conjunction with other assets. For this reason IAS 36 introduces the concept of a cash-generating unit (CGU) which is the smallest identifiable group of assets, which may include goodwill, that generates (largely) independent cash flows.

Frequency of testing for impairment:

Goodwill and any intangible asset that is deemed to have an indefinite useful life should be tested for impairment at least annually, as too should any intangible asset that has not yet been brought into use. In addition, at each reporting period end an entity must consider if there has been any indication that other assets may have become impaired and, if so, an impairment test should be done. If there are no indications of impairment, testing is not required.

(ii) Once an impairment loss for an individual asset has been identified and calculated it is applied to reduce the carrying amount of the asset, which will then be the base for future depreciation charges. The impairment loss should be recognized in profit or loss. However, if the asset has previously been revalued upwards, the impairment loss should first be set against any revaluation surplus. The application of impairment losses to a CGU is more complex. They should first be applied to eliminate any goodwill and then to the other assets on a pro rata basis to their carrying amounts. However, an entity should not reduce the carrying amount of an asset (other than goodwill) to below the higher of its fair value less costs to sell and its value in use if these are determinable.

(b) (i) The plant had a carrying amount of $240,000 on 1 October 20X4. The accident that may have caused an impairment occurred on 1 April 20X5 and an impairment test would be done at this date. The depreciation on the plant from 1 October 20X4 to 1 April 20X5 would be $40,000 ($640,000 \times 12\frac{1}{2}\% \times 6/12$) giving a carrying amount of $200,000 at the date of impairment. An impairment test requires the plant's carrying amount to be compared with its recoverable amount. The recoverable amount of the plant is the higher of its value in use of $150,000 or its fair value less costs to sell. If Wilderness trades in the plant it would receive $180,000 by way of a part exchange, but this is conditional on buying new plant which Wilderness is reluctant to do. A more realistic amount of the fair value of the plant is its current disposal value of only $20,000. Thus the recoverable amount would be its value in use of $150,000 giving an impairment loss of $50,000 ($200,000 – $150,000). The remaining effect on income would be that a depreciation charge for the last six months of the year would be required. As the damage has reduced the remaining life to only two years (from the date of the impairment) the remaining depreciation would be $37,500 ($150,000/ 2 years × 6/12).Thus extracts from the financial statements for the year ended 30 September 20X5 would be:

Statement of financial position

Non-current assets	$
Plant (150,000 – 37,500)	112,500

Statement of comprehensive income

Plant depreciation (40,000 + 37,500)	77,500
Plant impairment loss	50,000

(ii) There are a number of issues relating to the carrying amount of the assets of Mossel that have to be considered. It appears the value of the brand is based on the original purchase of the 'Quencher' brand. The company no longer uses this brand name; it has been renamed 'Phoenix'. Thus it would appear the purchased brand of 'Quencher' is now worthless. Mossel cannot transfer the value of the old brand to the new brand, because this would be the recognition of an internally developed intangible asset and the brand of 'Phoenix' does not appear to meet the recognition criteria in IAS 38. Thus prior to the allocation of the impairment loss the value of the brand should be written off as it no longer exists.

The inventories are valued at cost and contain $2 million worth of old bottled water (Quencher) that can be sold, but will have to be relabelled at a cost of $250,000. However, as the expected selling price of these bottles will be $3 million ($2 million × 150%), their net realisable value is $2,750,000. Thus it is correct to carry them at cost i.e. they are not impaired. The future expenditure on the plant is a matter for the following year's financial statements.

Applying this, the revised carrying amount of the net assets of Mossel's cash-generating unit (CGU) would be $25 million ($32 million – $7 million re the brand). The CGU has a recoverable amount of $20 million, thus there is an impairment loss of $5 million. This would be applied first to goodwill (of which there is none) then to the remaining assets pro rata. However the inventories should not be reduced as their fair value less cost to sell is in excess of their carrying amount. This would give revised carrying amounts at 30 September 20X5 of:

	$000
Brand	nil
Land containing spa (12,000 – (12,000/20,000 × 5,000))	9,000
Purifying and bottling plant (8,000 – (8,000/20,000 × 5,000))	6,000
Inventories	5,000
	20,000

17   LINNET

Key answer tips

Part (a) is a routine question on long-term construction contracts which should not present you with too many problems.

Your answer to part (b) should do more than calculate the inventory write down and state that the company should recognize a provision or a contingent liability. It is not clear how much of the loss in value of the inventory is due to the water leak or whether Myriad is liable to pay compensation to Securiprint and you should cover all the possibilities (meeting the requirement to discuss).

(a)   (i)   Long-term construction contracts span more than one accounting year-end. This leads to the problem of determining how the uncompleted transactions should be dealt with over the life of the contract. Normal sales are not recognized until the production and sales cycle is complete. Prudence is the most obvious concept that is being applied in these circumstances, and this is the principle that underlies the completed contract basis. Where the outcome of a long-term contract cannot be reasonably foreseen due to inherent uncertainty, the completed contracts basis should be applied. The effect of this is that revenue earned to date is matched to the cost of sales and no profit is taken.

The problem with the above is that for say a three-year contract it can lead to a situation where no profits are recognized, possibly for two years, and in the year of completion the whole of the profit is recognized (assuming the contract is profitable). This seems consistent with the principle that only realized profits should be recognized in profit or loss. The problem is that the overriding requirement is for financial statements to faithfully represent economic reality. In the above case it can be argued that the company has been involved in a profitable contract for a three-year period, but its financial statements over the three years show a profit in only one period. This also leads to volatility of profits which many companies feel is undesirable and not favoured by analysts.

An alternative approach is to apply the matching/accruals concept which underlies the percentage of completion method. This approach requires the percentage of completion of a contract to be assessed (there are several methods of doing this) and then recognising in profit or loss that percentage of the total estimated profit on the contract. This method has the advantage of more stable profit recognition and can be argued gives a fairer presentation than the completed contract method. A contrary view is that this method can be criticized as being a form of profit smoothing which, in other circumstances, is considered to be an (undesirable) example of creative accounting.

Accounting standards require the use of the percentage of completion method where the outcome of the contract is reasonably foreseeable. It should also be noted that where a contract is expected to produce a loss, the whole of the loss must be recognized as soon as it is anticipated.

(ii) **Linnet – statement of comprehensive income extract – year to 31 March 20X4** (see working below):

	$ million
Revenue	70
Cost of sales (64 +17)	(81)
Loss for period	(11)

Linnet – statement of financial position extracts – as at 31 March 20X4

Current assets

Gross amounts due from customers for contract work (w(iii))	59

Workings

	Cumulative 1 April 20X3 $ million	Cumulative 31 March 20X4 $ million	Amounts for year $ million
Revenue	150	(see below) 220	70
Cost of sales	(112)	(176)	(64)
Rectification costs	nil	(17)	(17)
Profit (loss)	38	(see below) 27	(11)

Progress payments received are $180 million. This is 90% of the work certified (at 29 February 20X4), therefore the work certified at that date was $200 million. The value of the further work completed in March 20X4 is given as $20 million, giving a total value of contract revenue at 31 March 20X4 of $220 million.

The total estimated profit (excluding rectification costs) is $60 million:

	$ million
Contract price	300
Cost to date	(195)
Estimated cost to complete	(45)
Estimated total profit	60

The degree of completion (by the method given in the question) is 220/300.

Therefore the profit to date (before rectification costs) is $44 million ($60 million × 220/300). Rectification costs must be charged to the period they were incurred and not spread over the remainder of the contract life. Therefore after rectification costs of $17 million the total reported contract profit to 31 March 20X4 would be $27 million.

With contract revenue of $220 million and profit to date of $44 million, this means contract costs (excluding rectification costs) would be $176 million. The difference between this figure and total cost incurred of $195 million is part of the $59 million of the gross amounts due from customers shown in the statement of financial position.

The gross amounts due from customers is cost to date ($195 million + $17 million) plus cumulative profit ($27 million) less progress billings ($180 million) = $59 million.

(b) This is a complex situation. The selling prices of some items of inventory after the reporting period end appear to be below their cost and this indicates that part of the closing inventory (at 31 March 20X4) may require writing down to net realisable value with the resultant loss recognized in the current year. This is an adjusting event after the end of the reporting period if the losses are due to circumstances that occurred before the year-end. However, if the losses are due to circumstances that developed in the period after the reporting period end they should be included in the following year's financial statements (to 31 March 20X5). If these losses (in 20X5) are material they should be brought to the attention of shareholders in the notes to the financial statements for the year to 31 March 20X4 as a non-adjusting event. Appling the above to the circumstances of the question would give the following analysis:

	$
Cost	48
Net realisable value (NRV)	41
Apparent loss	7 per pack

The NRV of $41 is the reduced selling price of A4 paper of $45 less the cost of getting the goods into a saleable condition of $4.

From the question it would appear that this loss is partly attributable to the remedial cost of the water leak. This is an adjusting event requiring a write down of $2 per pack of the relevant items. The net realisable value at the year-end would have been $46 (original selling price of $50 less $4 remedial costs), which is $2 below the cost of $48. The remainder of the loss, $5 ($50 – $45), is caused by the price reduction in response to competitive pressure in the period after the reporting period end. This is a non-adjusting event requiring appropriate disclosure if material.

The above ignores the effect of the information concerning the sale to Securiprint. If the 'marks' are due to the water leak or other flaw in manufacture, Linnet will probably be liable to pay compensation to Securiprint. This would be an actual liability requiring a provision to be made in the current year unless the amount cannot be determined reliably (the IASB says this should be rare). The provision would be for a refund of the cost of the goods sold and compensation for consequential losses caused by the faulty goods. If the marks were not due to the actions of Linnet then there would be no liability. It may be that at this early stage there is insufficient information to come to a conclusion as to who is at fault, but this represents at least a contingent liability on the part of Linnet and should be disclosed appropriately in the notes to the financial statements. The information may also indicate that other customers could have similar claims against Linnet.

A final point to consider is that if the above fault is not due to Securiprint, it may mean that all of the inventory affected by the water leak is still damaged (despite the remedial work). If so, this would be evidence that the value of the inventory is impaired and a further provision would be required to write down the inventory (probably to nil) in the current year. Clearly no more of this inventory should be sold until the problem is resolved.

18   BOWTOCK

Key answer tips

This is a friendly question covering three separate topics: deferred tax, leasing and events after the reporting period end. Questions involving several standards are usually easier than 25-mark questions that examine a single standard, so you must ensure that you have a broad knowledge of the whole syllabus, rather than a specialized knowledge of just a few topics.

The lease in part (b) is clearly a finance lease since the lease term is five years, which is also the useful life of the asset.

(a)   (i)   Accounting profit (as reported in a company's financial statements) differs from the profit figure used by the tax authorities to calculate a company's income tax liability for a given period. If deferred tax were ignored (flow through system), then a company's tax charge for a particular period may bear very little resemblance to the reported profit. For example if a company makes a large profit in a particular period, but, perhaps because of high levels of capital expenditure, it is entitled to claim large tax allowances for that period, this would reduce the amount of tax it had to pay. The result of this would be that the company reported a large profit, but very little, if any, tax charge. This situation is usually 'reversed' in subsequent periods such that tax charges appear to be much higher than the reported profit would suggest that they should be.

Many commentators feel that such a reporting system is misleading in that the profit after tax, which is used for calculating the company's earnings per share, may bear very little resemblance to the pre tax profit. This can mean that a government's fiscal policy may distort a company's profit trends. Providing for deferred tax goes some way towards relieving this anomaly, but it can never be entirely corrected due to items that may be included in the statement of comprehensive income, but will never be allowed for tax purposes (referred to as permanent differences in some jurisdictions). Where tax depreciation is different from the related accounting depreciation charges this leads to the tax base of an asset being different to its carrying value on the statement of financial position (these differences are called temporary differences) and a provision for deferred tax is made. This 'statement of financial position liability' approach is the general principle on which IAS 12 bases the calculation of deferred tax. The effect of this is that it usually brings the total tax charge (i.e. the provision for the current year's income tax plus the deferred tax) in proportion to the profit reported to shareholders.

The main area of debate when providing for deferred tax is whether the provision meets the definition of a liability. If the provision is likely to crystallize, then it is a liability, however if it will not crystallize in the foreseeable future, then arguably, it is not a liability and should not be provided for. The IASB takes a prudent approach and IAS 12 does not accept the latter argument.

(ii)   IAS 12 requires deferred tax to be calculated using the 'statement of financial position liability method'. This method requires the temporary difference to be calculated and the rate of income tax applied to this difference to give the deferred tax asset or liability. Temporary differences are the differences between the carrying amount of an asset and its tax base.

Carrying value at 30 September 20X3	$000	$000
Cost of plant		2,000
Accumulated depreciation at 30 September 20X3 $(2,000 - 400)/8$ years for 3 years		(600)
Carrying value		1,400

Tax base at 30 September 20X3		
Initial tax base (original cost)		2,000
Tax depreciation		
Year to 30 September 20X1 $(2,000 \times 40\%)$	800	
Year to 30 September 20X2 $(1,200 \times 20\%)$	240	
Year to 30 September 20X3 $(960 \times 20\%)$	192	(1,232)
Tax base 30 September 20X3		768

Temporary differences at 30 September 20X3 $(1,400 - 768)$	632
Deferred tax liability at 30 September 20X3 $(632 \times 25\%$ tax rate)	158
Statement of comprehensive income credit – year to 30 September 20X3 ((200 accounts depn – 192 tax depn) $\times$ 25%)	2

(b)

	$
Statement of comprehensive income extracts year to 30 September 20X3	
Depreciation of leased asset (W1)	10,400
Lease interest expense (W2)	2,672
Statement of financial position extracts as at 30 September 20X3	
Leased asset at cost	52,000
Accumulated depreciation $(7,800 + 10,400$ (W1))	18,200
Net book value	33,800
Non-current liabilities	
Obligations under finance leases (W2)	21,696
Current liabilities	
Accrued lease interest (W2)	1,872
Obligations under finance leases (W2)	9,504

Workings

(W1) Depreciation for the year ended 30 September 20X2 would be $7,800 ($52,000 $\times$ 20% $\times$ 9/12). Depreciation for the year ended 30 September 20X3 would be $10,400 ($52,000 $\times$ 20%)

(W2) The lease obligations are calculated as follows:

Cash price/fair value	52,000
Rental 1 January 20X2	(12,000)
	40,000
Interest to 30 September 20X2 (40,000 × 8% × 9/12)	2,400
Interest to 1 January 20X3 (40,000 × 8% × 3/12)	800
	43,200
Rental 1 January 20X3	(12,000)
Capital outstanding 1 January 20X3	31,200
Interest to 30 September 20X3 (31,200 × 8% × 9/12)	1,872
Interest to 1 January 20X4 (31,200 × 8% × 3/12)	624
	33,696

The lease interest expense for the year to 30 September 20X3 is $2,672 (800 + 1,872 from above), of which $1,872 is a current liability. The total capital amount outstanding at 30 September 20X3 is $31,200 (the same as at 1 January 20X3 as no further payments have been made). This must be split between current and non-current liabilities. Next year's payment will be $12,000 of which $2,496 (1,872 + 624) is interest. Therefore capital repaid in the next year will be $9,504 (12,000 – 2,496). This leaves capital of $21,696 (31,200 – 9,504) as a non-current liability.

(c) (i) Most events occurring after the reporting period end should be properly reflected in the following year's financial statements. There are two circumstances where events occurring after the reporting period end are relevant to the current year's financial statements. The first category, known as adjusting events, provides additional evidence of conditions that existed at the reporting period end. This usually means they help to determine the value of an item that may have been uncertain at the year-end. Common examples of this are post statement of financial position receipts from accounts receivable and sales of inventory. These receipts help to confirm the bad debt and inventory write down allowances.

The second category is non-adjusting events. As the name suggests these do not affect the amounts contained in the financial statements, but are considered of such importance that unless they are disclosed, users of financial statements would not properly be able to assess the financial position of the company. Common examples of these would be the loss of a major asset (say due to a fire) after the reporting period end or the sale of an investment (often a subsidiary) after the reporting period end.

(ii) **Inventory**

Sales of goods after the reporting period end are normally a reflection of circumstances that existed prior to the year end. They are usually interpreted as a confirmation of the value of inventory as it existed at the year end, and are thus adjusting events. In this case the sale of the goods after the year-end confirmed that the value of the inventory was correctly stated as it was sold at a profit. Goods remaining unsold at the date the new legislation was enacted are worthless. Whilst this may imply that they should be written off in preparing the financial statements to 30 September 20X3, this is not the case. What it is important to realize is that the event that caused the inventory to become worthless did not exist at the year end and its consequent losses should be reflected in the following accounting period. Thus there should be no adjustment to the value of inventory in the draft financial statements, but given that it is material, it should be disclosed as a non-adjusting event.

Construction contract

On first appearance this new legislation appears similar to the previous example, but there is a major difference. Profits on an uncompleted long term construction contract are based on assessment of the overall eventual profit that the contract is expected to make. This new legislation will mean the overall profit is $500,000 less than originally thought. This information must be taken into account when calculating the profit at 30 September 20X3. This is an adjusting event.

ACCA marking scheme				Marks
(a)	(i)	1 mark per valid point to maximum		5
	(ii)	Carrying value and tax base at 30 September 20X3		3
		Calculation of deferred tax at 30 September 20X3		2
		Deferred tax credit in statement of comprehensive income		2
			available	7
			maximum	6
(b)		Depreciation of leased asset		1
		Lease interest expense		1
		Net book value of leased asset		1
		Current liabilities: accrued lease interest		1
		Obligations under finance leases		1
		Non-current liabilities: obligations under finance leases		1
			available	6
			maximum	5
(c)	(i)	1 mark per valid point to maximum		4
	(ii)	Discussion of value of inventory up to		3
		Discussion of effect on construction contract up to		2
			maximum	5
			Maximum for question	25

19 MULTIPLEX

Key answer tips

Notice the key requirement word in each of the four parts of the question. In parts (a) and (b) it is *calculate* and in part (d) it is *prepare*. Part (c) is the odd one out as you are asked to *advise*.

(a) **Statement of comprehensive income extracts:**

	$000	$000
Loan stock interest paid ($80 million × 8%)		6,400
Required accrual of finance cost		1,844
Total finance cost for loan stock ($68,704,000 × 12%)		8,244

Statement of financial position extracts:

Non-current liabilities		
8% loan stock 20X4	68,704	
Accrual of finance costs	1,844	70,548
Equity and liabilities		
Share options		11,296

Workings

IAS 32 and 39, dealing with financial instruments, require compound or hybrid financial instruments such as convertible loan stock to be treated under the substance of the contractual agreement. For this type of instrument this means that its equity element and liability (debt) element must be separately identified and presented as such on the statement of financial position. There are several methods of calculating the split between the two elements. For example there are several option pricing models. However, given the limited information in the question, the split can only be calculated by a 'residual value of equity' approach. This involves calculating the present value of the cash flows attributable to a 'pure' debt instrument and treating the difference between this and the issue proceeds (the residue) as the equity component.

	Cash flow $m	Factor 12%	Discounted cash flow $000
Year 1 interest	6.4	× 0.89	5,696
Year 2 interest	6.4	× 0.80	5,120
Year 3 interest	6.4	× 0.71	4,544
Year 4 interest	6.4	× 0.64	4,096
Year 5 interest and capital	86.4	× 0.57	49,248
			68,704
Residual equity element (share options)			11,296
Proceeds of issue			80,000

(b)

	Assets: 1 Jan 20X0 $000	First impair- ment $000	Revised assets: 1 Feb 20X0 $000	Second impair- ment $000	Revised assets: 31 Mar 20X0 $000
Goodwill	200	(200)	nil		nil
Operating licence	1,200	(200)	1,000	(100)	900
Property – train stations/land	300	(50)	250	(50)	200
Rail track and coaches	300	(50)	250	(50)	200
Steam engines	1,000	(500)	500		500
	3,000	(1,000)	2,000	(200)	1,800

Notes

The first impairment loss of $1 million:

- $500,000 must be written off the engines as one of them no longer exists and is no longer part of the cash-generating unit

- the goodwill of $200,000 must be eliminated; and

- the balance of $300,000 is allocated pro rata to the remaining net assets (other than the engine which must not be reduced below its net selling price of $500,000), so (1,200/1,200 + 300 + 300) to the operating licence and so on.

The second impairment loss of $200,000:

- the first $100,000 is applied to the licence to write it down to its net selling price

- the balance is applied pro rata to assets other than those carried at their net selling prices i.e. $50,000 to both the property and the rail track and coaches.

Tutorial note: as Multiplex owns 100% of Steamdays, there is no grossing up of notional goodwill for the amount attributable to a minority interest.

(c)   Under IFRS 5 *Non-current Assets Held for Sale and Discontinued Operations* the engineering division meets the definition of a disposal group which must be treated in the financial statements in the same way as an asset 'held for sale'. As the division was not sold until after the year end then the directors must include it in the statement of financial position at the lower of the carrying amount and the fair value less costs to sell.

The current carrying value of the division is $46m ($66m – $20m) and the fair value less costs to sell is the agreed value of $30m. Therefore the division should be presented in the statement of financial position at 31 March 20X0 at a value of $30m below current assets. The impairment of $16m ($46m – $30m) must be recognized in the statement of comprehensive income.

As the division is classified as 'held for sale', represents a separate major line of business and is part of a single co-ordinated plant to dispose of this separate major line, then it meets the IFRS 5 definition of discontinued operations. Therefore in the statement of comprehensive income there should be a single amount comprising the total post-tax profit or loss of the division and the $16m impairment required to measure the division at fair value less costs to sell.

As the company is committed to the closure it should also recognize a provision for the cost of the closure (as required by IAS 37). The total provision should be made up of the following amounts:

	$m
Redundancies	2.0
Professional costs	1.5
Penalty costs	3.0
	6.5

The operating losses of $4.5 million in the period from 1 April 20X0 until the date of closure cannot be provided for at the date the closure is announced. IAS 37 *Provisions, Contingent Liabilities and Contingent Assets* prohibits this type of provision unless it relates to losses on 'onerous contracts'. There is no indication in the question that these future losses relate to onerous contracts.

(d)   **Statement of comprehensive income year to 31 March 20X0** $m

Contract revenue (W2)	18.0
Contract costs recognized (balancing figure)	(14.1)
Contract profit (W3)	3.9

Statement of financial position extracts as at 31 March 20X0 $m

Current assets
Gross amounts due from customers (W5)   11.0

Note to the financial statements

Contingent asset

The company is in the process of attempting to recover $2.5 million from a firm of civil engineers. The engineers were contracted to design the structure of a road bridge to be built by Multiplex. The engineers incorrectly specified certain materials to be used on the contract, which had to be replaced at a later date. The company's lawyers have advised that there is a good prospect of a successful recovery of these costs.

Workings

(W1) The percentage of completion is calculated as:

	at 31 March 19W9		at 31 March 20X0	
$\dfrac{\text{Work certified}}{\text{Contract price}}$	$\dfrac{\$12\text{ million}}{\$40\text{ million}}$	$= 30\%$	$\dfrac{\$30\text{ million}}{\$45\text{ million}}$	$= 66.7\%$ (or $^2/_3$)

The figure for 20X0 includes the variation to the contract.

(W2) The accumulated contract revenues at 31 March 20X0 would be $30 million (2/3 × $45 million). The contract revenue to be recognized in 20X0 would be $18 million i.e. accumulated revenue of $30 million less the contract revenue of $12 million reported in the previous year.

(W3) The accumulated profit at 31 March 20X0 would have been 2/3 of the revised estimated total profit of $15 million ($45 million contract price less $30 million costs) = $10 million. However the cost of the rectification work of $2.5 million must be charged to the year in which it occurs (i.e. the year to 31 March 20X0).

This gives a profit for the year of $3.9 million ($10 million − $3.6 million in 19W9 − $2.5 million rectification work).

(W4) The statement of comprehensive income for the year to 31 March 19W9 would be:

	$m
Contract revenue	12.0
Contract costs incurred (balancing figure)	(8.4)
	———
Profit ((40 − 28) × 30%)	3.6
	———

(W5) The gross amount due from customers is made up of:

Costs incurred to date	28.5
Plus recognized profits (3.6 + 3.9)	7.5
less Progress billings	(25.0)
	———
	11.0
	———

20 TORRENT

Key answer tips

The best way is to deal with the accounting for construction contracts is to work through one contract at a time, establishing whether over its life the contract is expected to generate profits (recognize only by the stage of completion method) or incur losses (recognize in full immediately). The requirement that unplanned rectification costs should be recognized in full in the year in which they are incurred (rather than being a normal cost which is spread over the life of the contract) is quite tricky.

(a) **Statement of comprehensive income for the year ended 31 March 20X6**

	Alpha	Beta	Ceta	Total
	$m	$m	$m	$m
Revenue (W1 – W3)	8	2.0	4.8	14.8
Cost of sales (W1 – W3)	(7)	(3.5)	(4.0)	(14.5)
Profit/(loss)	1	(1.5)	0.8	0.3

Statement of financial position at 31 March 20X6

Current assets

	Alpha	Beta	Ceta	Total
Gross amounts due from customers for contract work (W4)	1.0		4.8	5.8
Receivables – amounts recoverable on contracts ((14 – 12.6) and (2 – 1.8))	1.4	0.2		1.6
Current liabilities				
Gross amounts due to customers for contract work **(W4)**		(1.5)		(1.5)

Workings ($m)

(W1) **Alpha**

	At 31.3.05	At 31.3.06	Year to 31.3.06
Work invoiced	6.0 (5.4/90%)	14.0 (12.6/90%)	8
Cost of sales (β)	(4.5)	(11.5)	(7)
Profit	1.5	2.5	1

Profit is calculated as:

	At 31.3.05	At 31.3.06
% complete	30% (6/20 ×100)	70% (14/20 × 100)
Attributable profit	1.5 ((20 – 15) ×30%)	2.5 ((20 – 15) ×70%) – 1 rectification)

Rectification costs must be charged in the year in which they are incurred.

(W2) **Beta**

Due to the increase in the estimated cost, Beta is a loss-making contract and the whole of the loss must be provided for as soon as it is can be anticipated. The loss is expected to be $1.5 million ($7.5m – $6m). The revenue of the contract at 31 March 20X6 is $2 million ($1.8/90%), thus the cost of sales must be recorded as $3.5 million. As costs to date are $2 million, this means a provision of $1.5 million is required.

(W3) **Ceta**

Based on the costs to date at 31 March 20X6 of $4 million and the total estimated costs of $10 million, this contract is 40% complete. The estimated profit is $2 million ($12m – $10m); therefore the profit at 31 March 20X6 is $0.8 million ($2m × 40%). This gives an imputed revenue (and receivable) value of $4.8 million.

(W4) Gross amount due to/from customers

	Alpha $m	Beta $m	Ceta $m	Total $m
Contract cost incurred	12.5	2.0	4.0	18.5
Recognized profits/(losses)	2.5	(1.5)	0.8	1.8
Progress billings	(14.0)	(2.0)	(nil)	(16.0)
Due from customers	1.0		4.8	5.8
Due to customers		(1.5)		(1.5)

(b)   (i)   Savoir – EPS year ended 31 March 20X4:

The issue on 1 July 20X3 at full market value needs to be weighted:

Old shares (10/25c)   40m   3/12 =   10m
New shares   8m

                    48m × 9/12 =   36m

                          46m

Without the bonus issue this would give an EPS of 30c ($13.8m/46m × 100).

The bonus issue of one for four would result in 12 million new shares giving a total number of ordinary shares of 60 million. The dilutive effect of the bonus issue would reduce the EPS to 24c (30c × 48m/60m).

The comparative EPS (for 20X3) would be restated at 20c (25c × 48m/60m).

EPS year ended 31 March 20X5:

The rights issue of two for five on 1 October 20X4 is half way through the year. The theoretical ex rights value can be calculated as:

Holder of	100 shares worth $2.40 =	$240	
Subscribes for	40 shares at $1 each =	$40	
Now holds	140 worth (in theory)	$280	i.e. $2 each.

Weighting:

                        60m × 6/12 × 2.40/2.00 =   36 million

Rights issue (2 for 5)   24m

New total   84m × 6/12 =   42 million

Weighted average   78 million

EPS is therefore 25c ($19.5m/78m × 100).

The comparative (for 20X4) would be restated at 20c (24c × 2.00/2.40).

(ii)   The basic EPS for the year ended 31 March 20X6 is 30c ($25.2m/84m × 100).

Dilution

Convertible loan stock

On conversion loan interest of $1.2 million after tax would be saved ($20 million × 8% × (100% − 25%)) and a further 10 million shares would be issued ($20m/$100 × 50).

Directors' options

Options for 12 million shares at $1.50 each would yield proceeds of $18 million. At the average market price of $2.50 per share this would purchase 7.2 million shares ($18m/$2.50). Therefore the 'bonus' element of the options is 4.8 million shares (12m − 7.2m).

Using the above figures the diluted EPS for the year ended 31 March 20X6 is 26.7c ($25.2m + $1.2m)/(84m + 10m + 4.8m)).

21   QRS

Key answer tips

The two types of instruments in part (a) are the most important for this syllabus so you must know how to classify them.

In general, under the requirements of IAS 32 *Financial Instruments:Presentation,* financial instruments that fulfil the characteristics of a liability should be classified as such. Although preferred shares carry the description of 'shares' this does not mean that they can necessarily be classified as equity. In cases where the payment of the 'dividend' is a fixed sum that is normally paid in respect of each accounting period, the instrument is really a long-term liability and must be classified as such.

The convertible bonds would be classified as a compound, or hybrid, instrument by IAS 32; that is, they have characteristics of both debt and equity, and would therefore be presented partly as debt and partly as equity in the statement of financial position.Valuation of the equity element is often difficult. One method permitted by IAS 32 involves valuation of the liability element using an equivalent market rate of interest for non-convertible bonds, with equity as a residual figure.

Applying this approach to the proposed instrument, the following debt/equity split results:

	$
Present value of the capital element of the bond issue:	
$6 million × 0.735	4,410,000
Interest at present value:	
($6,000,000 × 6%) × (0.926 + 0.857 + 0.794 + 0.735)	
= $360,000 × 3.312	1,192,320
Value of liability element	5,602,320
Equity element (balancing figure)	397,680
Total value of instrument	6,000,000

Apart from the relatively small element of the hybrid instrument that can be classified as equity, the two proposed issues will be classified as debt under the provisions of IAS 32. If the directors wish to obtain finance through an issue of financial instruments that can be properly classified as equity, they should reconsider the rights issue proposal.

22 PX

(i) **Appropriate classification**

Securities of a listed entity

This investment has been acquired in order to be sold in the near future and so it meets the IAS 39 definition of an instrument 'held for trading'. Therefore it should be classified as a financial asset at fair value through profit or loss, as required by IAS 39.

Variable interest rate loan

This is a financial asset and PX intends to hold the loan until it is due for repayment (it has guaranteed not to assign the loan to a third party). The payments are also fixed and determinable and the repayment date is fixed. Therefore the loan should be classified as a held to maturity investment.

Portfolio of investments

These investments are not held for trading because there is no intention to sell them in the near future. They are not derivatives, nor do they fall into the other categories. Therefore they must be classified as available for sale financial assets.

(ii) **How the financial assets should be measured**

The following requirements apply:

- The listed securities are 'at fair value through profit or loss' and therefore are measured at fair value.

- The variable interest rate loan is measured at amortized cost (as a held to maturity investment).

- The investment portfolio is measured at fair value (as an available for sale financial asset).

23 TALL

(a) **MEMORANDUM**

To:	Assistant Management Accountant
From:	Management Accountant
Date:	xx-xx-xxxx
Subject:	Presentation of financial instruments

This memorandum explains the correct presentation of financial instruments in accordance with international accounting standards.

IAS 32 governs this area of accounting. The issuer of a financial instrument should classify it as a liability or as equity in accordance with the substance of the arrangement. Essentially one must look at the definitions of a financial liability and an equity instrument in IAS 32 and act accordingly.

The critical feature in identifying a financial liability is the existence of a contractual obligation on the issuer either to deliver cash or another financial asset to the holder, or to exchange instruments under conditions unfavourable to the issuer. The $1 bonds we have issued certainly qualify as a financial liability, since they are redeemable at a fixed price on a fixed date. The option to convert into equity shares is at the **holders'** discretion, so we have no power over this decision. There is a contractual obligation that we may have to fulfil, to pay cash in five years' time, thus the bonds should be shown as non-current liabilities on the statement of financial position, and not as part of equity.

Since the preference shares are mandatorily redeemable at a fixed future date, they also qualify as a financial liability. They should also be shown as non-current liabilities on the statement of financial position, and not as part of equity. The fact that they are legally shares is irrelevant to their IAS 32 classification which depends on the substance of the contractual arrangement involved.

Signed: Management Accountant

(b)   IAS 39 requires that a financial liability should initially be recognized at its cost ie the fair value of the consideration received for it. Subsequently, financial liabilities should be measured at amortized cost (except for liabilities held for trading, and other financial liabilities that are designated as being measured at fair value through profit or loss, which should be measured at fair value).

Capital instruments, such as bonds and redeemable preference shares, that qualify as financial liabilities like those discussed in part (a), should therefore be shown in each statement of financial position at their amortized cost. This is:

	$
The amount at which initially recognized	x
± effective interest rate	x
– repayments of interest/principal	(x)
	x

The annual movement in the carrying value of a financial liability should be reported in profit or loss as expense or income. For a bond, the expense will normally comprize two elements: the annual interest paid and the annual amortization of the premium payable on redemption. For zero interest bonds such as issued by Tall, there is no annual interest and the year's charge to profit or loss will comprise solely the year's amortization of the premium payable on redemption.

For zero dividend redeemable preference shares such as issued by Tall, the annual charge to profit or loss will similarly be solely the year's amortization of the premium payable on redemption. Note that this charge is shown as a finance cost expense in the statement of comprehensive income, not as a dividend cost in the statement of changes in equity. This is true for all costs relating to preference shares that qualify as financial liabilities. Any dividends paid on such preference shares are shown effectively as an interest expense in the statement of comprehensive income, since this reflects the substance of the contractual arrangement. It is only the dividends paid on shares that qualify as equity instruments that are taken directly to equity and disclosed in the statement of changes in equity.

24   TRIANGLE

Key answer tips

For this question you will need knowledge of IAS 37, IAS 10 and the IASB's Framework as it concerns the substance of transactions. Note that you are required to 'explain' the appropriate accounting treatment, therefore your answer should be largely in narrative form with quantification of the amounts where possible.

(i)   Future decontamination costs must be provided for in full at the time they become unavoidable. Where they are based on future values, they should be discounted to their present value (as has been done in this example). Rather than being immediately written off to the statement of comprehensive income, the decontamination costs are added to the cost of the related asset and amortized over the expected life of the asset. The current treatment of these costs by Triangle is incorrect. The depreciation charge must be based on the full cost of the plant which must include the decontamination costs. Also an imputed finance cost must be applied to the provision (often referred to as unwinding). Applying this, the extracts of the financial statements of Triangle at 31 March 20X5 would be:

Non-current assets	$ million
Plant at cost ($15 million + $5 million)	20.0
Depreciation at 10% per annum	(2.0)
	18.0
Non-current liabilities	
Provision	5.0
Accrued finance costs	0.4
	5.4
Statement of comprehensive income	
Depreciation	2.0
Accrued finance costs ($5 million × 8%)	0.4

(ii)   This is an example of an adjusting event after the end of the reporting period. To some extent the figures in the draft financial statements already reflect the effects of the fraud (up to the amount at the year end i.e. $210,000) in that presumably the cost of the materials paid for are included in cost of sales. However, the financial statements are incorrect in their presentation. As the fraud is considered material, $210,000 should be removed from the cost of sales and included as an operating expense (perhaps with separate disclosure). This will affect the gross profit and other ratios, though it will not affect the net profit. The further costs beyond the year end of $30,000 should be noted as a non-adjusting event (if material in their own right).

(iii) Triangle is of the opinion that the cost of the fraud may be covered by an insurance claim. However the insurance company is disputing the claim. This appears to be a contingent asset. If an outflow of resources is probable, a contingent asset should be noted in the financial statements. However if it is only possible, it should be ignored. As this claim is at an early stage and the company has not yet sought a legal opinion, it would be premature to consider the claim probable. In these circumstances the contingent asset should be ignored and the financial statements will be unaffected.

(iv)   Although this transaction has been treated as a sale, this is probably not its substance. The clause allowing Triangle to repurchase the inventory makes this a sale and repurchase agreement. Assuming Triangle acts rationally it will repurchase the inventory if its retail value at 31 March 20X8 is more than $7,320,500 ($5 million plus compound interest at 10% for four years) plus the accumulated storage costs (as these can be recovered from Factorall in the event that the inventory is not repurchased). There is no indication in the question as to what the inventory is likely to be worth on 31 March 20X8.

However it is unlikely that a finance company will really want to acquire this inventory (it is not its normal line of business) and thus it would not have entered into the contract unless it believed Triangle would repurchase the inventory. If the above is correct the substance of the transaction is that it is a secured loan rather than a sale. The required adjustments would therefore be:

– Remove $5 million from revenue (debit) and treat this as a long-term (four-year) loan.

– Remove $3 million from cost of sales and treat this as inventory.

– The receivable for the storage cost should be removed from trade receivables and added to the cost of the inventory.

– Accrued interest of $500,000 ($5 million × 10%) should be recognized in profit or loss and added to the carrying value of the loan.

25 PARTWAY

(a) (i) IFRS 5 *Non-current assets held for sale and discontinued operations* defines non-current assets held for sale as those assets (or a group of assets) whose carrying amounts will be recovered principally through a sale transaction rather than through continuing use. For this to be the case the assets must be available for immediate sale, subject only to conditions which are usual for sales of such assets, and the sale must be highly probable, eg it must be expected to be completed within 12 months of the classification as held for sale.

A discontinued operation is a component of an entity that has either been disposed of, or is classified as 'held for sale' and:

(i) represents a separate major line of business or geographical area of operations

(ii) is part of a single co-ordinated plan to dispose of such, or

(iii) is a subsidiary acquired exclusively for sale.

IFRS 5 says that a 'component of an entity' must have operations and cash flows that can be clearly distinguished from the rest of the entity and will in all probability have been a cash-generating unit (or group of such units) whilst held for use. This definition also means that a discontinued operation will also fall to be treated as a 'disposal group' as defined in IFRS 5. A disposal group is a group of assets (possibly with associated liabilities) that it is intended will be disposed of in a single transaction by sale or otherwise (closure or abandonment). Assets held for disposal (but not those being abandoned) must be presented separately (at the lower of cost or fair value less costs to sell) from other assets and included as current assets (rather than as non-current assets) and any associated liabilities must be separately presented under liabilities. The results of a discontinued operation should be disclosed separately as a single figure (as a minimum) as part of the profit for the year in the statement of comprehensive income with more detailed figures disclosed either in the statement of comprehensive income or in the notes.

The intention of this requirement is to improve the usefulness of the financial statements by improving the predictive value of the (historical) statement of comprehensive income. Clearly the results from discontinued operations should have little impact on future operating results. Thus users can focus on the continuing activities in any assessment of future income and profit.

(ii) The timing of the board meeting and consequent actions and notifications is within the accounting period ended 31 October 20X6. The notification of staff, suppliers and the press seems to indicate that the sale will be highly probable and the directors are committed to a plan to sell the assets and are actively locating a buyer. From the financial and other information given in the question it appears that the travel agencies' operations and cash flows can be clearly distinguished from its other operations. The assets of the travel agencies appear to meet the definition of non-current assets held for sale; however the main difficulty is whether their sale and closure also represent a discontinued operation. The main issue is with the wording of 'a separate major line of business' in part (i) of the above definition of a discontinued operation. The company is still operating in the holiday business, but only through Internet selling. The selling of holidays through the Internet compared with through high-street travel agencies requires very different assets, staff knowledge and training and has a different cost structure. It could therefore be argued that although the company is still selling holidays the travel agencies do represent a separate line of business. If this is the case, it seems the announced closure of the travel agencies appears to meet the definition of a discontinued operation.

(iii) **Partway statement of comprehensive income year ended:**

	31 October 20X6 $000	31 October 20X5 $000
Continuing operations		
Revenue	25,000	22,000
Cost of sales	(19,500)	(17,000)
Gross profit	5,500	5,000
Operating expenses	(1,100)	(500)
Profit/(loss) from continuing operations	4,400	4,500
Discontinued operations		
Profit/(loss) from discontinued operations	(4,000)	1,500
Profit for the period	400	6,000
Analysis of discontinued operations		
Revenue	14,000	18,000
Cost of sales	(16,500)	(15,000)
Gross profit/(loss)	(2,500)	3,000
Operating expenses	(1,500)	(1,500)
Profit/(loss) from discontinued operations	(4,000)	1,500

Note: other presentations may be acceptable.

(b) (i) Comparability is one of the four principal qualitative characteristics of useful financial information. It is a vital attribute when assessing the performance of an entity over time (trend analysis) and to some extent with other similar entities. For information to be comparable it should be based on the consistent treatment of transactions and events. In effect a change in an accounting policy breaks the principle of consistency and should generally be avoided. That said there are circumstances where it becomes necessary to change an accounting policy. These are mainly where it is required by a new or revised accounting standard, interpretation or applicable legislation or where the change would result in financial statements giving a reliable and more relevant representation of the entity's transactions and events.

It is important to note that the application of a different accounting policy to transactions or events that are substantially different to existing transactions or events or to transactions or events that an entity had not previously experienced does NOT represent a change in an accounting policy. It is also necessary to distinguish between a change in an accounting policy and a change in an estimation technique.

In an attempt to limit the problem of reduced comparability caused by a change in an accounting policy, the general principle is that the financial statements should be prepared as if the new accounting policy had always been in place. This is known as retrospective application. The main effect of this is that comparative financial statements should be restated by applying the new policy to them and adjusting the opening balance of each component of equity affected in the earliest prior period presented. IAS 8 *Accounting policies, changes in accounting estimates and errors* says that a change in accounting policy required by a specific Standard or Interpretation should be dealt with under the transitional provisions (if any) of that Standard or Interpretation (normally these apply the general rule of retrospective application). There are some limited exemptions (mainly on the grounds of impracticality) to the general principle of retrospective application in IAS 8.

(ii) This issue is one of the timing of when revenue should be recognized in the statement of comprehensive income. This can be a complex issue which involves identifying the transfer of significant risks, reliable measurement, the probability of receiving economic benefits, relevant accounting standards and legislation and generally accepted practice. Applying the general guidance in IAS 18 *Revenue*, the previous policy, applied before cancellation insurance was made a condition of booking, seemed appropriate. At the time the holiday is taken it can no longer be cancelled, all monies would have been received and the flights and accommodation have been provided. There may be some compensation costs involved if there are problems with the holiday, but this is akin to product warranties on normal sales of goods which may be immaterial or provided for based on previous experience of such costs. The appendix to IAS 18 specifically refers to payments in advance of the 'delivery' of goods and says that revenue should be recognized when the goods are delivered. Interpreting this for Partway's transaction would seem to confirm the appropriateness of its previous policy.

The directors of Partway wish to change the timing of recognition of sales because of the change in circumstances relating to the compulsory cancellation insurance. The directors are apparently arguing that the new 'transactions and events' are substantially different to previous transactions therefore the old policy should not apply. Even if this does justify revising the timing of the recognition of revenue, it is not a change of accounting policy because of the reasons outlined in (i) above.

An issue to consider is whether compulsory cancellation insurance represents a substantial change to the risks that Partway experiences. An analysis of past experience of losses caused by uninsured cancellations may help to assess this, but even if the past losses were material (and in future they will not be), it is unlikely that this would override the general guidance in the appendix to IAS 18 relating to payments made in advance of delivery. It seems the main motivation for the proposed change is to improve the profit for the year ended 31 October 20X6 so that it compares more favourably with that of the previous period.

To summarize, it is unlikely that the imposition of compulsory cancellation insurance justifies recognising revenue at the date of booking when a deposit is received, and, even if it did, it would not be a change in accounting policy. This means that comparatives would not be restated (which is something that would actually suit the suspected objectives of the directors).

26 SITUATIONS

(a) (i)   This is an example of a contingent liability. As it was only considered possible that AB would have to pay damages there has been no provision made for this liability. However under IFRS 3 XY must recognize the fair value of this contingent liability within net assets acquired for the purpose of the goodwill calculation.

(ii)   At the acquisition date there was no obligation to incur the integration costs and no liability should be recognized within net assets acquired (IFRS 3 and IAS 37).

(b)   Finance cost   =   Total payments payable in respect of an instrument *minus* Net proceeds on issue of the instrument

			$m
Total payments	=	Interest ($5 \times 4\% \times \$50m$)	10
		+ Repayment amount	60
			70

Assuming that the borrowings were issued at par:

			$m
Net proceeds on issue	=	Gross proceeds	50
		minus Direct costs of the issue	(0.5)
			49.5

∴ Total finance cost   =   70 – 49.5 = $20.5m

(c)   At the time of the initial acquisition of the investment it would have been designated as held-for-trading and included in the statement of financial position as such at a value of $51,000 (60,000 × 85c).

At 31 March 20X5 the investment would be remeasured to fair value of $52,500 (60,000 × 87.5c) and would appear in the statement of financial position at this value. The gain on the remeasurement of $1,500 would be recognized in profit or loss.

(d)   The results of a subsidiary that is held exclusively with a view to resale are not consolidated line by line in the normal way, provided that the subsidiary qualifies as 'held for sale' under IFRS 5 *Non-current Assets Held for Sale and Discontinued Operations.* To be classified as 'held for sale' management must be committed to the sale, the disposal must be highly probable and the sale must be expected to take place within 12 months of the date of acquisition (i.e. before December 20X6). In these circumstances the subsidiary is treated as a discontinued operation and its result is presented as a one-line adjustment to profit for the year from continuing activities.

Tutorial note: such as subsidiary is consolidated in the statement of financial position, but with all its assets and all its liabilities presented as two line items. They are not consolidated line by line.

(e) As this is a hybrid financial instrument it should be recognized in the statement of financial position as partly debt and partly capital. The measurement of the equity element is the residual value once the present value of the liability element has been computed using the 6% interest rate for such debt without conversion terms.

	$
Present value of principal (10,000 × 50 × 0.747)	373,500
Present value of interest payments (500,000 × 5% × 4.212)	105,300
Debt element	478,800
Equity element (balance)	21,200
	500,000

27 WINGER

Key answer tips

Read the information in the question carefully. There are several potential problem areas:

– the goods sold on sale or return must be brought back into inventory (W1);

– the profit on the sale of the buildings has been incorrectly calculated (W1); and

– the proposed prior period adjustment (W1).

Remember to leave enough time to answer part (c) and to relate the issue of non-depreciation to the scenario in the main part of the question; simply re-stating the requirements of IAS 16 will not gain full marks.

(a) **Winger**

Statement of comprehensive income for year to 31 March 20X0

	$000	$000
Revenue (358,450 – 27,000 (W1))		331,450
Cost of sales (W1)		(223,550)
Gross profit		107,900
Distribution expenses		(28,700)
Administration expenses		(15,000)
		64,200
Finance costs (W3) (4,000 + 7,200)		(11,200)
Profit before tax		53,000
Income tax expense (15,000 – 2,200)		(12,800)
Profit for the period		40,200

(b) **Winger – Statement of financial position as at 31 March 20X0**

Non-current assets	$000	$000
Property, plant and equipment (W5)		354,000
Current assets		
Inventories (28,240 + 22,500 (W1))	50,740	
Trade accounts receivable (55,000 – 27,000 (W1))	28,000	
Cash	10,660	89,400
		———
Total assets		443,400
		———
Equity and liabilities:		
Equity		
Equity shares of 25c each		150,000
Reserves:		
Retained earnings ((W8)		129,800
		———
		279,800
Non-current liabilities		
8% Loan notes	50,000	
Leasing obligations (W4)	47,200	97,200
Current liabilities		
Trade and other payables (W6)	51,400	
Income tax	15,000	
	———	
		66,400
		———
Total equity and liabilities		443,400
		———

Workings

(W1) **Cost of sales**	$000
Per question	185,050
Additional inventory on sale or return at cost (see below)	(22,500)
Depreciation (W2)	46,000
Loss on abandonment of research project (W8)	30,000
Profit on disposal of property (W8)	(15,000)
	———
	223,550
	———

As the period allowed for the return of the goods has not expired, they cannot be treated as a sale and must therefore be brought back into inventory at their cost. A mark-up of 20% (1/5) on cost is equivalent to a profit of 1/6 on selling price, therefore the profit in these sales is $27 million × 1/6 = $4.5 million. The cost of these goods is therefore $22.5 million.

The directors are incorrect in the calculation of the profit on the sale of the building. IAS 16 *Property, Plant and Equipment* states that the profit on the disposal of an asset is the difference between the carrying value of the asset and its (net) sale proceeds. Thus the profit will be $15 million reported in the statement of comprehensive income. A consequence of the sale is that the revaluation surplus, which would have been $30 million, is now realized and should be transferred to retained earnings in the statement of changes in equity.

The directors are also mistaken in their opinion of the treatment of the deferred development expenditure. The reason for it having to be written off is because its value has become impaired due to adverse legislation and not to a change in accounting policy. It is now effectively worthless. As there has not been a change in the company's accounting policy, it cannot be treated as a prior period adjustment; it must be written off to the statement of comprehensive income.

(W2) Depreciation

Property:	$000
Heating system (20,000/10 years)	2,000
Lifts (30,000/15 years)	2,000
Building (100,000/50 years)	2,000
	6,000
Owned plant (154,800 – 34,800) × 20%	24,000
Leased plant (W4) (20% × 80,000)	16,000
	46,000

(W3) Finance costs

Loan note interest (2,000 + 2,000 accrued)	4,000
Interest on finance lease (W4)	7,200
	11,200

(W4) Finance lease

The cash price of leased plant of $80 million should be capitalized and included as plant and equipment. As the lease has a five-year life, straight-line depreciation for the year to 31 March 20X0 will be 20% of $80 million = $16 million. Interest implicit in the lease is 12% pa, details of lease obligations are:

	$000
Obligation 1 April 19W9	80,000
Less first payment	(20,000)
Balance outstanding during year	60,000
Interest at 12% pa (charged to statement of comprehensive income)	7,200
Total obligation at 31 March 20X0	67,200

This must be split between a current liability of $20 million (payable on 1 April 20X0) and a long-term liability of the balance of $47.2 million.

(W5) Property, plant and equipment at 31 March 20X0

	$000	$000
Property at cost	200,000	
Depreciation (W2)	(6,000)	194,000
Owned plant at cost	154,800	
Leased plant	80,000	
	234,800	
Depreciation (W2) – owned plant (34,800 + 24,000)	(58,800)	
– leased plant	(16,000)	160,000
		354,000

(W6) **Current liabilities**

	$000
Trade accounts payable	29,400
Accrued loan note interest	2,000
Leasing obligation (W4)	20,000
	51,400

(W7) **Retained earnings**

	$000
Profit for the year	40,200
Dividends – Interim	(12,000)
Retained profit for the period	28,200
Revaluation surplus now realized	30,000
Retained earnings b/f	71,600
Retained earnings c/f	129,800

(c) **Non-depreciation of buildings**

It has long been the opinion of many directors that to charge depreciation on an asset that is increasing in value seems to defy economic logic. This belief largely arises from a misunderstanding of the purpose of depreciation, which is to allocate the depreciable amount of an asset over the periods expected to benefit. Depreciation is not intended to be part of a valuation model.

IAS 16 requires the depreciable amount of an asset to be charged over its useful life. The definition of the depreciable amount of an asset is its cost (or other substituted amount) less its estimated residual value and IAS 16 requires residual values to be reviewed at each year end. So valuation changes up to the reporting period end are taken into account. A further justification for non-depreciation is that the useful life of some properties is so long that to charge depreciation would be immaterial. IAS 16 does not directly address this argument, but it may have some validity, as there is an overriding principle that IFRSs only relate to material amounts. However, immateriality must not only apply to the depreciation for the year, but also to the accumulated depreciation in the statement of financial position. Over a period of time the lack of accumulated depreciation in the statement of financial position would become a material misstatement, thus the 'long life' argument also loses its validity. On the basis of the above it would appear that Winger's previous policy of non-depreciation was inappropriate and not in compliance with IAS 16.

28 ALLGONE

Key answer tips

The sale to Funders (point (i)) is in substance a loan and should be treated as such. The 'extraordinary item' (point (iv)) should be treated as a prior period adjustment as the fraud occurred in the previous year.

(a) **Allgone Statement of comprehensive income – Year to 31 March 20X3**

	$000
Revenue (236,200 – 8,000 (see below))	228,200
Cost of sales (W1)	(150,000)
Gross profit	78,200
Operating expenses	(12,400)
Finance costs (W2)	(3,850)
Profit before tax	61,950
Taxation (W3)	(13,100)
Profit for the period	48,850
Other comprehensive income	
Gain on property revaluation	40,000
Available-for-sale financial assets (12,000 × (2.5 – 2.25)/2.50)	(1,200)
Total comprehensive income for the period	87,650

The sale of goods to Funders is an attempt to 'window dress' the statement of financial position by improving its liquidity position. It is in substance a (short term) loan with a finance cost of $250,000.

(b) **Allgone – Statement of Changes in Equity – Year to 31 March 20X3**

	Ordinary shares $000	Irredeemable preference shares $000	Revaluation reserve $000	Retained earnings $000	Total $000
Balance at 1 April 20X2	60,000	20,000	5,000	4,350	89,350
Prior period error (see below)				(32,000)	(32,000)
Restated balance	60,000	20,000	5,000	(27,650)	57,350
Transfer to realized profits re building (W4)			(1,000)	1,000	
Total comprehensive income for the period			38,800	48,850	87,650
Dividends – Preference				(2,000)	(2,000)
Balance at 31 March 20X3	60,000	20,000	42,800	20,200	143,000

The discovery of the major fraud is not an extraordinary item. As it occurred in previous years it should be treated as a prior period error.

(c)   **Allgone – Statement of financial position as at 31 March 20X3**

	$000	$000
Non-current assets		
Software (W4)		2,000
Property, plant and equipment (W4)		175,000
Investments (12,000 – 1,200 (per (a))		10,800
		187,800
Current assets		
Inventory (W1)	14,300	
Trade receivables	23,000	37,300
Total assets		225,100
Equity and liabilities:		
Ordinary shares of 25c each		60,000
10% Irredeemable preference shares		20,000
Equity		80,000
Reserves:		
Retained earnings	20,200	
Revaluation reserve (W4)	42,800	
		63,000
		143,000
Non-current liabilities (W5)		44,800
Current liabilities		
Trade payables	16,200	
Bank overdraft	350	
In substance loan from Funders	8,000	
Accrued finance costs (1,200 + 250 (W2))	1,450	
Taxation	11,300	
		37,300
Total equity and liabilities		225,100

Workings

(W1) **Cost of sales:**

	$000
Opening inventory	19,450
Purchases	127,850
Depreciation (W4) – software	2,000
– building	3,000
– plant	12,000
Closing inventory (8,500 – 200 + 6,000 see below)	(14,300)
	150,000

The slow moving inventory requires a write down to net realisable value of $200,000 ($500,000 – $300,000). The cost of the goods of the sale and repurchase agreement ($6 million) should be treated as inventory.

(W2) Finance costs:

	$000
Per question	2,400
Accrued loan note interest (see below)	1,200
Accrued facilitating fee for in substance a loan (see below)	250
	3,850

The loan notes have been in issue for nine months, but only six months' interest has been paid. Accrued interest of $1,200,000 $((40,000 \times 12\% \times 9/12) - 2,400)$ is required.

The substance of the sale and repurchase agreement is that it is a loan with effective interest of $250,000, the facilitating fee. Therefore this has been treated as a finance cost.

(W3) Taxation:

	$000
Provision for year	11,300
Deferred tax (see below)	1,800
	13,100

The difference between the tax base of the assets and their carrying value of $16 million would require a statement of financial position provision for deferred tax of $4.8 million (at 30%). The opening provision is $3 million, thus an additional charge of $1.8 million is required.

(W4) Non-current assets/depreciation/revaluation:

Land and buildings	Buildings	Land
	$000	$000
Cost 1 April 19W7	80,000	20,000
Five years' depreciation (80,000 × 5/40)	(10,000)	
Net book value prior to revaluation	70,000	
Valuation 1 April 20X2	105,000	25,000
Revaluation surplus	35,000	5,000
Depreciation year to 31 March 20X3 (105,000/35 years)	3,000	
Plant depreciation ((84,300 – 24,300) × 20%)	12,000	

Summarising:	Cost/ valuation	Accumulated depreciation	Net book value
	$000	$000	$000
Land and building (25 + 105)	130,000	3,000	127,000
Plant and equipment	84,300	36,300	48,000
Property, plant and equipment	214,300	39,300	175,000
Software (10/5)	10,000	8,000	2,000

(W5) **Non-current liabilities:**

Deferred tax (3,000 + 1,800) (W3)	4,800
12% loan note	40,000
	44,800

29   TOURMALET

Key answer tips

IFRS 5 requires that the post tax results of the discontinued operations are shown as a single amount on the face of the statement of comprehensive income. In this question we have no information about the tax effects of the closure, therefore only the figures given can be shown.

(a)   The sale of the plant has been incorrectly treated on two counts. Firstly even if it were a genuine sale it should not have been included in sales and cost of sales, rather it should have been treated as the disposal of a non-current asset. Only the profit or loss on the disposal would be included in profit or loss (requiring separate disclosure if material). However even this treatment would be incorrect. As Tourmalet will continue to use the plant for the remainder of its useful life, the substance of this transaction is a secured loan. Thus the receipt of $50 million for the 'sale' of the plant should be treated as a loan. The rentals, when they are eventually paid, will be applied partly as interest (at 12% per annum) and the remainder will be a capital repayment of the loan. In the statement of comprehensive income an accrual for loan interest of 12% per annum on $50 million for four months ($2 million) is required.

(b)   **Tourmalet – Statement of comprehensive income for the year ending 30 September 20X3**

	$000
Continuing operations	
Revenue (313,000 – 50,000 – 15,200 (discontinued)	247,800
Cost of sales (W1 – 16,000 discontinued**)**	(128,800)
Gross profit	119,000
Distribution expenses	(26,400)
Administrative expenses (W2)	(20,000)
Finance costs (W3)	(3,800)
Loss on investment properties (10,000 – 9,800)	(200)
Investment income	1,200
Profit before tax	69,800
Income tax expense (9,200 – 2,100)	(7,100)
Profit for the period from continuing operations	62,700
Discontinued operations	
Loss for the period from discontinued operations (15,200 – 16,000 – 3,200 – 1,500) (W4)	(5,500)
Profit for the period	57,200

(c)   **Tourmalet Statement of changes in equity – Year to 30 September 20X3**

	Ordinary shares	Revaluation reserve	Retained earnings	Total
	$000	$000	$000	$000
At 1 October 20X2	50,000	18,500	47,800	116,300
Profit for period			57,200	57,200
Transfer to realized profit		(500)	500	
Ordinary dividends paid			(2,500)	(2,500)
At 30 September 20X3	50,000	18,000	103,000	171,000

Note: IAS 32 *Financial Instruments: Presentation* says redeemable preference shares have the substance of debt and should be treated as non-current liabilities and not as equity. This also means that preference dividends are treated as a finance cost in the statement of comprehensive income.

Workings

(W1) **Cost of sales:**

	$000
Opening inventory	26,550
Purchases	158,450
Transfer to plant (see (a))	(40,000)
Depreciation **(W2)**	25,800
Closing stock (28,500 – (4,500 – 2,000) see below)	(26,000)
	144,800

The slow moving inventory should be written down to its estimated realisable value. Despite the optimism of the Directors, it would seem prudent to base the realisable value on the best offer so far received (i.e. $2 million).

(W2) **Non-current assets depreciation**

	$000
Buildings $120/40 years	3,000
Plant – per trial balance ((98,600 – 24,600) × 20%)	14,800
Plant – plant treated as sold (40,000/5 years)	8,000
	25,800

Note: investment properties do not require depreciating under the fair value model in IAS 40. Instead they are revalued each year with the surplus or deficit being recognized in profit or loss.

For information only:

In the statement of financial position	Cost/valuation	Accumulated depreciation	Net book value
	$000	$000	$000
Land and buildings	150,000	12,000	138,000
Plant – per trial balance	98,600	39,400	59,200
Plant incorrectly treated as sold	40,000	8,000	32,000
			229,200

(W3) **Finance costs: statement of comprehensive income**

	$000
Accrued interest on in-substance loan (see (a))	2,000
Preference dividends (30,000 × 6% – half accrued)	1,800
	3,800

(W4) The penalty on the lease has been accrued for as it would appear to be unlikely that the permission for change of use will be granted. The $1.5m has therefore been included in the loss from discontinuing operations.

Note: this statement of financial position is provided for information only. It does not form part of the answer or marking scheme.

Tourmalet – Statement of financial position as at 30 September 20X3

	$000	$000
Non-current assets (W2)		229,200
Investment properties		9,800
		239,000
Current assets		
Inventory (W1)	26,000	
Trade receivables	31,200	
Bank	3,700	60,900
Total assets		299,900
Equity and liabilities		
Equity:		
Ordinary shares of 20c each		50,000
Retained earnings	103,000	
Revaluation reserve (see (c))	18,000	121,000
		171,000
Non-current liabilities		
6% Redeemable preference shares	30,000	
In-substance loan (see (a))	50,000	80,000
Current liabilities		
Trade payables	35,300	
Accrued penalty cost (W4)	1,500	
Accrued finance costs (W3)	2,900	
Taxation	9,200	
		48,900
Total equity and liabilities		299,900

30   HARRINGTON

Key answer tips

In the statement of comprehensive income most of the adjustments are reflected in cost of sales but there are other adjustments for investment income, loan interest and taxation as well. In part (b) take care with the share capital and share premium as the rights issue has already been recorded, therefore you will need to work backwards to find the opening balances.

(a)   Harrington:

Restated statement of comprehensive income – Year to 31 March 20X5	$000
Revenue (13,700 – 300 plant sale proceeds)	13,400
Cost of sales (W1)	(8,910)
Gross profit	4,490
Operating expenses	(2,400)
Investment income (1,320 – 1,200 increase in market value)	120
Loan interest (25 + 25 per (c))	(50)
Profit before tax	2,160
Income tax expense (55 + 260 + (350 – 280 deferred tax))	(385)
Profit for the period	1,775
Other comprehensive income	
Gain on property revaluation (W2)	1,800
Total comprehensive income for the period	3,575

(b)   **Statement of changes in equity – Year to 31 March 20X5**

	Ordinary shares	Share premium	Revaluation reserve	Retained profits	Total
	$000	$000	$000	$000	$000
At 1 April 20X4	1,600	40	Nil	2,990	4,630
Rights issue (see below)	400	560			960
Total comprehensive income for the period			1,800	1,775	3,575
Transfer to realized profit (W2)			(80)	80	nil
Ordinary dividends paid				(500)	(500)
At 31 March 20X5	2,000	600	1,720	4,345	8,665

The number of 25c ordinary shares at the year end is 8 million ($2 million × 4). This is after a rights issue of 1 for 4. Thus the number of shares prior to the issue would be 6.4 million (8 million × 4/5) and the rights issue would have been for 1.6 million shares. The rights issue price is 60c each which would be recorded as an increase in share capital of $400,000 (1.6 million × 25c) and an increase in share premium of $560,000 (1.6 million × 35c).

(c)   **Statement of financial position as at 31 March 20X5**

	$000	$000
Non-current assets		
Property, plant and equipment (6,710 + 1,350 (W2)		8,060
Investments (1,200 × 110%)		1,320
		9,380
Current assets		
Inventory	1,750	
Trade receivables	2,450	
Bank	350	4,550
Total assets		13,930
Equity and liabilities:		
Ordinary shares of 25c each		2,000
Reserves (see (b)):		
Share premium	600	
Revaluation reserve	1,720,	
Retained earnings	4,345	6,665
		8,665
Non-current liabilities		
10% loan note (issued 20X2)	500	
Deferred tax (1,400 × 25%)	350	850
Current liabilities		
Trade payables	4,130	
Accrued loan interest ((500 × 10%) – 25 paid)	25	
Current tax payable	260	4,415
Total equity and liabilities		13,930

Workings (all figures in $000):

(W1) **Cost of sales:**

Per question	9,200
Profit on sale of plant ((900 – 630 (W3)) – 300 proceeds)	(30)
Depreciation – plant (W3)	450
– buildings (W2)	290
Capitalized expenses net of error (W2)	(1,000)
	8,910

(W2) **Land and buildings: cost/revaluation depreciation**

	Cost/revaluation	Depreciation
Self constructed (see below)	1,000	50 (20-year life)
Revalued	6,000	240 (see below)
	7,000	290

The carrying value of the land and buildings at 31 March 20X5 is $6,710,000 (7,000 – 290).

Depreciation on the building element will be $240 (4,800/20 years). The revaluation of the land and buildings will create a revaluation reserve initially of $1,800 (6,000 – (1,000 + 3,200)), however a transfer of $80 ((4,800 – 3,200)/20 building element of the revaluation) to retained earnings is required.

Self constructed asset:

Purchased materials	150
Direct labour	800
Supervision	65
Design and planning costs	20
Error in construction (10 + 25)	(35)
	1,000

Note: the cost of the error cannot be capitalized; it must therefore be written off.

(W3) **Plant**

	Cost	Depreciation 31 March 20X4	Carrying value
Per statement of financial position	5,200	3,130	
Disposal	(900)	(630)	
	4,300	2,500	1,800

Depreciation for the current year will be $450,000 (25% reducing balance), giving a net book value at 31 March 20X5 of $1,350,000.

31   CHAMBERLAIN

Key answer tips

The main complication is for the construction contract. This construction contract started at the beginning of the current year, so there are no balances b/f.

(a)   **Chamberlain – Statement of comprehensive income – Year to 30 September 20X4**

	$000
Revenue (246,500 + 50,000 (W1))	296,500
Cost of sales (W2)	(151,500)
Gross profit	145,000
Operating expenses	(29,000)
Profit before interest and tax	116,000
Interest expense (1,500 + 1,500 accrued)	(3,000)
Profit before tax	113,000
Income tax (22,000 – (17,500 – 14,000))	(18,500)
Profit for the period	94,500

(b) **Chamberlain – Statement of financial position as at 30 September 20X4**

	$000	$000
Non-current assets		
Property, plant and equipment (W3)		442,000
Intangible assets (40,000 – 25,000)		15,000
		457,000
Current assets		
Inventory	38,500	
Amounts due from construction contracts (W1)	25,000	
Trade receivables	48,000	
Bank	12,500	124,000
Total assets		581,000
Equity and liabilities		
Capital and reserves:		
Ordinary share capital		200,000
Retained profits – 1 October 20X3	162,000	
– Year to 30 September 20X4	94,500	
Less dividends paid	(8,000)	248,500
		448,500
Non-current liabilities (W4)		64,000
Current liabilities		
Trade payables	45,000	
Accrued finance costs	1,500	
Taxation	22,000	68,500
Total equity and liabilities		581,000

Workings (all figures in $000)

(W1) **Construction contract:**

	$000
Contract price	125,000
Estimated cost	(75,000)
Estimated total profit	50,000
Contract cost for year (35,000 – 5,000 inventory on site)	30,000
Estimated cost	75,000
Percentage complete (30,000/75,000)	40%

Year to 30 September 20X4

Contract revenue – included in sales (125,000 × 40%)	50,000
Contract costs – included in cost of sales (35,000 – 5,000)	(30,000)
Amounts due from customers:	
Cost to date plus profit taken (35,000 + 20,000)	55,000
Less progress billings received	(30,000)
	25,000

(W2) **Cost of sales:**

Opening inventory	35,500
Purchases	78,500
Contract costs (W1)	30,000
Research costs	25,000
Depreciation (W3) – buildings	6,000
– plant	15,000
Closing inventory	(38,500)
	151,500

(W3) **Non-current assets/depreciation:**

Buildings:

A cost of $240,000 (403,000 – 163,000 for the land) over a 40 year life gives annual depreciation of $6,000 per annum.

This gives accumulated depreciation at 30 September 20X4 of $66,000 (60,000 + 6,000) and a net book value of $337,000 (403,000 – 66,000).

Plant:

The carrying value prior to the current year's depreciation is $120,000 (180,000 – 60,000). Depreciation at 12.5% on the reducing balance basis gives an annual charge of $15,000. This gives a carrying value at 30 September 20X4 of $105,000 (120,000 – 15,000). Therefore the carrying value of property, plant and equipment at 30 September 20X4 is $442,000 (337,000 + 105,000).

(W4) **Non-current liabilities**

6% loan note	50,000
Deferred tax	14,000
	64,000

32 PETRA

Key answer tips

Part (a), the statement of comprehensive income, requires most of the work for this question. Set up workings for cost of sales, non-current assets and development expenditure. Remember to put the adjustments you make for the statement of comprehensive income into the statement of financial position as well. You need to recognize that the plant is a 'held for sale' asset. Part (c) is a standard calculation that you need to be able to do.

(a) **Petra – Statement of comprehensive income for the year ended 30 September 20X5**

	$000
Revenue (197,800 – 12,000 (W1))	185,800
Cost of sales (W2)	(128,100)
Gross profit	57,700
Other income – commission received (W1)	1,000
	58,700
Distribution costs	(17,000)
Administration costs	(18,000)
Interest expense (1,500 + 1,500)	(3,000)
Profit before tax	20,700
Income tax expense (4,000 +1,000 + (17,600 – 15,000))	(7,600)
Profit for the period	13,100

(b)   **Petra – Statement of financial position as at 30 September 20X5**

Non-current assets	Cost	Acc depn	Carrying amount
	$000	$000	$000
Property, plant and equipment (W3)	150,000	44,000	106,000
Development costs (W4)	40,000	22,000	18,000
	190,000	66,000	124,000

Current assets			
Inventories		21,300	
Trade receivables		24,000	
Bank		11,000	
		56,300	
Held for sale assets – plant (W3)		6,900	63,200
Total assets			187,200

Equity and liabilities:			
Ordinary shares of 25c each			40,000
Reserves:			
Share premium		12,000	
Retained earnings (34,000 + 13,100)		47,100	59,100
			99,100
Non-current liabilities			
6% loan note		50,000	
Deferred tax		17,600	67,600

Current liabilities			
Trade payables		15,000	
Accrued interest		1,500	
Current tax payable		4,000	20,500
Total equity and liabilities			187,200

(c)   **Basic EPS:**

A nominal value of 25c per share would mean that the $40 million share capital represented 160 million shares. The basic EPS would thus be 8.2 cents ($13.1 million /160 million shares)

Diluted EPS:

The existence of the directors' share options requires the disclosure of a diluted EPS. The dilution effect of the options is: Proceeds from options when exercised $7.2 million. This is equivalent to buying 8 million shares at full market value (7.2 million/90c). Thus the dilutive number of shares is 16 million (24 million – 8 million).

Diluted EPS is 7.4 cents ($13.1 million /(160 + 16 million shares))

Workings (figures in brackets are $000)

(W1) **Agency sales:**

Petra has treated the sales it made on behalf of Sharma as its own sales. The advice from the auditors is that these are agency sales. Thus $12 million should be removed from revenue and the cost of the sales of $8 million and the $3 million 'share' of profit to Sharma should also be removed from cost of sales. Petra should only recognize the commission of $1 million as income. The answer has included this as other income, but it would also be acceptable to include the commission in revenue.

(W2) **Cost of sales:**

	$000
Cost of sales (114,000 – (8,000 + 3,000) (W1))	103,000
Depreciation (W3) – buildings	2,000
– plant	6,000
Amortization (W3) – development expenditure	8,000
Impairment of development expenditure (W3)	6,000
Impairment of plant held for sale (W3)	3,100
	128,100

(W3) **Non-current assets/depreciation:**

The buildings will have a depreciation charge of $2 million (100,000 – 40,000)/30 years) giving accumulated depreciation at 30 September 20X5 of $18 million (16,000 + 2,000).

IFRS 5 *Non-current assets held for sale and discontinued operations* requires plant whose carrying amount will be recovered principally through sale (rather than use) to be classified as 'held for sale'. It must be shown separately in the statement of financial position and carried at the lower of its carrying amount (at the date of classification) and its fair value less estimated costs to sell. Assets classified as held for sale should not be depreciated. Applying this:

	Cost	Depn at 1 Oct 20X4	Carrying amount
	$000	$000	$000
Plant and equipment per trial balance	66,000	26,000	40,000
Plant held for sale	(16,000)	(6,000)	(10,000)
Plant held for continuing use	50,000	20,000	30,000
Land and buildings	100,000	16,000	84,000
Property, plant and equipment	150,000	36,000	114,000

The continuing use plant will have a depreciation charge of $6 million ((50,000 – 20,000) × 20%) giving accumulated depreciation at 30 September 20X5 of $26 million. The total accumulated depreciation for property, plant and equipment at 30 September 20X5 will be $44 million (18,000 + 26,000).

Plant held for sale must be valued at $6.9 million ($7.5 selling price less commission of $600,000 ($7.5 × 8%)) as this is lower than its carrying amount of $10 million. Thus an impairment charge of $3.1 million is required.

(W4) Development expenditure:

This has suffered an impairment as a result of disappointing sales. The impairment loss should be calculated after charging amortization of $8 million (40,000/5 years) for the current year. Thus the impairment charge will be $6 million ((40,000 – (8,000 b/f + 8,000 current year)) – 18,000). The carrying amount of $18 million will then be written off over the next two years.

33 TINTAGEL

Key answer tips

The question is very clear in saying what you have to do. In part (a), start with the draft figures provided, then go through each of points (i) to (vi) in turn to state the adjustments necessary. In part (b), we take the statement of financial position provided in the question as the proforma into which to slot in your corrected figures.

(a)

		$000	$000
Retained earnings at 1 April 20X3			52,500
Reversal of provision plant overhaul (W4)			6,000
			58,500
Profit for the year to 31 March 20X4		47,500	
Lease rental charge added back (W1)		3,200	
Lease interest (W1)		(800)	
Depreciation (W2) – building	2,600		
– owned plant	22,000		
– leased plant	2,800		
		(27,400)	
Loss on investment property (15,000 – 12,400)		(2,600)	
Write down of inventory (W3)		(2,400)	
Unrecorded trade payable		(500)	
Reversal of provision for plant overhaul (W4)		6,000	
Increase in deferred tax (22.5 – 18.7)		(3,800)	
Loan note interest (0.6 + 0.3 (W5))		(900)	18,300
Retained earnings at 31 March 20X4			76,800

(b) **Tintagel – Statement of financial position as at 31 March 20X4**

	$000	$000
Non-current assets		
Freehold property (126,000 – 2,600 (W2))		123,400
Plant – owned (110,000 – 22,000 (W2))		88,000
– leased (11,200 – 2,800 (W2))		8,400
Investment property		12,400
		232,200
Current assets		
Inventory (60,400 – 2,400 (W3))	58,000	
Trade receivables and prepayments	31,200	
Bank	13,800	103,000
Total assets		335,200

	$000	$000
Equity and liabilities		
Capital and Reserves:		
Ordinary shares of 25c each		150,000
Reserves:		
Share premium	10,000	
Retained earnings – 31 March 20X4 (part (a))	76,800	86,800
		236,800
Non-current liabilities		
Deferred tax	22,500	
Finance lease obligations (W1)	5,600	
8% Loan note (14,100 + 300 (W5))	14,400	
		42,500
Current liabilities		
Trade payables (47,400 + 500 (W3))	47,900	
Accrued loan note interest (W5)	600	
Finance lease obligation (W1)	3,200	
Taxation	4,200	55,900
Total equity and liabilities		335,200

Workings

(W1) **Finance lease:**

The lease has been incorrectly treated as an operating lease. Treating it as a finance lease gives the following figures:

	$000
Cash price/recorded cost	11,200
First instalment (reversed in statement of comprehensive income)	(3,200)
Capital outstanding at 1 April 20X3	8,000
Interest at 10% p.a. to 31 March 20X4 (current liability)	800

The capital outstanding of $8 million must be split between current and non-current liabilities. The second instalment payable on 1 April 20X4 will contain $800,000 of interest (8,000 × 10%), therefore the capital element in this payment will be $2.4 million and this is a current liability. This leaves $5.6 million (8,000 – 2,400) as a non-current liability.

(W2) **Non-current assets depreciation:**

	$000
Buildings (130,000 × 2%)	2,600
Non-leased plant (110,000 × 20%)	22,000
Leased plant (11,200 × 25%)	2,800

(W3) The damaged and slow moving inventory should be written down to its estimated realisable value. This is $3.6 million ($4 million less sales commission at 10%). Therefore the required write down is $2.4 million ($6 million – $3.6 million).

The unrecorded invoice would be an addition to purchases therefore a deduction from profit.

(W4) A provision for a future major overhaul does not meet the definition of a liability in IAS 37 *Provisions, Contingent Liabilities and Contingent Assets* and must be reversed; this will increase the current year's profit and the previous year's profit by $6 million each.

(W5) International accounting standards require issue costs, discounts on issue and premiums on redemptions of loan instruments to be included as part of the finance costs: The net proceeds are $14.1 million (($15 million × 95%) less $0.15 million issue costs) per the suspense account. The finance cost and liability amounts are computed as:

	$000
Initial carrying value	14,100
Interest at 6% for first 6 months	846
	14,946

Of this $600,000 is represented by the cash payment to be made on 1 April 20X4 (current liability) and the $14.346 million remainder is a long-term liability.

34 DARIUS

Key answer tips

Remember that redeemable shares are classified as liabilities, so the dividend on them is presented within finance costs, rather than as a deduction from retained earnings. Surpluses/deficits on investment properties accounted for under the fair value model are always recognized in profit or loss, not in other comprehensive income. IAS 16 revaluation surpluses on PPE are recognized in other comprehensive income, however. The plant held for sale must not be depreciated but written down if fair value less costs to sell are less than the carrying value.

(a) **Darius statement of comprehensive income for the year ended 31 March 20X6**

	$000
Revenue	213,800
Cost of sales (W1)	(152,000)
Gross profit	61,800
Operating expenses	(22,400)
Investment income	1,200
Loss on investment property (16,000 – 13,500)	(2,500)
Finance costs (5,000 – (20,000 × 4 × 4c ord div)	(1,800)
Profit before tax	36,300
Income tax expenses (W2)	(6,400)
Profit for the period	29,900
Other comprehensive income	
Gain on property revaluation	21,000
Total comprehensive income for the period	50,900

(b)   **Darius statement of financial position at 31 March 20X6**

	$000	$000
Non-current assets		
Property, plant and equipment (W3)		76,600
Investment property		13,500
		90,100
Current assets		
Inventories (10,500 – 300 (W1))	10,200	
Trade receivables	13,500	
	23,700	
Asset held for sale	5,700	
		29,400
Total assets		119,500
Equity and liabilities		
Ordinary share capital of 25c each		20,000
Revaluation reserve		21,000
Retained earnings (17,500 + 29,900 – (20,000 × 4 × 4c ord div))		44,200
Equity		85,200
Non-current liabilities		
Deferred tax (W2)	3,600	
10% Redeemable preference shares of $1 each	10,000	
		13,600
Current liabilities		
Trade payables	11,800	
Current tax	8,000	
Bank overdraft	900	
		20,700
Total equity and liabilities		119,500

Workings

(W1) **Cost of sales**	$000
Per question	143,800
Inventory write down (800 – (950 – 450))	300
Depreciation	
– building (48,000/15)	3,200
– plant (W3)	2,400
Write down of plant held for sale (6,000 × 95% – 8,000)	2,300
	152,000

(W2) **Tax**

Deferred tax	
Balance b/f	5,200
Balance c/f (12,000 × 30%)	3,600
Written back	1,600
Current tax	(8,000)
	(6,400)

(W3) **Property, plant and equipment**

	$000
Plant	
Cost b/f	36,000
Accumulated depreciation b/f	(16,800)
Carrying amount	19,200
Depreciation charge for year – 12.5%	(2,400)
Carrying amount c/f	16,800
Land and building (63,000 – 3,200 **(W1)**)	59,800
Carrying amount	76,600

35 TADEON

Key answer tips

Most of the work for this question is done in the statement of comprehensive income and the adjustments there lead through to the statement of financial position. So make sure that when you make an adjustment in the statement of comprehensive income that you also remember to adjust the appropriate statement of financial position figures.

(a) **Tadeon – Statement of comprehensive income – Year to 30 September 20X6**

	$000	$000
Revenue		277,800
Cost of sales (w (i))		(144,000)
Gross profit		133,800
Operating expenses (40,000 + 1,200 (w (ii)))		(41,200)
Investment income		2,000
Finance costs – finance lease (w (ii))	(1,500)	
– loan (w (iii))	(2,750)	(4,250)
Profit before tax		90,350
Income tax expense (w (iv))		(36,800)
Profit for the period		53,550
Other comprehensive income		
Gain on property revaluation (20,000 – 4,000 (w (v)))		16,000
		69,550

(b)   **Tadeon – Statement of financial position as at 30 September 20X6**

	$000	$000
Non-current assets		
Property, plant and equipment (w (v))		299,000
Investments at amortized cost		42,000
		341,000
Current assets		
Inventories	33,300	
Trade receivables	53,500	86,800
Total assets		427,800
Equity and liabilities		
Capital and reserves:		
Equity shares of 20 cents each fully paid (150,000 + 50,000 w (vi))		200,000
Reserves		
Share premium (w (vi))	28,000	
Revaluation reserve (w (v))	16,000	
Retained earnings (w (vii))	42,150	86,150
		286,150
Non-current liabilities		
2% Loan note (w (iii))	51,750	
Deferred tax (w (iv))	14,800	
Finance lease obligation (w (ii))	10,500	77,050
Current liabilities		
Trade payables	18,700	
Finance lease obligation (w (ii))	6,000	
Bank overdraft	1,900	
Income tax payable (w (iv))	38,000	64,600
Total equity and liabilities		427,800

Workings (note figures in brackets are in $000)

	$000
(i) Cost of sales:	
Per trial balance	118,000
Depreciation (12,000 + 5,000 + 9,000 w (v))	26,000
	144,000

(ii)   Vehicle rentals/finance lease:

The total amount of vehicle rentals is $6.2 million of which $1.2 million are operating lease rentals and $5 million is identified as finance lease rentals. The operating rentals have been included in operating expenses.

	$000
Finance lease	
Fair value of vehicles	20,000
First rental payment – 1 October 20X5	(5,000)
Capital outstanding to 30 September 20X6	15,000
Accrued interest 10% (current liability)	1,500
Total outstanding 30 September 20X6	16,500

In the year to 30 September 20X7 (i.e. on 1 October 20X6) the second rental payment of $6 million will be made, of this $1.5 million is for the accrued interest for the previous year, thus $4.5 million will be a capital repayment. The remaining $10.5 million (16,500 – (4,500 + 1,500)) will be shown as a non-current liability.

(iii) Although the loan has a nominal (coupon) rate of only 2%, amortization of the large premium on redemption, gives an effective interest rate of 5.5% (from question). This means the finance charge to the statement of comprehensive income will be a total of $2.75 million (50,000 × 5.5%). As the actual interest paid is $1 million an accrual of $1.75 million is required. This amount is added to the $50 million carrying amount of the loan in the statement of financial position to give a liability of $51.75 million.

(iv) Income tax and deferred tax

	$000
The statement of comprehensive income charge is made up as follows:	
Current year's provision	38,000
Deferred tax (see below)	(1,200)
	———
	36,800
	———

There are $74 million of taxable temporary differences at 30 September 20X6. With an income tax rate of 20%, this would require a deferred tax liability of $14,8 million (74,000 × 20%). $4 million ($20m × 20%) is in respect of the revaluation of the leasehold property (and recognized within other comprehensive income and then debited to the revaluation reserve), thus the effect of deferred tax on profit or loss is a credit of $1.2 million (14,800 – 4,000 – 12,000 b/f).

(v) Non-current assets/depreciation:

Non-leased plant

This has a carrying amount of $96 million (181,000 – 85,000) prior to depreciation of $12 million at 12½% reducing balance to give a carrying amount of $84 million at 30 September 20X6.

The leased vehicles will be included in non-current assets at their fair value of $20 million and depreciated by $5 million (four years straight-line) for the year ended 30 September 20X6 giving a carrying amount of $15 million at that date.

The 25 year leasehold property is being depreciated at $9 million per annum (225,000/25 years). Prior to its revaluation on 30 September 20X6 there would be a further year's depreciation charge of $9 million giving a carrying amount of $180 million (225,000 – (36,000 + 9,000)) prior to its revaluation to $200 million. Thus $20 million would be transferred to a revaluation reserve. The question says the revaluation gives rise to $20 million of the deductible temporary differences, at a tax rate of 20%, this would give a credit to deferred tax of $4 million which is recognized within other comprehensive income and then debited to the revaluation reserve to give a net balance of $16 million.

Summarising:

	Cost/valuation	Accumulated depreciation	Carrying amount
	$000	$000	$000
25 year leasehold property	200,000	nil	200,000
Non-leased plant	181,000	97,000	84,000
Leased vehicles	20,000	5,000	15,000
	401,000	102,000	299,000

(vi)   Suspense account

The called up share capital of $150 million in the trial balance represents 750 million shares (150m/0.2) which have a market value at 1 October 20X5 of $600 million (750m × 80 cents). A yield of 5% on this amount would require a $30 million dividend to be paid.

A fully subscribed rights issue of one new share for every three shares held at a price of 32c each would lead to an issue of 250 million (150m/0.2 × 1/3). This would yield a gross amount of $80 million, and after issue costs of $2 million, would give a net receipt of $78 million. This should be accounted for as $50 million (250m × 20 cents) to equity share capital and the balance of $28 million to share premium.

The receipt from the share issue of $78 million less the payment of dividends of $30 million reconciles the suspense account balance of $48 million.

(vii) Retained earnings

	$000
At 1 October 20X5	18,600
Year to 30 September 20X6	53,550
less dividends paid (w (vi))	(30,000)
	42,150

36   UPDATE

Key answer tips

Consider what the diluted earnings per share figure actually tells (and does not tell) a prospective investor.

(i)   The ordinary dividends for the year to 31 March 20X3 are:

	$
Interim (12 million (3 million × $1/25c) × 3c)	360,000
Final (12 million × ((5 + 1) ÷ 5 for rights issue) × 6c)	864,000
	1,224,000
Profits attributable to ordinary shares (see (ii))	2,475,000
Dividend cover (2,475,000/1,224,000)	2.02 times

The dividend cover is the number of times the current year's ordinary dividends could have been paid out of the current year's profit attributable to ordinary shareholders. It is an indication of the company's dividend policy, i.e. a company having a dividend cover of three has paid out one third of its profit as dividends. In terms of maintainable dividends, the dividend cover is a basic measure of risk; the higher the dividend cover the less is the risk that dividends would be reduced if profits suffer a downturn. Conversely, a low dividend cover means that future dividends are more vulnerable to a deterioration in profit. A dividend cover of less than one means the company has used previous years' retained earnings to pay the current year's dividend.This is not a good sign and is not sustainable in the long term.

(ii)   All items in arriving at the profit for the financial year are included in the calculation of the earnings per share.

Profits attributable to the ordinary shares are after the deduction of the following dividends on the non-redeemable preference shares:

	$
8% on $1 million for full year	80,000
New issue 6% on $1 million for six months	30,000
Preference dividends	110,000
Profits attributable to ordinary shares (2,585,000 – 110,000)	$2,475,000

Weighted average number of shares in issue: Calculation of theoretical ex-rights price:	$
100 shares at $2.40 would be worth	240
Rights to 20 shares at $1.50 each costing	30
120 shares now worth	270

This gives a theoretical ex-rights value of $2.25 per share ($270/120)

Weighted average calculation:	
$12,000,000 \times \$2.4/\$2.25 \times {}^{3}/_{12}$	3,200,000
14,400,000 (12 million × ((5 + 1) ÷ 5 for rights issue)) $\times {}^{9}/_{12}$	10,800,000
Weighted average number	14,000,000

Earnings per share is 17.7c ($2,475,000/14,000,000 × 100)

Restated earnings per share for the year to 31 March 20X2 is 22.5c (24 × 2.25/2.40)

(iii)   Fully diluted earnings per share

On conversion the loan stock would create an extra 800,000 new shares ($2 million × 40/$100).The effect on profit would be a saving of interest of $140,000 ($2 million × 7%) before tax and $98,000 after tax (140,000 × (100% – 30%))

The directors' warrants would create an additional 750,000 new shares without any effect on profit. Fully diluted earnings per share is 16.5c ((2,475,000 + 98,000)/(14,000,000 + 800,000 + 750,000)).

The basic earnings per share is a measure of past performance. The diluted earnings per share figure is more forward looking and is intended to act as a warning to existing and prospective shareholders. Although it is still based on past performance, it does give effect to potential ordinary shares outstanding during the period. Its disclosure is required where circumstances exist that would cause the eps to be lower if those circumstances had crystallized. It is not a prediction of the future earnings per share figures, as these will be based on the future profits and the number of shares in issue in the future.

The diluted EPS is more a 'theoretical' value, as it is unlikely that the profit in the period when the circumstances crystallize will be the same as the current year's profit. The convertible loan stock in the question is a good example of diluting circumstance. On conversion the share entitlement will cause the number of shares in issue in the future to be greater than the present (assuming loan stockholders opt for conversion). There will be a compensating increase in profit as a result of the non-payment of interest but overall the expected conversion will cause a dilution.

37   A

Key answer tips

The calculations in this question are not particularly difficult but you have to be organized in your workings to make sure that you have presented them all for the examiner to see. Part (c) presents the opportunity to gain some easy marks so long as you make sure you remember the specific query of the investor in question.

(a)   **Earnings per share**

20X8: $\dfrac{1,030.0}{1,009.6}$ = 102c

20X7: $\dfrac{880}{500} \times \dfrac{3.37}{3.50}$ = 169c

Workings

Weighted average number of shares in issue:

Date	No. of shares in issue (millions)	Weighted average (millions)
1/10/X7 – 31/3/X8	$500 \times 6/12 \times 3.5/3.37$	259.6
1/4/X8 – 30/9/X8	$1,500 \times 6/12$	750.0
		1,009.6

Theoretical ex rights price

	$
1 share @ $3.50	3.50
2 shares @ $3.30	6.60
	10.10

Theoretical ex rights price = $10.10 ÷ 3 = $3.37

Bonus fraction: $\dfrac{\text{Actual cum} - \text{rights price}}{\text{Theoretical ex} - \text{rights price}} = \dfrac{3.50}{3.37}$

(b) **REPORT**

To: Mr B

From: A Management Accountant

Subject: The change in the earnings per share of A

Date: 25 November 20X8

As requested, I have attempted to identify the key factors which may have led to the reduction in the earnings per share (EPS) of A since 30 September 20X7. My comments are based on the statements of comprehensive income and statements of financial position of A for the two years ended 30 September 20X8.

EPS is normally regarded as a key measure of a company's profitability. However, although EPS has fallen, revenue has increased by 17.6% ((10,000 – 8,500) as % of 8,500)and net profit after tax has also increased by 17%((1,030 – 880) as % of 880). The net profit percentage has remained at 10.3% for both years.

Looking at the statement of comprehensive income in more detail, the gross profit margin has fallen slightly from 40% to 37%, but there has been a corresponding slight fall in operating expenses, from 21.2% of sales to 19% of sales.

The decrease in earnings per share has arisen, not because the company is less profitable, but because there has been a substantial issue of new shares. It appears that the company has used the extra capital to finance the acquisition of a large intangible asset and possibly also additional tangible non-current assets.

In theory, these new assets should eventually generate increased profits and cause EPS to return to a higher level. However, this is not yet happening. Return on shareholders' equity (which measures the profit available for equity shareholders as a proportion of their investment) has fallen from 52.7% to 20.2%. As the company's profitability has remained the same throughout the period, the company must be generating relatively less revenue from its assets than before. This is confirmed by the fact that the asset turnover ratio has fallen from 2.3 times to 1.4 times, showing that A is now only generating $1.40 of revenue for every $1 of capital employed.

Workings: Ratios

	20X8	20X7
Gross profit percentage		
$\dfrac{\text{Gross profit}}{\text{Revenue}}$	$\dfrac{3,700}{10,000} \times 100\% = 37\%$	$\dfrac{3,400}{8,500} \times 100\% = 40\%$
Net profit percentage		
$\dfrac{\text{Profit after tax}}{\text{Revenue}}$	$\dfrac{1,030}{10,000} \times 100\% = 10.3\%$	$\dfrac{880}{8,500} \times 100\% = 10.3\%$
Operating expenses/sales		
$\dfrac{\text{Operating expenses}}{\text{Revenue}}$	$\dfrac{1,900}{10,000} \times 100\% = 19\%$	$\dfrac{1,800}{8,500} \times 100\% = 21.2\%$

Return on shareholders' equity

$\dfrac{\text{Profit after tax}}{\text{Shareholders' funds}}$	$\dfrac{1,030}{5,100} \times 100\% = 20.2\%$	$\dfrac{880}{1,670} \times 100\% = 52.7\%$

Asset turnover

$\dfrac{\text{Revenue}}{\text{Capital employed}}$	$\dfrac{10,000}{7,100} = 1.4 \text{ times}$	$\dfrac{8,500}{3,670} = 2.3 \text{ times}$

(c)   **The relevance of earnings per share**

Earnings per share (EPS) is regarded as a key measure of a company's performance and is also used to calculate the price earnings ratio. The price earnings ratio (P/E ratio) measures the market price of a share in relation to its EPS and is used as an indicator of market confidence in a company. Both EPS and the P/E ratio may be used to compare the performance of similar companies for the purpose of making investment decisions.

To some extent, EPS influences the market price of a share. However, it has several important limitations as a performance measure. It may be based on earnings which include large or unusual items, so that it becomes volatile, making it difficult for users of the financial statements to assess underlying trends in performance. It does not take account of inflation. Most importantly, it only measures profitability, although there are many other aspects of financial performance. For example, A has become less profitable, but also less risky as an investment, as net current liabilities (2,290 – 2,320) have become net current assets (2,900 – 2,800) and gearing has fallen from 54% to 28% (W).

In conclusion, the market price of a share is influenced by many different factors, including the strength of the company's statement of financial position, its cash flows, its ability to compete with other businesses, and its ability to adapt to changing economic conditions.

Workings

	20X8	20X7

Gearing

$\dfrac{\text{Long - term loans}}{\text{Capital employed}}$	$\dfrac{2,000}{7,100} \times 100\% = 28\%$	$\dfrac{2,000}{3,670} \times 100\% = 54\%$

38   EARNIT

Key answer tips

Make sure that you can both do the calculations and discuss their relevance for investors.

(a)   **Earnings per share for the year ended 31 March 20Y0**

Basic:	$\dfrac{\$34m}{525m}$	=	6.48 cents

Diluted:	$\dfrac{\$34m}{552.5m}$	=	6.15 cents

Workings

(W1) **Weighted average number of ordinary shares in issue**

Date	No. of shares in issue (million)	Weighted average (million)
1 April – 30 September	$500 \times 6/12$	250
1 October – 31 March	$(500 + 50$ re exercised options$) \times 6/12$	275
		___
		525

(W2) **Weighted average number of potential ordinary shares**

	Million	Million
Weighted average number of ordinary shares in issue **(W1)**		525.0
Number of shares under option:		
1 April – 30 September $(100 \times 6/12)$	50.0	
1 October – 31 March $((100 - 50 + 70) \times 6/12)$	60.0	
	___	
	110.0	
Number of shares that would have been issued at fair value		
$(110 \times 1.50$ subscription price$/2.00$ average market price$)$	(82.5)	
	___	27.5
		___
		552.5

(b) **The usefulness of basic and diluted earnings per share to an equity shareholder**

Basic earnings per share measures the earnings (profit) in relation to each equity share and is regarded as a key measure of performance.

IAS 33 *Earnings per share* sets out the method of calculation and required disclosures. Therefore shareholders can compare the return on their investment for the current period with previous periods. Shareholders can also compare the earnings underlying their investment with the earnings underlying investments in similar entities.

Earnings per share is used to calculate the price earnings ratio, which represents the market's view of the future prospects of a share. The price earnings ratio enables shareholders to judge the cost of a share relative to the earnings that it produces.

Diluted earnings per share alerts equity shareholders to the possibility that there may be additional equity shares in future periods as the result of the exercise of existing capital instruments such as options and warrants. If this is the case, their earnings per share may be reduced. This applies to Earnit, which has issued options for shares which are likely to be exercised (because the shares can be subscribed for below the current market price). Diluted earnings per share shows the earnings per share if all the options were exercised. This is 5.1% ((6.48 – 6.15) as % of 6.48) lower than basic earnings per share and this indicates that there is a small risk associated with the shares.

The usefulness of earnings per share may be limited by the following factors:

(i) It is not necessarily a predictor of future earnings per share because it is based on historical information. It only measures past performance. This also applies to diluted earnings per share as calculated in accordance with IAS 33 and for this reason it is only of limited use as a 'warning signal'.

(ii) The profits figure is affected by an entity's choice of accounting policies. Therefore it may not always be appropriate to compare the earnings per share of different companies.

(iii) It does not take account of inflation. Apparent growth in profits may not be true growth.

(iv) It only measures profitability, which is only one aspect of overall performance. In the longer term, cash flow, gearing and working capital management may be equally important influences on the return on an equity investment.

39   JKL

(a) **Basic and diluted earnings per share**

Basic earnings per share: $\dfrac{2,763,000}{6,945,922\,(W3)} = 39.8c$

Diluted EPS: $\dfrac{2,858,200\,(W4)}{9,045,922\,(W5)} = 31.6c$

(W1) **Calculate the theoretical ex-rights price after the rights issue**

	¢
4 shares×145¢	580
1 share×125¢	125
Theoretical value of holding of 5 shares	705
Theoretical ex-rights price of 1 share after rights issue: 705/5	141

(W2) **Calculate bonus fraction**

$$\frac{\text{Fair value of one share before rights issue}}{\text{Theoretical ex - rights price of one share (W1)}} = \frac{145}{141}$$

(W3) **Weighted average number of shares in issue in the year to 31 August 20X4**

	Number of shares
1 September 20X3 – 1 February 20X4	
6,000,000 × 145/141×5/12	2,570,922
1 February 20X4 – 31 August 20X4	
7,500,000×7/12	4,375,000
	6,945,922

(W4) **Adjustment to profits for calculation of diluted EPS**

	$
Profits	2,763,000
Add: Interest after tax	
(2,000,000 × 7%)×(1−0.32)	95,200
Adjusted profits	2,858,200

(W5) **Adjustment to number of shares for calculation of diluted EPS**

Note: Use the most advantageous (for loan stockholders) conversion rate.

	Number of shares
Weighted average shares in issue in year to 31 August 20X4 (W3)	6,945,922
Add: Dilutive effect 2,000,000/100×105	2,100,000
Diluted shares	9,045,922

(b) Much of the information contained in financial statements refers to events that have occurred in the past, and so it is of relatively restricted usefulness in making decisions. Diluted earnings per share, however, can be quite useful to investors and potential investors in that it incorporates some information about likely future events. Where potentially dilutive financial instruments have been issued, it is helpful to investors to be able to appreciate the impact full dilution would have upon the earnings of the business. However, it should be appreciated that only some elements of the calculation relate to the future. One of the key elements of the calculation, the basic earnings for the period, relates to events that have already taken place and that may not be replicated in the future.

BUSINESS COMBINATIONS

40   HALOGEN

Key answer tips

(a)   This is a standard consolidated statement of financial position question, with a complication in the form of development costs in the subsidiary's statement of financial position at the date of acquisition. These costs have been sold to the parent company, a transaction that should be accounted for like any other inter-group sale of non-current assets.

(b)   There are two aspects to consider. Should Lockstart be consolidated under IAS 27, and if so, should it be separately disclosed under IFRS 5?

(a)   **Consolidated statement of financial position of Halogen as at 31 March 20X1**

	$ million	$ million
Assets		
Non-current assets		
Property, plant and equipment (910 + 330 + 10 + 8)	1,258	
Goodwill (W2)	150	
Development expenditure (100 – 8 (W5))	92	
Investments ((700 – 480 (W3))) + 60)	280	
		1,780
Current assets		
Inventory (W4)	341	
Trade receivables (264 + 84 – 12 (W4))	336	
Bank	25	702
Total assets		2,482

	$ million	$ million
Equity and liabilities		
Equity shares $1 each		1,000
Share premium	300	
Retained earnings (W6)	501	
Revaluation reserve ((60 + 10 in year) + (75% × 8 in year))	76	877
		1,877
Minority interest (W5)		120
Equity		1,997
Non-current liabilities		
10% Debenture		60
Current liabilities		
Trade payables (178 + 44)	222	
Taxation (94 + 35)	129	
Overdraft (86 – 12 (W4))	74	425
Total equity and liabilities		2,482

Workings (Note: all figures in $ million)

(W1) Net assets of subsidiary

	At acquisition $m	*At reporting period end* $m
Share capital	200	200
Revaluation reserve	40	40
Retained earnings	180	240
Fair value adjustments – dev exp (28 – 8)	20	20
	440	500

(W2) Goodwill

	$m
Cost of investment (W3)	480
Net assets acquired 75% × 440 W1)	330
Goodwill	150

(W3) Cost of investment

The cost of investments in Stimulus is:

75 million (200 million × 75% holding/2) new shares at $5 each	=	$375 million
Cash paid (200 million × 75% holding/2 × $1.40)	=	$105 million
		$480 million

(W4) Current asset adjustments

	$m
Inventory:	
Amounts per question (224 + 120)	344
Less unrealized profit in inventory (26 × 30/130 × ½)	(3)
	341

The cash in transit will reduce the overdraft and trade receivables of Halogen by $12 million.

(W5) Minority interest

	$m
Net assets at balance sheet **(W1)**	500
Unrealized profit on sale (36 – 8)	(28)
Revaluation of land	8
	480
Minority share 25% × 480	120

The unrealized profit (in Stimulus' reserves) on the sale of its development expenditure to Halogen is its transfer value ($36 million) less its carrying value (£8 million). This $28 million is made up of a fair value adjustment of $20 million ($28 – £8) and $8 million unrealized profit (included in the carrying value of development expenditure) on the sale to Halogen.

(W6) Retained earnings

	$m
Halogen	480
Less: unrealized profit in stock (W4)	(3)
Stimulus – share post-acquisition 75% × ((240 – 28 (W5)) – 180)	24
	516
	50)

(b) There is a view in the accounting profession that a statement of comprehensive income prepared under the concept of 'current operating income' has some merit. The principal advantage of this method of reporting is said to be that it reports the results of those parts of a business that can be expected to be operating in the future and this forms a useful basis from which to predict the future profit and income streams of the entity. Whilst this view may have some benefits, the accounting profession has rejected it mainly because it would lead to incomplete reporting and the introduction of greater subjectivity. It would give management scope to report selectively certain aspects of performance.

The directors of Halogen are partly correct in interpreting the usefulness of IFRS 5, in that by identifying and separately reporting discontinued operations and assets and liabilities of subsidiaries held for sale this does help the predictive/forecasting process. However, it is important to realize that IFRS 5 does not permit the omission of the results of those parts of the business that have been (or are about to be) discontinued, which is what the directors of Halogen are proposing.

IAS 27 *Consolidated and Separate Financial Statements* does not allow any subsidiary to be excluded from the consolidation process. The Standard prevents managers from selectively excluding the results of subsidiaries that have made losses or have a poor liquidity position. Subsidiaries must continue to be consolidated up to the date of their disposal. It seems the directors of Halogen may be attempting to avoid reporting the losses of Lockstart. This they cannot do. There is however some value in ascertaining those parts of a business that will not affect group profits in the future.

Provided the future disposal meets the criteria in IFRS 5 to be reported as a discontinued operation, Lockstart's results should be presented in the statement of comprehensive income as a single-line adjustment to profit from continuing operations. (Although the sale has not yet taken place, it is possible that Lockstart meets the definition of a disposal group held for sale, in which case it might be possible to classify it as a discontinued operation.) Thus the directors' current treatment of excluding Lockstart from the consolidated financial statements is incorrect and they should be advised to redraft the group financial statements to include its results, possibly as part of discontinued operations, and there may need to be further provisions for some of the future costs associated with the disposal and for impairment losses.

Tutorial note: Lockstart's total assets and total liabilities would be presented as single line items in the consolidated statement of financial condition.

41 HIGHMOOR

Key answer tips

The parent company has agreed to pay an additional contingent consideration if the new subsidiary makes a profit. Note (iv) of the question tells us that the subsidiary has in fact reported losses, so no contingent consideration need be provided.

(a) **Consolidated Statement of financial position of Highmoor as at 30 September 20X3**

	$ million	$ million
Assets		
Non-current assets		
Tangible (585 + 172)		757
Intangible:		
Software (W6)		24
Investments (225 – 160 shares – 50 loan (W5) + 13)		28
		809
Current assets		
Inventory (85 + 42)	127	
Accounts receivable (95 – 4 in transit (W5) + 36)	127	
Tax asset	80	
Bank (20 + 9 in transit (W5))	29	363
Total assets		1,172
Equity and liabilities		
Equity attributable to owners of the parent		
Ordinary shares $1 each		400
Retained earnings (W4)		326
		726
Minority interest (W3)		43
		769
Non-current liabilities		
12% loan notes		35
Current liabilities		
Accounts payable (210 + 71)	281	
Overdraft	17	
Taxation	70	368
Total equity and liabilities		1,172

Workings (Note: all figures in $ million)

(W1) **Net assets in subsidiary**

	At acquisition	At reporting period end
	$m	$m
Share capital	100	100
Profit and loss reserve	150	115
	250	215

(W2) **Goodwill**

	$m
Cost of investment	160
Net assets at acquired (80% × 250) (W1)	200
Excess of net assets acquired over consideration given	40

The contingent consideration has not been included in the above calculation. IFRS 3 *Business Combinations* only requires contingent consideration to be included in the cost of an acquisition if it is probable that the amount will be paid and it can be measured reliably. The additional $96 million (i.e. 100 × 80% × $1.20 per share) is only payable if Slowmoor makes a profit within two years of acquisition. In the year since acquisition the company made a loss of $35 million and the directors of Highmoor are now less confident of the future prospects of Slowmoor. This seems to indicate that it is unlikely that any further consideration will be paid and the above treatment is justified.

The excess of net assets acquired over consideration given of $40 million will be recognized immediately in profit or loss.

(W3) **Minority interest**

20% × 215 (W1) = $43 million

(W4) **Retained earnings**

	$m
Highmoor	330
Excess of net assets acquired over consideration given	40
Unrealized profit (W6)	(16)
Slowmoor – group share post acquisition losses 80% × 35	(28)
	326

(W5) **Elimination of loan and accrued interest**

After removing the purchase consideration of $160 million **(W2)** for Slowmoor, the balance of Highmoor's investments will include an unadjusted amount of $50 million as a loan to Slowmoor. The cash in transit of $9 million from Slowmoor should be applied $4 million to cancel the accrued interest receivable and the balance of $5 million to the investment (loan). When this adjustment is made the remaining investment in Slowmoor and the loan will cancel each other out.

(W6) The net book value of the software in Slowmoor's books is $40 million (50 less 20%). If the software had been depreciated on its original cost of $30 million it would have a book value of $24 million ($30 less $6 million depreciation at 20% per annum). Thus there is an unrealized profit on the sale of the software by Highmoor of $16 million ($40 million – $24 million).

(b) The consideration given for a business may be less than the fair value of the net assets acquired. Intuitively it does not make sense for a vendor to sell net assets for less than they are worth. This view is reflected by the IASB which is rather sceptical about the existence of what is often described as negative goodwill. They say where an acquisition appears to create negative goodwill, a careful check of the value of the assets acquired and whether any liabilities have been omitted is required.

The consideration may be less than the net assets acquired for several reasons; the most obvious is that there has been a bargain purchase. This may occur through the vendor being in a poor financial position and needing to realize assets quickly, or it may be due to good negotiating skills on the part of the acquirer, or the vendor may not realize how much the assets are really worth.

A more controversial situation is where a company, in determining the amount of consideration it is willing to pay for a business, will take into account the cost of anticipated future losses and post acquisition reorganization expenditure that it believes will be required. The effect of this is that it would reduce the consideration offered/paid. As these costs cannot generally be recognized as a liability at the date of purchase, this can lead to the consideration being lower than the recognisable net assets.

In relation to the acquisition of Slowmoor the following are questionable issues:

– Highmoor may be trying to deliberately create losses at Slowmoor to avoid paying the further consideration. An example of this may be the transfer price of the software.

The additional consideration of $96 million, if payable, would change the excess of consideration over net assets into goodwill of $56 million.

– The tax asset of Slowmoor may be questionable. Accounting standards are quite restrictive over the recognition of tax assets.

42 HIGHVELDT

Key answer tips

Part (a) of this question requires the three standard workings for the consolidated statement of financial position – goodwill, minority interest and consolidated reserves. These should be well known to students but as the rest of the consolidated statement of financial position is not required there are more complications than in a normal statement of financial position question. Read carefully through each of the notes (i) to (vi) and think about how they will affect your figures. There are not only fair value adjustments to make but also an accounting policy adjustment with regards to the development expenditure. Note the deferred element of the consideration which should be discounted and the unwinding of the discount shown as a reduction of consolidated profits.

Leave enough time for part (b) which is 5 easy marks on the advantages to users of consolidated financial statements.

(a) (i) **Goodwill**

		$m
Cost of investment		
	Cash (75% × 80m × $3.50)	210
	Deferred consideration (108 × 1/1.08)	100
		310
Less: net assets at acquisition 75% × 296 **(W2)**		222
Recognized goodwill at 1 April 20X4		88
Amount attributable to minority interest (25/75)		29
Notional goodwill		117
Impairment		(29)
Notional goodwill after impairment		88
Recognized goodwill after impairment (75%)		66

(ii) **Minority interest**

	$m
Net assets at reporting period end	
25% × 350 **(W2)**	87.5
Less: unrealized profit in inventory 25% × 2m **(W3)**	(0.5)
	87.0

(iii) **Consolidated share premium**

	$m
Parent only	80

Consolidated revaluation reserve

	$m
Parent	45
Subsidiary – post-acquisition (75% × 4m)	3
	48

Consolidated retained earnings

	$m
Parent	350.0
Add: interest receivable (60m × 10%)	6.0
Less: unwinding of discount on deferred consideration 100 × 8%	(8.0)
	348.0
Subsidiary – group share post acquisition (ex 4 re land and buildings taken to revaluation reserve)	
75% × ((350 – 296) – 4) **(W2)**	37.5
Less: unrealized profit in inventory 75% × 2m **(W3)**	(1.5)
Less: impairment of goodwill (part i)	(22.0)
	362.0

Workings

(W1) **Group structure**

> Highveldt
>
> 1 April 20X4   75%
>
> Samson

(W2) **Net assets**

	At acquisition		At reporting period end
	$m		$m
Share capital	80		80
Share premium	40		40
Retained earnings	134		210
	254		330
Fair value adjustments:			
Land and buildings	20		24
Brand	40	$\times 9/10$	36
Research and development	(18)		(40)
	296		350

The brand should be recognized in the consolidated statement of financial position even though it is not included in Samson's own statement of financial position. As the brand has been professionally valued then it can be 'reliably measured' and should be included in the consolidated statement of financial position.

(W3) **Unrealized profit in inventory**

Profit = $6m

Still in stock = 1/3 × $6m = $2m

(b) The objective of consolidated financial statements is to show the financial performance and position of the group as if it was a single economic entity. There is a view that, as the entity financial statements of the parent company contain the investments in subsidiaries as non-current assets, they reflect the assets of the group as a whole. The more traditional view is that entity financial statements do not provide users with sufficient information about subsidiaries for them to make a reliable assessment of the performance of the group as a whole. The following illustrates benefits of consolidated financial statements:

–   they identify the nature and classification of the subsidiary's assets. For example, the investment in a subsidiary may be almost entirely in intangible assets or conversely they may be substantially land and buildings. Such a distinction is of obvious importance to users.

–   the amount of the subsidiary's debt could not be assessed from the parent's entity financial statements. In effect the subsidiary's assets and liabilities are netted off when it is shown as an investment. This means group liquidity and gearing cannot be properly assessed.

–   the cost of the investment does not reflect the size of a company. For example a parent company may show an investment in a subsidiary at a cost of $10 million. This may represent the purchase of a subsidiary that has $10 million of assets and no liabilities. Alternatively this could be a subsidiary that has $100 million in assets and $90 million of liabilities.Clearly the latter subsidiary would be a much larger company than the former.

– the cost of the investment may be a fair representation of its value at the date of purchase, but with the passage of time (assuming the subsidiary is profitable), its value will increase. This increase would not be reflected in the original cost, but it would be reflected in the consolidated net assets of the subsidiary (and the increase in group reserves).

– the cost of the investment might represent all of the ownership of the subsidiary or only just over half of it i.e. there would be no indication of the minority interest.

To summarize, in the absence of a consolidated statement of financial position, users would have no information on the current value of a subsidiary, its size, the composition of its net assets and how much of it was owned by the group.

43   HEPBURN

Key answer tips

Notice that in part (b) there are two parts to the requirement: comment on the directors' treatment *and* state how the investment should be accounted for. The answer must address both requirements. You are not required to describe the mechanics of consolidation.

(a)   **Hepburn**

Consolidated statement of comprehensive income year to 31 March 20X0

	$000
Sale revenues $(1,200 + (1,000 \times 6/12) - 100$ intra-group sales)	1,600
Cost of sales (W1)	(890)
Gross profit	710
Operating expenses $(120 + (88 \times 6/12))$	(164)
Finance costs $(12 \times 6/12)$	(6)
Profit before tax	540
Income tax expense $(100 + (40 \times 6/12))$	(120)
Profit for the period	420
Attributable to:	
Owners of the parent	400
Minority interests $(200 \times 20\% \times 6/12)$	20
	420

Consolidated statement of financial position at 31 March 20X0

	$000	$000
Non-current assets		
Property, plant and equipment (620 + 660 + 125)		1,405
Intangible: Goodwill (W2)		200
Investments (20 + 10)		30
		1,635
Current assets		
Inventory (240 + 280 – 10)	510	
Accounts receivable (170 + 210 – 56 (W5))	324	
Bank (20 + 40 + 20 (W5))	80	914
Total assets		2,549
Equity and liabilities:		
Equity shares of $1 each (400 + 300 (W2))		700
Reserves:		
Share premium (W2)	600	
Retained earnings (W3)	480	1,080
		1,780
Minority interest (W4)		195
		1,975
Non-current liabilities		
8% Loan notes		150
Current liabilities		
Accounts payable (210 + 155 – 36 (W5))	329	
Taxation (50 + 45)	95	424
		2,549

Workings

(W1) **Cost of sales**

	$000
Hepburn	650
Salter (660 × 6/12)	330
Intra-group sales	(100)
URP in inventory (100 × 50% × 25/125))	10
	890

(W2) **Goodwill**

Hepburn issued five shares for every two shares it acquired in Salter.

Therefore Hepburn issued ((150,000/2 × 5) × 80%) = 300,000 shares at a value of $3 each for a total consideration of $900,000.

This would be recorded in Hepburn's books as equity share capital of $300,000 and share premium of $600,000.

	$000	$000
Investment at cost (300 × $3)		900
Net assets acquired	150	
– Equity shares of Salter		
– Retained earnings at acquisition	600	
(700 – (200 × 6/12))		
– Fair value adjustment of land	125	
	———	
Group share 80%	875	700
	———	———
Goodwill on consolidation		200
		———

(W3) **Consolidated reserves**

	$000
Hepburn's reserves	410
Share of Salter's post acquisition profits (200 × 6/12 × 80%)	80
URP in inventory (W1)	(10)
	———
	480
	———

(W4) **Minority interest**

Minority share (850 + 125) × 20%	195

(W5) **Elimination of current accounts**

The difference on the current accounts is due to cash in transit of $20,000. A summary of the intra-group cancellations is:

	$000	$000
Cash/bank	20	
Accounts payable	36	
Accounts receivable		56
	———	———
	56	56
	———	———

(b)   It seems that the directors of Hepburn are trying to argue against the investment in Woodbridge being classified as one in an associated company. The ownership of the total equity is 25%, giving Hepburn the right to 25% of any dividends Woodbridge may pay. If this were the basis on which the assessment of associated company status is made, it may be that given the lack of involvement in the operating policies of Woodbridge, the directors may be able to rebut the normal presumption that Woodbridge is an associate by virtue of its 25% holding.

The directors do however appear to be misunderstanding the basis of determining subsidiary company status. IAS 27 *Consolidated and Separate Financial Statements* bases its definition of a subsidiary on control rather than ownership. In the case of Woodbridge, Hepburn in fact owns 6,000 of the 10,000 voting shares, and, in the absence of any other information, this would constitute control of Woodbridge by virtue of its 60% of voting rights. Thus, far from being an associate of Hepburn, Woodbridge is in fact a subsidiary, irrespective of the fact that control may be passive. Therefore Woodbridge's results should be consolidated by Hepburn from the date of its acquisition.

It may be that the motive for the directors' position is that they wish to improve group profits by avoiding consolidation of Woodbridge's losses. This raises the further point that these losses may indicate that the value of the investment in this subsidiary has been impaired under IAS 36 *Impairment of Assets*. If so, it will be necessary to perform an impairment test, which involves calculating the recoverable amount of the investment. The directors may have to write down the value of the investment (in Hepburn's own (entity) financial statements) to its recoverable amount, and also write down the consolidated assets of Woodbridge.

44 HILLUSION

Key answer tips

Part (b) asks you why it is necessary to eliminate unrealized profits. You do not need to discuss the double entry techniques for dealing with intra-group adjustments, nor the reasons why they arise. You are also specifically asked to refer to the circumstances described in the question. These include the high level of intra-group sales and the fact that there is no charge for administration costs.

(a) **Hillusion**

Consolidated statement of comprehensive income for the year to 31 March 20X3

	$000	$000
Revenue ((60,000 + (24,000 $\times^9/_{12}$)) – 12,000 intra-group sales)		66,000
Cost of sales (W1)		(46,100)
		———
Gross profit		19,900
Operating expenses (6,000 + (200 $\times$ $^9/_{12}$))	(6,150)	
Loan interest ((200 $\times$ $^9/_{12}$) – 75 intra-group)	(75)	
	———	(6,225)
		———
Profit before tax		13,675
Taxation (3,000 + (600 $\times$ $^9/_{12}$))		(3,450)
		———
Profit for the period		10,225
		———
Attributable to:		
Owners of the parent		9,895
Minority interest (((3,000 $\times$ $^9/_{12}$) – 600 depreciation adjust **(W1)**) $\times$ 20%)		330
		———
		10,225
		———

Consolidated statement of financial position at 31 March 20X3

Tangible non-current assets (19,320 + 8,000 + 3,200 – 600)
depreciation adjustment (W1)   29,920
Goodwill (W3)   1,200
                                                                 _____
                                                                  31,120
Current assets (W6)   21,750
                                                                 _____
Total assets   52,870
                                                                 _____

Equity and liabilities
Equity attributable to owners of the parent
Ordinary shares of $1 each   10,000
Retained earnings (W5)   26,420
                                                                 _____
                                                                  36,420
Minority interest (W4)   2,600
                                                                 _____
                                                                  39,020

Non-current liabilities
10% Loan notes (2,000 – 1,000 intra-group)   1,000
Current liabilities (W6)   12,850
                                                                 _____
Total equity and liabilities   52,870
                                                                 _____

Workings in $000

(W1) **Cost of sales**

	$000
Hillusion	42,000
Skeptik (20,000 × $^9/_{12}$)	15,000
Intra-group sales	(12,000)
URP in inventory	500
Additional depreciation	600
	_____
	46,100

The unrealized profit (URP) in inventory is calculated as:

Intra-group sales are $12 million of which Skeptik has sold on $10 million leaving $2 million ($^1/_6$) still in inventory at the year-end. The cost of the sales made by Hillusion to Skeptik was $9 million giving Hillusion a profit of $3 million (12m – 9m). The unrealized element is $500,000 ($3 million × $^1/_6$).

The fair value adjustment to the tangible non-current assets is $3.2 million. At the date of acquisition they have a remaining life of four years. Additional depreciation would be $800,000 per annum which requires apportioning by $^9/_{12}$ = $600,000

(W2) **Net assets in subsidiary**

	At acquisition	At reporting period end
	$000	$000
Share capital	2,000	2,000
Retained earnings ((8,400 – 3,000) + 3/12 × 3,000)	6,150	8,400
Fair value adjustment (depn (W1))	3,200 × 39/48	2,600
	_____	_____
	11,350	13,000

(W3) Goodwill

	$000
Investment at cost	10,280
Net assets at acquisition (80% × 11,350 **(W2)**)	(9,080)
Goodwill on consolidation	1,200

(W4) Minority interest (statement of financial position)

	$000
20% × 13,000 (W2)	2,600

(W5) Consolidated retained earnings:

	$000
Hillusion's reserves	25,600
Skeptik's post acquisition (80% × 13,000 – 11,350 (W2))	1,320
URP in inventory (W1)	(500)
	26,420

(W6) Current assets and current liabilities

Current assets:	$000
Hillusion	15,000
Skeptik	8,000
URP in inventory	(500)
Intra-group balance	(750)
	21,750

Creditors payable within one year:	
Hillusion	10,000
Skeptik	3,600
Intra-group balance	(750)
	12,850

(b)   The main reason why intra-group unrealized profits must be eliminated on consolidation is to achieve the main objective of group financial statements which is to show the position of the group as if it were a single economic entity. As such, a group cannot trade with itself, nor can it make a profit out of itself. In a similar way it cannot increase its sales or its net assets by transferring assets and liabilities between members of the group.

As a simple illustrative example, but for the requirement to eliminate intra-group profits, a group could buy an item of inventory; sell it to another member of the group (at a profit), who in turn could sell it to another member of the group and so on. The result would be that each member of the group would make a profit which would then be combined to form a large group profit. This would be 'balanced' by an inflated inventory value in the statement of financial position (in practice this effect would be limited by the application of the lower of cost and net realisable value principle of valuing inventory). Such accounting would not give a fair presentation of the results and position.

The main problem with using Skeptik entity financial statements to assess its performance is that it is a related party of its parent, Hillusion. Related party transactions can distort the true economic performance and financial position of a company. In this case, the related party relationship extends to complete control of Skeptik by Hillusion.

From the information in the question, it can be seen that most of Skeptik's trading is from goods it buys from Hillusion. (Sales of non-group sourced goods are only $9 million (out of $24 million).) It may be that these have been transferred at a favourable price allowing Skeptik to achieve a higher level of sales and make a higher than normal profit. Ultimately this course of action is no real detriment to the group as a whole as most of Skeptik's profits (and all of them if it were 100% owned) are consolidated into the group profit. In a similar manner the fact that Hillusion does not make any charge for Skeptik's administration costs acts to increase Skeptik's profit. If Skeptik was to be purchased by an external party, all these beneficial effects would cease and Skeptik's profit would then be much lower. It could be observed that Hillusion may be 'massaging' Skeptik's financial statements with a view to obtaining a favourable price on its future sale. Hillusion's past record of success in selling previous businesses at a considerable profit after only a short period of ownership supports this view.

45   HORSEFIELD

Key answer tips

Part (b) represents 5 easy marks. Make sure that you leave enough time to attempt it properly and that you answer the question fully. The requirement word discuss is a clue that the Examiner is looking for more than a restatement of the definition in IAS 28.

(a)   **Consolidated statement of financial position of Horsefield as at 31 March 20X2**

	$000	$000
Non-current assets		
Property, plant and equipment (8,050 + 3,600)		11,650
Goodwill (W2)		1,170
Licence (W1)		120
Investments		
Associated company (W5)	717	
Others (4,000 + 910 – 3,240 (Sandfly) – 630 (Anthill) + 120 (fair value (W1)))	1,160	1,877
		14,817
Current assets		
Inventory (830 + 340)	1,170	
Accounts receivable (520 + 290 – 40 cash in transit)	770	
Bank (240 + 40 cash in transit)	280	2,220
Total assets		17,037
Equity and liabilities		
Equity attributable to owners of the parent:		
Ordinary shares of $1 each		5,000
Retained earnings (W4)		8,593
		13,593
Minority interest (W3)		364
		13,957
Non-current liabilities		
10% Loan notes (500 + 240)		740
Current liabilities		
Accounts payable (620 + 1,060)	1,680	
Taxation (220 + 250)	470	
Overdraft	190	2,340
Total equity and liabilities		17,037

Workings (*Note:* all figures in $000)

(W1) **Net assets in subsidiary**

	At acquisition $000	At reporting period end $000
Share capital	1,200	1,200
Retained earnings	800	2,200
Fair value adjustment – Inv property	120	120
– Licence (amortization 2/6)	180	120
	2,300	3,640

(W2) **Goodwill**

	$000
Cost of investment ($3 × 1,200 × 90%)	3,240
Net assets acquired (90% × 2,300 (W1))	2,070
Goodwill	1,170

(W3) **Minority interest**

10% × 3,640 (W1) = $364,000

(W4) **Retained earnings**

	$000
Horsefield	7,300
Unrealized profit (65,000 × 30/130 × 2/3 × 30%)	(3)
Sandfly – group share post acquisition 90% × (3,640 – 2,300) (W1)	1,206
Anthill – group share post acquisition 30% × (600 × 6/12)	90
	8,593

(W5) **Associated company – carrying value in consolidated statement of financial position**

	$000
Investment at cost	630
Post acquisition profit (W4)	90
	720
Unrealized profit in inventory (W4)	(3)
	717

(b)   In order for an investment to be classified as an investment in an associated company the investor must have 'significant influence' over the investee. Significant influence is presumed to exist where there is a holding of 20% or more of the voting power unless the investor can clearly demonstrate that this is not the case. Conversely a holding of less than 20% is presumed not to be an associate, unless it can be clearly demonstrated that the investor can exercise significant influence. The voting rights can be held directly or through subsidiaries. IAS 28 *Investments in Associates* excludes subsidiaries and joint ventures from the definition of an associate. Presumably this is for clarity as the definition of a subsidiary would also meet the definition of an associate, and whilst joint ventures are in many ways similar to associates, they are covered by a different International Standard and may require a different accounting treatment.

Somewhat controversially IAS 28 says that a majority holding by one investor does not preclude another investor having significant influence. An investing company owning a majority holding in another company normally has control over the investee and would thus class it as a subsidiary. In normal circumstances it is difficult to see how a company could be controlled by one entity and be significantly influenced by a different entity unless 'control' was passive. The 20% test is not definitive and the following other evidence should be considered.

Does the investing company:

– have representation on the Board of the investee?

– participate in the policy making processes (operational and financial); have material transactions with the investee?

– interchange managerial personnel with the investee; or provide technical expertise to the investee?

46 HAPSBURG

Key answer tips

One of the main complications in part (a) is the deferred consideration. As you are given a discount factor for three years' time this is a big hint that you must discount the deferred consideration element when calculating the goodwill. There are further added complications with the unwinding of the discount on this deferred consideration and the fair value of the plant but otherwise the adjustments required are fairly straightforward. Make sure that you write enough in part (b) to deserve the 5 marks available. A quick 10-line note will not be enough.

(a) **Consolidated Statement of financial position of Hapsburg as at 31 March 20X4**

	$000	$000
Non-current assets		
Goodwill (W3)		16,000
Property, plant and equipment (41,000 + 34,800 + 3,750 (W2))		79,550
Investments:		
– in associate (W7)	15,900	
– ordinary (3,000 + 1,500 (fair value increase))	4,500	20,400
		115,950
Current assets		
Inventory (9,900 + 4,800 – 300 (W4))	14,400	
Trade receivables (13,600 + 8,600)	22,200	
Cash (1,200 + 3,800)	5,000	41,600
Total assets		157,550

	$000	$000
Equity and liabilities		
Ordinary share capital (20,000 + 16,000)		36,000
Reserves:		
Share premium (8,000 + 16,000)	24,000	
Retained earnings (W6)	12,000	36,000
		72,000
Minority interests (W5)		9,150
Non-current liabilities		
10% Loan note (16,000 + 4,200)	20,200	
Deferred consideration (18,000 + 1,800 (W3)	19,800	
		40,000
Current liabilities:		
Trade payables (16,500 + 6,900)	23,400	
Taxation (9,600 + 3,400)	13,000	36,400
Total equity and liabilities		157,550

Workings – Note: all working figures in $000.

(W1) The 80% (24m/30m shares) holding in Sundial gives Hapsburg control and means it is a subsidiary and should be consolidated. The 30% (6m/20m shares) holding in Aspen is likely to give Hapsburg significant influence rather than control and thus it should be equity accounted.

(W2) **Net assets**

	At acquisition	*At reporting period end*
	$000	$000
Sundial		
Share capital	30,000	30,000
Share premium	2,000	2,000
Retained earnings (8,500 – 4,500)	4,000	8,500
	36,000	40,500
Fair value – Plant (15,000 – 10,000) 5,000 × ¾	5,000	3,750
– Investment (4.500 – 3,000)	1,500	1,500
	42,500	45,750
Aspen		
Share capital	20,000	20,000
Retained earnings		
(8,000 – 6,000 + (6/12 × 6,000))	5,000	8,000
	25,000	28,000

(W3) Goodwill on acquisition

	$000
Cost of investment:	
Shares 24m × 2/3 × $2 ($1 share capital, $1 share premium)	32,000
Cash 24m × $1 × 0.75	18,000
	50,000
Net assets acquired 80% × 42,500 (W2)	34,000
Goodwill	16,000

Unwind discount on deferred consideration

Debit Consolidated retained earnings (W6) (18,000 × 10%)	1,800
Credit Deferred consideration	1,800

(W4) Unrealized profit in inventory

	$000
Aspen (associate) selling to Hapsburg (parent)	
(2.5m × 4m -2.4m/4m) × 30% =	300
Debit Consolidated retained earnings	300
Credit Consolidated inventory	300

(W5) Minority interest

	$000
Net assets at reporting period end 20% × 45,750 (W2)	9,150

(W6) Consolidated retained earnings

	$000
Hapsburg	10,600
Post acquisition in Sundial	
(45,750 – 42,500 (W2)) × 80%	2,600
Post acquisition in Aspen	
(28,000 – 25,000 (W2)) × 30%	900
Less: unwinding of discount (W3)	(1,800)
Less: unrealized profit in inventory (W4)	(300)
	12,000

(W7) Investment in associate

	$000
Cost	15,000
Post acquisition profits (28,000 – 25,000× 30% (W2)	900
	15,900

(b)　In recent years many companies have increasingly conducted large parts of their business by acquiring substantial minority interests in other companies. There are broadly three levels of investment. Below 20% of the equity shares of an investee would normally be classed as an ordinary financial asset investment, measured according to the IFRS 39 *Financial Instruments: Recognition and Measurement* rules for the particular category of asset.

A holding of above 50% normally gives control and would create subsidiary company status and consolidation is required. Between these two, in the range of over 20% up to 50%, the investment would normally be deemed to be an associate (note: the level of shareholding is not the only determining criterion). The relevance of this level of shareholding is that it is presumed to give significant influence over the operating and financial policies of the investee (but this presumption can be rebutted). If such an investment were treated as an ordinary investment, the investing company would have the opportunity to manipulate its profit. The most obvious example of this would be by exercising influence over the size of the dividend the associated company paid. This would directly affect the reported profit of the investing company. Also, as companies tend not to distribute all of their profits as dividends, over time the cost of the investment in the statement of financial position may give very little indication of its underlying value.

Equity accounting for associated companies is an attempt to remedy these problems. In the statement of comprehensive income any dividends received from an associate are replaced by the investor's share of the associate's results. In the statement of financial position the investment is initially recorded at cost and subsequently increased by the investor's share of the retained earnings of the associate (any other gains such as the revaluation of the associate's assets would also be included in this process). This treatment means that the investor would show the same profit irrespective of the size of the dividend paid by the associate and the statement of financial position more closely reflects the worth of the investment.

The problem of off balance sheet finance relates to the fact that it is the net assets that are shown in the investor's statement of financial position. Any share of the associate's liabilities is effectively hidden because they have been offset against the associate's assets. As a simple example, say a holding company owned 100% of another company that had assets of $100 million and debt of $80 million; both the assets and the debt would appear on the consolidated statement of financial position. Whereas if this single investment was replaced by owning 50% each of two companies that had the same statements of financial position (i.e. $100 million assets and $80 million debt), then under equity accounting only $20 million ((100 – 80) × 50% × 2) of net assets would appear on the statement of financial position thus hiding the $80 million of debt. Because of this problem, it has been suggested that proportionate consolidation is a better method of accounting for associated companies, as both assets and debts would be included in the investor's statement of financial position.

IAS 28 *Investments in Associates* does not permit the use of proportionate consolidation of associates.

47   HEDRA

Key answer tips

Take care with the deferred consideration and the tax losses. Not only is the deferred consideration part of the cost of Salvador but it is also a liability. The tax losses are a deferred tax asset of the group but this asset is only the tax losses at the tax rate not the full amount of tax losses. Remember also that Hedra has not yet recorded the acquisition of Aragon, therefore Hedra's share capital and share premium must be adjusted.

Consolidated statement of financial position of Hedra as at 30 September 20X5:

	$m	$m
Non-current assets		
Property, plant and equipment (358 + 240 + 12 + 25 +15 (W2))		650
Goodwill (W3)		80
Investment in associate (W4)		220
Other investments		45
		995
Current assets		
Inventories (130 + 80)	210	
Trade receivables (142 + 97)	239	
Cash and bank	4	453
Total assets		1,448
Equity and liabilities		
Equity attributable to the parent		
Ordinary share capital (400 + 80 (40 × 2)) (W4)		480
Reserves:		
Share premium (40 + (200 − (40 × 2)) (W4)	160	
Revaluation (15 + 12 + (5 × 60%) (W2)	30	
Retained earnings (W6)	261	451
		931
Minority interest (W5)		112
		1,043
Non-current liabilities		
Deferred tax (45 − 10)		35
Current liabilities		
Bank overdraft	12	
Trade payables (118 + 141)	259	
Deferred consideration (W3)	49	
Current tax payable	50	370
Total equity and liabilities		1,448

Workings

(W1) Group structure

Investment in Salvador =	72m/120m	=	60% – consolidate
Investment in Aragon =	40m/100m	=	40% – equity account

(W2) Net assets in Salvador

	At acquisition $m	At reporting period end $m
Share capital	120	120
Share premium	50	50
Retained earnings	20	60
Fair value adjustments:		
Land and buildings	20	25
Plant (depn ¼)	20	15
Deferred tax asset (40 × 25%)	10	10
	240	280

(W3) Goodwill

	$m	$m
Cost of investment – cash		195
deferred		49
		244
Net assets acquired (60% × 240 (W1))		144
Goodwill at acquisition		100
Notional goodwill, grossed up for minority interest (100 × 100/60)	166	
Recoverable amount	(133)	
Impairment – 60% recognized	33	(20)
Goodwill in statement of financial position		80

(W4) Investment in associate

	$m	$m
Cost of investment (40m × 2 × $2.50)		200
Net assets at acquisition		
Share capital	100	
Retained earnings		
(200 + ((300 – 200) × 6/12))	250	
	350	
Group share 350 × 40%		140
Goodwill		60

	$m
Investment in associate	
Cost	200
Group share of post acquisition profit	
(40% × ((300 – 200) × 6/12))	20
	220

OR

	$m
Investment in associate	
Share of net assets (40% × 400)	160
Goodwill	60
	220

(W5) Minority interest

Minority share of net assets at reporting period end (40% × 280 (W2))	$112m

(W6) Consolidated retained earnings

	$m	$m
Hedra		240
Salvador – post acquisition (60 – 20)	40	
Additional depreciation	(5)	
	35	
Group share 60%		21
Aragon (W4)		20
Impairment of goodwill		(20)
		261

48 HOLDRITE, STAYBRITE AND ALLBRITE

Key answer tips

Part (a) contains a routine calculation of goodwill, being the difference between the fair value of the consideration paid and the fair value of the net assets acquired. In part (b), note that both the subsidiary and the associate were acquired half-way into the current year, so only half a year's post-acquisition profits can be included in group profits in the consolidated statement of comprehensive income.

(a) **Goodwill in Staybrite – at 1 April 20X4:**

	$000	$000
Consideration		
Shares (10,000 × 75% × 2/3 × $6)		30,000
8% loan notes (10,000 × 75% × $100/250)		3,000
		33,000
Less		
Equity shares	10,000	
Share premium	4,000	
Pre acq reserves (7,500 + (9,000 × $^6/_{12}$))	12,000	
Fair value adjustment (3,000 + 5,000)	8,000	
	34,000 × 75%	(25,500)
Goodwill		7,500

Goodwill on the purchase of shares in Allbrite – at 1 April 20X4:

	$000
Consideration	
Shares (5,000 × 40% × 3/4 × $6)	9,000
Cash (5,000 × 40% × $1)	2,000
	11,000
Less	
Equity shares	5,000
Share premium	2,000
Pre acq reserves (6,000 + (4,000 × 6/12))	8,000
15,000 × 40%	(6,000)
Goodwill	5,000

(b) **Holdrite Group Consolidated statement of comprehensive income for the year ended 30 September 20X4**

	$000
Revenue (75,000 + (40,700 × 6/12) − 10,000)	85,350
Cost of sales (W1)	(48,750)
Gross profit	36,600
Operating expenses (W2)	(15,730)
Profit from operations	20,870
Income from associate (4,000 × 6/12 × 40%)	800
	21,670
Finance cost	(170)
Profit before tax	21,500
Income tax expense	
(4,800 + (3,000 × 6/12))	
	(6,300)
Profit for the period	15,200
Attributable to:	
Owners of the parent	14,200
Minority interest (W3)	1,000
	15,200

(c) **Holdrite Group Movement on consolidated retained earnings attributable to Holdrite for the year ended 30 September 20X4**

	$000
Profit for the period	14,200
Dividend paid	(5,000)
	9,200
Retained earnings b/f	18,000
Retained earnings c/f	27,200

Workings

(W1) **Cost of sales**

	$000
Holdrite	47,400
Staybrite (19,700 × 6/12)	9,850
Additional depreciation of plant	500
Intra group purchases	(10,000)
Unrealized profit in inventory (4,000 × 25%)	1,000
	48,750

(W2) **Operating expenses**

	$000
Holdrite	10,480
Staybrite (9,000 × 6/12)	4,500
Impairment of Staybrite's recognized goodwill (1,000 × 75%)	750
	15,730

(W3) **Minority Interest**

	$000
$9,000 \times 6/12$	4,500
Less additional depreciation	(500)
	4,000
$\times 25\%$	1,000

Tutorial note: The retained profits carried forward can be proved as:

	$000
Holdrite $(18,000 + 12,150 - 5,000)$	25,150
Staybrite $(75\% \times 9,000 \times {}^6\!/_{12})$	3,375
Allbrite $(40\% \times 4,000 \times {}^6\!/_{12})$	800
Additional depreciation of plant $(75\% \times 500)$	(375)
Unrealized profit in inventory (W1)	(1,000)
Impairment of goodwill (W2)	(750)
	27,200

49   HYDAN

Key answer tips

A slightly unusual question, in that the post acquisition result has already been calculated. It is also unusual that this result is a loss. The intra-group sales, unrealized profit and fair value adjustments are pretty standard. Remember to leave enough time for part (b). The key is to identify the significant changes in gross profit margin and operating expenses after the acquisition date and then discuss the likely effects on those interested in the results of Systan itself, such as the 40% minority interest.

(a)   **Consolidated statement of comprehensive income of Hydan for the year ended 31 March 20X6**

	$000
Revenue $(98 + 35.2 - 30$ intra-group$)$	103,200
Cost of sales (W1)	(77,500)
Gross profit	25,700
Operating expenses $(11.8 + 8 + 0.375$ goodwill impair (W3)$)$	(20,175)
Interest receivable $(0.35 - 0.2 \ (4 \times 10\% \times 6/12)$ intra-group$)$	150
Finance costs	(420)
Profit before tax	5,255
Income tax expenses $(4.2 - 1$ relief$)$	(3,200)
Profit for the period	2,055
Attributable to:	
Owners of Hydan (β)	3,455
Minority interest (W4)	(1,400)
	2,055

Consolidated statement of financial position at 31 March 20X5

Non-current assets

Property, plant and equipment (18.4 + 9.5 + 1.2 (fv) – 0.3 (fv depn) (W2))	28,800
Goodwill (W3)	2,625
Investments (16 – 10.8 cost of investment (W3) – 4 intra-group	1,200
	32,625
Current assets (18 + 7.2 – 1 intra-group – 0.2 UPR (W1))	24,000
Total assets	56,625

Equity and liabilities

Equity attributable to the parent

Ordinary share capital of $1 each	10,000
Share premium	5,000
Retained earnings (W5)	17,525
	32,525
Minority interest (W4)	3,800
Total equity	36,325
Non-current liabilities	
7% bank loan	6,000
Current liabilities (11.4 + 3.9 – 1 intra-group)	14,300
Total equity and liabilities	56,625

Workings

(W1) Cost of sales

	$000
Hydan	76,000
Systan	31,000
Intra-group sales	(30,000)
URP on inventories (4 × 5%)	200
Additional depreciation re fv adjustment	300
	77,500

(W2) Net assets in Systan

	At acquisition $000	At reporting period end $000
Share capital	2,000	2,000
Share premium	500	500
Retained earnings:		
– brought forward (6.3 – 3.6 pre acq profit + 3 post acq loss)	5,700	5,700
– current period (3.6 – 3)	3,600	600
Fair value adjustment (1.2 – 0.3)	1,200	900
Unrealized profit on inventory (W1)	–	(200)
	13,000	9,500

(W3) Goodwill re Systan

	$000
Cost of investment ($9 × 60% × 2,000)	10,800
Less: share of net assets acquired:	
60% × 13,000 (W2)	7,800
	3,000
Less: 12.5% impairment	(375)
	2,625

(W4) Minority interest

	$000
In statement of comprehensive income:	
Post-acquisition loss	(3,000)
Additional cost of sales (0.2 + 0.3 (w1))	(500)
Adjusted post-acquisition loss	(3,500)
40% thereof	(1,400)
In statement of financial position	
40% × 9,500 (w2)	3,800

(W5) Consolidated retained earnings

	$000
Hydan	20,000
Systan – 60% × (3,500) (w4)	(2,100)
Goodwill impairment (w3)	(375)
	17,525

(b) Although Systan's revenue has increased since its acquisition by Hydan, its operating performance appears to have deteriorated markedly. Its gross profit margin has fallen from 25% (6m/24m) in the six months prior to the acquisition to only 11.9% (4.2m/35.2m) in the post-acquisition period. The decline in gross profit is worsened by a huge increase in operating expenses in the post-acquisition period. These have gone from $1.2 million pre-acquisition to $8 million post-acquisition. Taking into account the effects of interest and tax a $3.6 million first half profit (pre-acquisition) has turned into a $3 million second half loss (post-acquisition).

Whilst it is possible that some of the worsening performance may be due to market conditions, the major cause is probably due to the effects of the acquisition. The question states Hydan has acquired a controlling interest in Systan, so the two companies are related parties. Since the acquisition most of Systan's sales have been to Hydan. This is not surprising as Systan was acquired to secure supplies to Hydan. The terms under which the sales are made are now determined by the management of Hydan, whereas they were previously determined by the management of Systan.The question says sales to Hydan yield a consistent gross profit of only 5%. This is very low and much lower than the profit margin on sales to Hydan prior to the acquisition and also much lower than the few sales that were made to third parties in the post acquisition period. It may also be that Hydan has shifted the burden of some of the group operating expenses to Systan – this may explain the large increase in Systan's post acquisition operating expenses. The effect of these (transfer pricing) actions would move profits from Systan's books into those of Hydan.

The implications of this are quite significant. Initially there may be a tendency to think the effect is not important as on consolidation both companies' results are added together, but other parties are affected by these actions. The most obvious is the significant (40%) minority interest; they are effectively having some of their share of Systan's profit and statement of financial position value taken from them. It may also be that the management and staff of Systan may be losing out on profit related bonuses. Finally, any party using Systan's entity financial statements, for whatever purpose, would be basing any decisions they make on potentially misleading information.

50 HOSTERLING

Key answer tips

Parts (a) and (b) are relatively easy marks. Note that in part (a) you are asked to calculate the goodwill at acquisition so before any impairment. When preparing the statement of comprehensive income remember that you are dealing with losses in the associate.

(a) **Goodwill arising on acquisition of Sunlee – at 1 October 20X5:**

	$000	$000
Consideration		
Shares (20,000 × 80% × 3/5 × $5)		48,000
Less		
Equity shares	20,000	
Pre acq reserves	18,000	
Fair value adjustments ((22,000 – 18,000) + (20,000 – 17,000) + (35,000 – 30,000))	12,000	
	―――	
	50,000× 80%	(40,000)
	―――	
Goodwill		8,000
		―――

(b) **Carrying amount of Amber 30 September 20X6 (prior to impairment loss):**

	$000
At cost	
Cash (6,000 × $3)	18,000
6% loan notes (6,000 × $100/100)	6,000
	―――
	24,000
Less	
Post acquisition losses (20,000 × 40% × 3/12)	(2,000)
	―――
	22,000
	―――

(c)   **Hosterling Group**

Consolidated statement of comprehensive income for the year ended 30 September 20X6

	$000
Revenue (105,000 + 62,000 – 18,000 intra group)	149,000
Cost of sales (see working)	(89,000)
	———
Gross profit	60,000
Distribution costs (4,000 + 2,000)	(6,000)
Administrative expenses (7,500 + 7,000)	(14,500)
Finance costs (1,200 + 900)	(2,100)
Impairment losses:	
Goodwill	(1,600)
Investment in associate (22,000 (per (b)) – 21,500)	(500)
Share of loss from associate (per (b))	(2,000)
	———
Profit before tax	33,300
Income tax expense (8,700 + 2,600)	(11,300)
	———
Profit for the period	22,000
	———
Attributable to:	
Owners of the parent	19,600
Minority Interest ((13,000 – 1,000 depreciation adjustment) × 20%)	2,400
	———
	22,000
	———

Note: the dividend from Sunlee is eliminated on consolidation.

Working

	$000
Cost of sales	
Hosterling	68,000
Sunlee	36,500
Intra group purchases	(18,000)
Additional depreciation of plant ((35,000 – 30,000)/5 years)	1,000
Unrealized profit in inventories (7,500 × 25%/125%)	1,500
	———
	89,000
	———

51   AJ

Key answer tips

The only real complication in this question is the fact that AJ owns loan notes in BK as well as equity shares: Dr Non-current liabilities, Cr Other financial assets. You need to do the full goodwill calculation in order to arrive at the impairment loss to be written off to consolidated reserves.

(a)   **How the investments will be treated**

AJ owns 80% of the ordinary shares in BK.This suggests that AJ is able to control the operating and financial policies of BK. Therefore BK is a subsidiary of AJ and AJ must prepare consolidated financial statements using the purchase method.

AJ also owns 40% of the ordinary shares of CL. On the face of it, this suggests that AJ has significant influence over the operating and financial policies of CL, but cannot control them. Most of the remaining shares in CL are owned by three other investors, which suggests that no other investor has overall control. In addition, AJ only has the power to appoint one director to the board. All these factors indicate that CL is an associate of AJ and AJ should include its investment in CL in its consolidated financial statements using equity accounting.

(b) **Consolidated statement of financial position at 31 March 20X5**

	$000	$000
Assets		
Non-current assets		
Property, plant and equipment (12,500 + 4,700 + 195 (W2))		17,395
Goodwill (W3)		1,700
Investment in associate (W4)		4,560
Other financial assets (W5)		4,100
		27,755
Current assets		
Inventories (7,200 + 8,000 − 200 (W2))	15,000	
Trade receivables (6,300 + 4,300)	10,600	
Cash	800	
		26,400
		54,155
Equity and liabilities		
Equity		
Share capital	10,000	
Reserves (W6)	13,156	
Equity attributable to owners of the parent		23,156
Minority interests (W7)		1,199
		24,355
Non-current liabilities: Loan notes (10,000 + 3,000 − 2,000)		11,000
Current liabilities		
Trade payables (8,900 + 6,700)	15,600	
Tax liabilities (1,300 + 100)	1,400	
Short term borrowings (600 + 1,200)	1,800	
		18,800
		54,155

Workings

(W1) **Group structure**

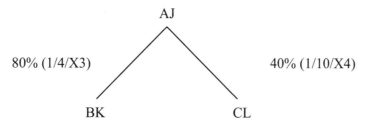

(W2) Net assets of subsidiary and associate

	BK		CL	
	Acquisition	Reporting period end	Acquisition	Reporting period end
	$000	$000	$000	$000
Share capital	5,000	5,000	2,500	2,500
Reserves	1,500	1,000	3,900	4,300
Fair value adjustment (1,115 – 920)	195	195		
Provision for unrealized profit (25/125 × 1,000)		(200)		
	6,695	5,995	6,400	6,800

(W3) Goodwill (BK)

	$000
Cost of combination	7,500
Less: net assets acquired: (80% × 6,695)	(5,356)
	2,144
Impairment loss (balancing figure	(444)
	1,700

(W4) Investment in associate

	$000
Cost of investment	4,400
Share of post-acquisition profit (40% × 6,800 – 6,400 **(W2)**)	160
	4,560

Alternative calculation:

Share of net assets at reporting period end (40% × 6,800 (W2))	2,720
Goodwill (see below)	1,840
	4,560

Goodwill

Cost of investment	4,400
Share of net assets acquired: (40% × 6,400)	(2,560)
	1,840

(W5) Other financial assets

	$000
Investments	18,000
Less:	
BK (shares (W3))	(7,500)
BK (loan notes)	(2,000)
CL (W4)	(4,400)
	4,100

(W6) Consolidated reserves

		$000	$000
AJ			14,000
BK:	At reporting period end (W2)	5,995	
	At acquisition (W2)	(6,695)	
		(700)	
	Group share (80%)		(560)
CL:	At reporting period end (W2)	6,800	
	At acquisition (W2)	(6,400)	
		400	
	Group share (40%)		160
			13,600
	Less: impairment loss (W1)		(444)
			13,156

(W7) Minority interests

	$000
Net assets at reporting period end (20% × 5,995)	1,199

ANALYSING AND INTERPRETING FINANCIAL STATEMENTS

52   COMPARATOR

Key answer tips

Be careful with your time allocation for answering this question. The bulk of your time should be spent in writing the report required in part (c). Only 6 marks are offered for calculating ratios. All the remaining marks are for explanation and interpretation.

(a)   Ratios are used to assess the financial performance of a company by comparing the calculated figures to various other sources. This may be to previous years' ratios of the same company, to the ratios of a similar rival company, to accepted norms (say of liquidity ratios) or, as in this example, to industry averages. The problems inherent in these processes are several. Probably the most important aspect of using ratios is to realize that they do not give the answers to the assessment of how well a company has performed; they merely raise the questions and direct the analyst into trying to determine what has caused favourable or unfavourable indicators. In many ways it can be said that ratios are only as useful as the skills of the person using them. It is also true that any assessment should also consider other information that may be available including non-financial information.

More specific problem areas are:

–   Accounting policies: if two companies have different accounting policies, it can invalidate any comparison between their ratios. For example return on capital employed is materially affected by revaluations of assets. Comparing this ratio for two companies where one has revalued its assets and the other carries them at depreciated historic cost would not be very meaningful. Similar examples may involve depreciation methods, inventory valuation policies, etc.

– Accounting practices: this is similar to differing accounting policies in its effects. An example of this would be the use of debt factoring. If one company collects its accounts receivable in the normal way, then the calculation of the accounts receivable collection period would be a reasonable indication of the efficiency of its credit control department. However if a company chose to factor its accounts receivable (i.e. 'sell' them to a finance company) then the calculation of its collection period would be meaningless. A more controversial example would be the engineering of a lease such that it fell to be treated as an operating lease rather than a finance lease.

– Statement of financial position averages: many ratios are based on comparing statement of comprehensive income items with statement of financial position items. The ratio of accounts receivable collection period is a good example of this. For such ratios to have any meaning, there is an assumption that the year-end statement of financial position figures are representative of annual norms. Seasonal trading and other factors may invalidate this assumption. For example the level of accounts receivable and inventory of a toy manufacturer could vary largely due to the nature of its seasonal trading.

– Inflation can distort comparisons over time.

– The definition of an accounting ratio. If a ratio is calculated by two companies using different definitions, then there is an obvious problem. Common examples of this are gearing ratios (some use debt/equity, others may use debt/debt + equity). Also where a ratio is partly based on a profit figure, there can be differences as to what is included and what is excluded from the profit figure. Problems of this type include the treatment of finance costs.

– The use of norms can be misleading. A desirable range for the current ratio may be say between 1.5 and 2 : 1, but all businesses are different. This would be a very high ratio for a supermarket (with few accounts receivable), but a low figure for a construction company (with high levels of work in progress).

– Looking at a single ratio in isolation is rarely useful. It is necessary to form a view when considering ratios in combination with other ratios.

A more controversial aspect of ratio analysis is that management have sometimes indulged in creative accounting techniques in order that the ratios calculated from published financial statements will show a more favourable picture than the true underlying position. Examples of this are sale and repurchase agreements, which manipulate liquidity figures, and off balance sheet finance which distorts return on capital employed.

Inter firm comparisons:

Of particular concern with this method of using ratios is:

– They are themselves averages and may incorporate large variations in their composition. Some inter firm comparison agencies produce the ratios analysed into quartiles to attempt to overcome this problem.

– It may be that the sector in which a company is included may not be sufficiently similar to the exact type of trade of the specific company. The type of products or markets may be different.

– Companies of different sizes operate under different economies of scale, this may not be reflected in the industry average figures.

- The year end accounting dates of the companies included in the averages are not going to be all the same. This highlights issues of statement of financial position averages and seasonal trading referred to above. Some companies try to minimize this by grouping companies with approximately similar year-ends together as in the example of this question, but this is not a complete solution.

(b) **Calculation of specified ratios:**

	Comparator	Sector average
Return on capital employed (186 + 34 loan interest/(335 + 300))	34.6%	22.1%
Net asset turnover (2,425/(335 + 300))	3.8 times	1.8 times
Gross profit margin (555/2,425 × 100)	22.9%	30%
Net profit (before tax) margin (186/2,425 × 100)	7.7%	12.5%
Current ratio (595/500)	1.19 : 1	1.6 : 1
Quick ratio (320/500)	0.64 : 1	0.9 : 1
Inventory holding period (275/1,870 × 365)	54 days	46 days
Accounts receivable collection period (320/2,425 × 365)	48 days	45 days
Accounts payable payment period (350/1,870 × 365) (based on cost of sales)	68 days	55 days
Debt to equity (300/335 × 100)	90%	40%
Dividend yield (see below)	2.5%	6%
Dividend cover (96/90)	1.07 times	3 times

The workings are in $000 (unless otherwise stated) and are for Comparator's ratios.

The dividend yield is calculated from a dividend per share figure of 15c ($90,000/150,000 × 4) and a share price of $6.00.

Thus the yield is 2.5% (15c/$6.00 × 100%).

(c) **REPORT**

Subject: Analysis of Comparator's financial performance compared to sector average for the year to 30 September 20X3

Operating performance

The return on capital employed of Comparator is impressive being more than 50% higher than the sector average. The components of the return on capital employed are the asset turnover and profit margins. In these areas Comparator's asset turnover is much higher (nearly double) than the average, but the net profit margin after exceptionals is considerably below the sector average. However, if the exceptionals are treated as one off costs and excluded, Comparator's margins are very similar to the sector average.

This short analysis seems to imply that Comparator's superior return on capital employed is due entirely to an efficient asset turnover i.e. Comparator is making its assets work twice as efficiently as its competitors. A closer inspection of the underlying figures may explain why its asset turnover is so high. It can be seen from the note to the statement of financial position that Comparator's non-current assets appear quite old. Their net book value is only 15% of their original cost. This has at least two implications; they will need replacing in the near future and the company is already struggling for funding; and their low net book value gives a high figure for asset turnover. Unless Comparator has underestimated the life of its assets in its depreciation calculations, its non-current assets will need replacing in the near future. When this occurs its asset turnover and return on capital employed figures will be much lower.

This aspect of ratio analysis often causes problems and to counter this anomaly some companies calculate the asset turnover using the cost of non-current assets rather than their net book value as this gives a more reliable trend. It is also possible that Comparator is using assets that are not on its statement of financial position. It may be leasing assets that do not meet the definition of finance leases and thus the assets and corresponding obligations are not recognized on the statement of financial position.

A further issue is which of the two calculated margins should be compared to the sector average (i.e. including or excluding the effects of the exceptionals). The gross profit margin of Comparator is much lower than the sector average. If the exceptional losses were taken in at trading account level, which they should be as they relate to obsolete inventory, Comparator's gross margin would be even worse. As Comparator's net margin is similar to the sector average, it would appear that Comparator has better control over its operating costs. This is especially true as the other element of the net profit calculation is finance costs and as Comparator has much higher gearing than the sector average, one would expect Comparator's interest to be higher than the sector average.

Liquidity

Here Comparator shows real cause for concern. Its current and quick ratios are much worse than the sector average, and indeed far below expected norms. Current liquidity problems appear due to high levels of accounts payable and a high bank overdraft. The high levels of inventory contribute to the poor quick ratio and may be indicative of further obsolete inventory (the exceptional item is due to obsolete inventory). The accounts receivable collection figure is reasonable, but at 68 days, Comparator takes longer to pay its accounts payable than do its competitors. Whilst this is a source of 'free' finance, it can damage relations with suppliers and may lead to a curtailment of further credit.

Gearing

As referred to above, gearing (as measured by debt/equity) is more than twice the level of the sector average. Whilst this may be an uncomfortable level, it is currently beneficial for shareholders. The company is making an overall return of 34.6%, but only paying 8% interest on its loan notes. The gearing level may become a serious issue if Comparator becomes unable to maintain the finance costs. The company already has an overdraft and the ability to make further interest payments could be in doubt.

Investment ratios

Despite reasonable profitability figures, Comparator's dividend yield is poor compared to the sector average. From the extracts of the changes in equity it can be seen that total dividends are $90,000 out of available profit for the year of only $96,000 (hence the very low dividend cover).It is worthy of note that the interim dividend was $60,000 and the final dividend only $30,000. Perhaps this indicates a worsening performance during the year, as normally final dividends are higher than interim dividends.Considering these factors it is surprising the company's share price is holding up so well.

Summary

The company compares favourably with the sector average figures for profitability, however the company's liquidity and gearing position is quite poor and gives cause for concern. If it is to replace its old assets in the near future, it will need to raise further finance.With already high levels of borrowing and poor dividend yields, this may be a serious problem for Comparator.

Yours faithfully

53   RYTETREND

Key answer tips

Although you are specifically asked for ratios in part (b), most of the marks can be gained through observation and analysis. As well as the statement of comprehensive income and statement of financial position, you should refer to the statement of cash flows that you prepared in part (a). This highlights a central issue: the heavy expenditure on non-current assets during the year.

(a)   **Rytetrend – Statement of cash flows for the year to 31 March 20X3**

	$000	$000
Cash flows from operating activities		
[*Note:* figures in brackets are in $000]		
Operating profit per question		3,860
Capitalization of installation costs		
less depreciation (300 – 20%) (W1)		240
Adjustments for:		
Depreciation of non-current assets (W1)	7,410	
Loss on disposal of plant (W1)	700	
	———	8,110
Increase in warranty provision (500 – 150)		350
Decrease in inventory (3,270 – 2,650)		620
Decrease in receivables (1,950 – 1,100)		850
Increase in payables (3,300 – 2,260)		1,040
		———
Cash generated from operations		15,070
Interest paid		(460)
Income taxes paid (W2)		(910)
		———
Net cash from operating activities		13,700
Net cash used in investing activities		
Purchase of non-current assets (W1)		(15,550)
Cash flows from financing activities:		
Issue of ordinary shares (1,500 + 1,500)	3,000	
Issue of 6% loan note	2,000	
Repayment of 10% loan notes	(4,000)	
Ordinary dividends paid	(600)	
	———	
Net cash from financing activities		400
		———
Net decrease in cash and cash equivalents		(1,450)
Cash and cash equivalents at beginning of period		400
		———
Cash and cash equivalents at end of period		(1,050)
		———

Workings

(W1) **Non-current assets – cost**

	$000
Balance b/f	27,500
Disposal	(6,000)
Balance c/f (37,250 + 300 re installation)	(37,550)
Cost of assets acquired	(16,050)
Trade in allowance	500
Cash flow for acquisitions	(15,550)

Depreciation	
Balance b/f	(10,200)
Disposal (6,000 × 20% × 4 years)	4,800
Balance c/f (12,750 + (300 × 20%))	12,810
Difference – charge for year	7,410

Disposal	
Cost	6,000
Depreciation	(4,800)
Net book value	1,200
Trade in allowance	(500)
Loss on sale	700

(W2) **Tax paid:**

Tax provision b/f	(630)
Statement of comprehensive income tax charge	(1,000)
Tax provision c/f	720
Difference – cash paid	(910)

(b) **REPORT**

Subject: The financial performance of Rytetrend for the year ended 31 March 20X3

Operating performance

(i) Revenue up $8.3 million representing an increase of 35.3% on 20X2 figure of $23.5 million.

(ii) Costs of sales up by $6.5 million (40.6% increase on 20X2 figure of $16 million).

Overall the increase in activity has led to an increase in gross profit of $1.8 million, however the gross profit margin has eased slightly from 31.9% in 20X2 to 29.2% in 20X3. Perhaps the slight reduction in margins gave a boost to sales.

(iii) Operating expenses have increased by $840,000, an increase of 18.3% on 20X2 figure of $4.6 million but this is considerably lower than the increase in revenue.

(iv) Interest costs reduced by $40,000. It is worth noting that the composition of them has changed. It appears that Rytetrend has taken advantage of a cyclic reduction in borrowing cost and redeemed its 10% loan notes and (partly) replaced these with lower cost 6% loan notes. From the interest cost figure, this appears to have taken place half way through the year. Although borrowing costs on long-term finance have decreased, other factors have led to a substantial overdraft which has led to further interest of $200,000.

(v) The accumulated effect is an increase in profit before tax of $1 million (up 41.7% on 20X2) which is reflected by an increase in dividends of $200,000.

(vi) The company has invested heavily in acquiring new non-current assets (over $15 million – see statement of cash flows). The refurbishment of the equipment may be responsible for the increase in the company's sales and operating performance.

Analysis of financial position

(vii) Inventory and receivables have both decreased markedly. Inventory is now at 43 days (2,650/22,500 × 365) from 75 days (3,270/16,000 × 365), this may be due to new arrangements with suppliers or that the different range of equipment that Rytetrend now sells may offer less choice requiring lower inventory. Receivables are only 13 days (1,100/31,800 × 365) (from 30 days (1,950/23,500 × 365)). This low figure is probably a reflection of a retailing business.

(viii) Although payables have increased significantly, they still represent only 54 days ((3,300/22,500 × 365) based on cost of sales) which is almost the same as in 20X2 (2,260/16,000 × 365).

(ix) A very worrying factor is that the company has gone from net current assets of $2,580,000 to net current liabilities of $1,820,000. This is mainly due to a combination of the above mentioned item: decreased inventory and receivables and increased trade payables leading to a fall in cash balances of $1,450,000. That said, traditionally acceptable norms for liquidity ratios are not really appropriate to a mainly retailing business.

(x) Long-term borrowing has fallen by $2 million; this has lowered gearing from 20% (4,000/(4,000 + 15,880)) to only 9% (2,000/(2,000 + 20,680)). This is a very modest level of gearing.

The statement of cash flows

This indicates very healthy cash flows generated from operations of $15,070,000, more than sufficient to pay interest costs, taxation and dividends. The main reason why the overall cash balance has fallen is that new non-current assets (costing over $15 million) have largely been financed from operating cash flows (only $1 million net of new capital has been raised). If Rytetrend continues to generate operating cash flows in the order of the current year, its liquidity will soon get back to healthy levels.

54 BIGWOOD

Key answer tips

Be sure that you know the IAS 7 format for the statement of cash flows before the exam, so that you can quickly slot in the required figures to earn full marks. Part (b) tells you exactly what is required. Make sure that you refer to your statement of cash flows from part (a) as instructed.

(a) **Bigwood – Statement of cash flows for the year to 30 September 20X4:**

Cash flows from operating activities

	$000	$000
Note: figures in brackets are in $000		
Net profit before tax		700
Adjustments for:		
depreciation – non-current assets (W1)	3,800	
loss on disposal of fixtures (W1)	1,250	
interest expense	300	5,350
Operating profit before working capital changes		6,050
Increase in inventory (2,900 – 1,500)		(1,400)
Increase in trade receivables (100 – 50)		(50)
Increase in trade payables (3,100 – 2,150)		950
Cash generated from operations		5,550
Interest paid		(300)
Income tax paid (W2)		(480)
Net cash from operating activities		4,770
Cash flow from investing activities		
Purchase of Property, plant and equipment (W1)	(10,500)	
Disposal costs of fixtures (W1)	(50)	
Net cash used in investing activities	–––––	(10,550)
Cash flows from financing activities		
Issue of ordinary shares (2,000 + 1,000)	3,000	
Long term loans (3,000 – 1,000)	2,000	
Equity dividend paid	(600)	
Net cash from financing activities	–––––	4,400
Net decrease in cash and cash equivalents		(1,380)
Cash and cash equivalents at beginning of period		450
Cash and cash equivalents at end of period		(930)

Workings (all figures in $000)

(W1) **Property, plant and equipment – cost**

Balance b/f	9,500
Disposal	(3,000)
Balance c/f	(17,000)
Difference cash purchase	(10,500)

Depreciation	
Balance b/f	(3,000)
Disposal (3,000 – 1,200)	1,800
Balance c/f	5,000
Difference charge for year	3,800

Disposal	
Cost	3,000
Depreciation	(1,800)
Net book value	1,200
Cost of disposal	50
Total loss on disposal	(1,250)

(W2) **Income tax paid:**

Provision b/f	(450)
Statement of comprehensive income tax charge	(250)
Provision c/f	220
Difference cash paid	(480)

(b) **REPORT**

Subject: The financial performance of Bigwood for the two years ended 30 September 20X4

Operating performance

Bigwood's overall performance as measured by the return on capital employed has deteriorated markedly. This ratio is effectively a composite of the company's profit margins and its asset utilization. The expansion represented by the acquisition of the five new stores has considerably increased investment in net assets. The asset turnover (a measure of asset utilization) has fallen from 3.3 times to just 2.1 times. This is a relatively large fall and is partly responsible for the deteriorating performance. However, it should be borne in mind that it often takes some time before new investment generates the same level of sales as existing capacity so it may be that the situation will improve in future years.

Of more concern in the current year is the deteriorating gross profit margin of the company's clothing sales. This has fallen from 18.6% to 9.4%. The effect of this is all the more marked because sales of clothing (in the current year) represents nearly 70% (16,000 as % of 13,000) of revenue. It should also be noted that the inventory holding period of clothing has also increased significantly from 39 days in 20X3 to 68 days in the current year. This may be a reflection of a company policy to increase inventory levels in order to attract more sales, but it may also be an indication that there is some slow-moving or obsolete inventory. The clothing industry is notoriously susceptible to fashion changes; the new designs may not have gone down well with the buying public. By contrast the profit margin on food sales has increased substantially (from 25% to 32.1%) as indeed have the sales themselves (up 75% on last year). These improvements have helped to offset the weaker performance of clothing sales.

A more detailed analysis shown by the ratios in the appendix confirms the position. The expansion has created a 35% increase in the sales floor area, but the proportionate increase in revenue is only 17.3%. Breaking this down between the two sectors shows that the clothing sector is responsible for this deterioration; an increase in capacity of 37% has led to an increase in sales of only 2.6%, whereas a more modest increase of 20% in the food floor area has led to a remarkable increase of 75% in food sales.In the current year food retailing has generated sales of $1,167,000 per square metre, whereas clothing sales per square metre has fallen from $446,000 to $333,000. When the relative profit margins of clothing and food are considered it can be seen that food retailing has been far more profitable than clothing retailing and this gap in margins has increased during the current year.

This deterioration in trading margins has continued through to net profit margins (falling from 7.1% to only 2.0%). It can be observed that operating expenses have increased considerably, but this is to be expected and is probably in line with the increase in the number of stores.

In summary, the increase in capacity has focused on clothing rather than food retailing. On reflection this seems misguided as the performance of food retailing was superior to that of clothing (in 20X3) and this has continued (even more so) during the current year.

Liquidity/solvency

The increase in the investment in new stores and the refurbishment of existing stores has been largely financed by increasing long term loans by $2 million and issuing $3 million of equity. The effect of this is an increase in gearing from 17% to 28%. Although the level of gearing is still modest, the interest cover has fallen from a very healthy 25 times to a worrying low 3.3 times. The investment has also taken its toll on the bank balance falling from $450,000 in hand to an overdraft of $930,000. This probably explains why the company has stretched its payment of accounts payable to 59 days in 20X4 from 50 days in 20X3.

The company's current liquidity position has deteriorated slightly from 0.77 : 1 to 0.71 : 1. No quick ratios have been given, nor would they be useful. Liquidity ratios are difficult to assess for retailing companies. Most of the sales generated by such companies are for cash (thus there will be few trade receivables) and normal liquidity benchmarks are not appropriate. The statement of cash flows reveals cash flows generated from operations of $5,550,000. This is a far more reliable indicator of the company's liquidity position. The $5,550,000 is more than adequate to service the tax and the dividend payments. Indeed the operating cash flows have contributed significantly to the financing of the expansion programme.

Share price and dividends

Bigwood's share price has halved from $6.00 to $3.00 during the current year. The dilution effect of the share issue at $1.50 per share (2 million shares for $3 million) would account for some of this fall (to approximately $4.20), but the further fall probably represents the market's expectations of the company's performance. It is worth noting that the company has maintained its dividends at $600,000 despite an after tax profit of only $450,000. Whilst this dividend policy cannot be maintained indefinitely (at the current level of profits), the directors may be trying to convey to the market a feeling of confidence in the future profitability of the company. It may also be a reaction designed to support the share price. It should also be noted that although the total dividend has been maintained, the dividend per share will have decreased due to the share issue during the year.

Summary

The above analysis of performance seems to give mixed messages, the company has invested heavily in new and upgraded stores, but operating performance has deteriorated and the expansion may have been mis-focused. This appears to have affected the share price adversely. Alternatively, it may be that the expansion will take a little time to bear fruit and the deterioration may be a reflection of the current state of the economy. Cash generation remains sound and if this continues, the poor current liquidity position will soon be reversed.

Appendix

The following additional ratios can be calculated:

	Clothing		Food		Overall	
Increase in sales area	(13,000/35,000)	37%	(1,000/5,000)	20%	(14,000/40,000)	35%
Increase in revenue	(400/15,600)	2.6%	(3,000/4,000)	75%	(3,400/19,600)	17.3%

	Sales per sq mtr 20X4		Sales per sq mtr 20X3	
		$000		$000
Overall	(23,000/54)	426	(19,600/40)	490
Clothing	(16,000/48)	333	(15,600/35)	446
Food	(7,000/6)	1,167	(4,000/5)	800

55   MINSTER

Key answer tips

The question asks you to analyse the performance of the company from the statement of cash flows you have prepared and the financial statements given. There is therefore no need to calculate any ratios.

(a)   **Statement of cash flows of Minster for the Year ended 30 September 20X6:**

	$000	$000
Cash flows from operating activities		
Profit before tax		142
Adjustments for:		
Depreciation of property, plant and equipment	255	
Amortization of software (180 – 135)	45	300
Investment income		(20)
Finance costs		40
		462
Working capital adjustments		
Decrease in trade receivables (380 – 270)	110	
Increase in amounts due from construction contracts (80 – 55)	(25)	
Decrease in inventories (510 – 480)	30	
Decrease in trade payables (555 – 350)	(205)	(90)
Cash generated from operations		372
Interest paid (40 – (150 × 8%) re unwinding of environmental provision)		(28)
Income taxes paid (w (ii))		(54)
Net cash from operating activities		290
Cash flows from investing activities		
Purchase of – property, plant and equipment (w (i))	(410)	
– software	(180)	
– investments (150 – (15 + 125))	(10)	
Investment income received (20 – 15 gain on investments)	5	
Net cash used in investing activities		(595)
Cash flows from financing activities		
Proceeds from issue of equity shares (w (iii))	265	
Proceeds from issue of 9% loan note	120	
Dividends paid (500 × 4 × 5 cents)	(100)	
Net cash from financing activities		285
Net decrease in cash and cash equivalents		(20)
Cash and cash equivalents at beginning of period (40 – 35)		(5)
Cash and cash equivalents at end of period		(25)

Note: interest paid may be presented under financing activities and dividends paid may be presented under operating activities.

Workings (in $000)

(i) Property, plant and equipment:

Carrying amount b/f	940
Non-cash environmental provision	150
Revaluation	35
Depreciation for period	(255)
Carrying amount c/f	(1,280)
Difference is cash acquisitions	(410)

(ii) Taxation:

Tax provision b/f	(50)
Deferred tax b/f	(25)
Statement of comprehensive income charge	(57)
Tax provision c/f	60
Deferred tax c/f	18
Difference is cash paid	(54)

(iii) Equity shares

Balance b/f	(300)
Bonus issue (1 for 4)	(75)
Balance c/f	500
Difference is cash issue	125

Share premium	
Balance b/f	(85)
Bonus issue (1 for 4)	75
Balance c/f	150
Difference is cash issue	140

Therefore the total proceeds of cash issue of shares are $265,000 (125 + 140).

(b) **REPORT**

Subject: The financial position of Minster for the year ended 30 September 20X6

Minster shows healthy operating cash inflows of $372,000 (prior to finance costs and taxation). This is considered by many commentators as a very important figure as it is often used as the basis for estimating the company's future maintainable cash flows. Subject to (inevitable) annual expected variations and allowing for any changes in the company's structure this figure is more likely to be repeated in the future than most other figures in the statements of cash flows which are often 'one-off' cash flows such as raising loans or purchasing non-current assets. The operating cash inflow compares well with the underlying profit before tax $142,000. This is mainly due to depreciation charges of $300,000 being added back to the profit as they are a non-cash expense. The cash inflow generated from operations of $372,000 after the reduction in net working capital of $90,000 is more than sufficient to cover the company's taxation payments of $54,000, interest payments of $28,000 and the dividend of $100,000 and leaves an amount to contribute to the funding of the increase in non-current assets. It is important that these short term costs are funded from operating cash flows; it would be of serious concern if, for example, interest or income tax payments were having to be funded by loan capital or the sale of non-current assets.

There are a number of points of concern. The dividend of $100,000 gives a dividend cover of less than one (85/100 = 0.85) which means the company has distributed previous year's profits. This is not a tenable situation in the long-term. The size of the dividend has also contributed to the lower cash balances (see below). There is less investment in both inventory levels and trade receivables. This may be the result of more efficient inventory control and better collection of receivables, but it may also indicate that trading volumes may be falling. Also of note is a large reduction in trade payable balances of $205,000. This too may be indicative of lower trading (i.e. less inventory purchased on credit) or pressure from suppliers to pay earlier. Without more detailed information it is difficult to come to a conclusion in this matter.

Investing activities:

The statement of cash flows shows considerable investment in non-current assets, in particular $410,000 in property, plant and equipment. These acquisitions represent an increase of 44% of the carrying amount of the property, plant and equipment as at the beginning of the year. As there are no disposals, the increase in investment must represent an increase in capacity rather than the replacement of old assets. Assuming that this investment has been made wisely, this should bode well for the future (most analysts would prefer to see increased investment rather than contraction in operating assets). An unusual feature of the required treatment of environmental provisions is that the investment in non-current assets as portrayed by the statement of cash flows appears less than if statement of financial position figures are used. The statement of financial position at 30 September 20X6 includes $150,000 of non-current assets (the discounted cost of the environmental provision), which does not appear in the cash flow figures as it is not a cash 'cost'. A further consequence is that the 'unwinding' of the discounting of the provision causes a financing expense in the statement of comprehensive income which is not matched in the statement of cash flows as the unwinding is not a cash flow. Many commentators have criticized the required treatment of environmental provisions because they cause financing expenses which are not (immediate) cash costs and no 'loans' have been taken out. Viewed in this light, it may be that the information in the statement of cash flows is more useful than that in the statement of comprehensive income and statement of financial position.

Financing activities:

The increase in investing activities (before investment income) of $600,000 has been largely funded by an issue of shares at $265,000 and raising a 9% $120,000 loan note. This indicates that the company's shareholders appear reasonably pleased with the company's past performance (or they would not be very willing to purchase further shares). The interest rate of the loan at 9% seems quite high, and virtually equal to the company's overall return on capital employed of 9.1% (162/(1,660 + 120)). Provided current profit levels are maintained, it should not reduce overall returns to shareholders.

Cash position:

The overall effect of the year's cash flows has worsened the company's cash position by an increased net cash liability of $20,000. Although the company's short term borrowings have reduced by $15,000, the cash at bank of $35,000 at the beginning of the year has now gone. In comparison to the cash generation ability of the company and considering its large investment in non-current assets, this $20,000 is a relatively small amount and should be relieved by operating cash inflows in the near future.

Summary

The above analysis shows that Minster has invested substantially in new non-current assets suggesting expansion. To finance this, the company appears to have no difficulty in attracting further long-term funding. At the same time there are indications of reduced inventories, trade receivables and payables which may suggest the opposite i.e. contraction. It may be that the new investment is a change in the nature of the company's activities (e.g. mining) which has different working capital characteristics. The company has good operating cash flow generation and the slight deterioration in short term net cash balance should only be temporary.

Yours ....

56 PENDANT

Key answer tips

(a) You are given two statements of financial position but no statement of comprehensive income. You must therefore reconstruct the statement of comprehensive income from the information you are given, in order to derive the first figure in the statement of cash flows, the profit for the year.

(b) Don't calculate any ratios, as told. Just identify the important features of the statement of cash flows you have produced in part (a)

(a) **Statement of cash flows of Pendant for the year to 31 March 20X1**

	$000	$000
Cash flows from operating activities		
Operating profit (profit before interest and tax (W1))		176
Adjustments for:		
Depreciation – leasehold buildings	20	
– 'purchased' plant (W3)	193	
– leased plant (140 – 30)	110	323
Profit of disposal of – freehold (800 – 580)	(220)	
– plant (from question)	(18)	(238)
Operating profit before working capital changes		261
Decrease in inventory (540 – 490)		50
Increase in trade receivables (787 – 584)		(203)
Increase in trade payables (663 – 602)		61
Cash generated from operations		169
Interest paid (35 + 10) (W1)		(45)
Income taxes paid (W2)		(321)
Net cash used in operating activities		(197)
Cash flows from investing activities		
Purchase of property, plant and equipment (W4)	(630)	
Proceeds from the sale of property, plant and equipment (W4)	875	
Software development (300 – 100)	(200)	
Interest received (from question)	15	
Net cash from investing activities		60
Cash flows from financing activities		
Proceeds from issue of equity shares (100 + 70)	170	
Payments of finance lease liabilities (W5)	(230)	
Sale of government securities (180 – 30 + 27 profit)	177	
Dividends paid	(150)	
Net cash used in financing		(33)
Net decrease in cash and cash equivalents		(170)
Cash and cash equivalents b/f		125
Cash and cash equivalents c/f		(45)

Workings

(W1) In the absence of a statement of comprehensive income the figure for the operating profit before interest and tax has to be derived from the statements of financial position plus the information given in the notes. The basic technique is to start with the change in the retained earnings, which would equal the retained profit or loss for the year, and work back to the profit before interest and tax. In this case there is a decrease in retained earnings indicating a small retained loss for the period.

	$000
Decrease in retained earnings (1,084 – 1,092)	(8)
Dividends paid	150
Income taxes (from question)	31
Interest – payable on finance lease (from question)	35
– bank overdraft (from question)	10
– receivable (from question)	(15)
Profit on sale of Government securities (from question)	(27)
Profit before interest and income tax	176

(W2) **Income tax**

Tax provision b/f	(213)
Deferred tax b/f	(172)
Statement of comprehensive income charge (from question)	(31)
Tax provision c/f	83
Deferred tax c/f	12
Difference is cash paid	(321)

(W3) **'Purchased' plant**

	$000	$000
Cost b/f		620
Disposals		(200)
Balance c/f		(550)
Difference is cash purchases		(130)
Cost of disposal		200
Proceeds		(75)
Profit on disposal		18
Difference is accumulated depreciation on disposal		143
Depreciation b/f		200
Less – disposal (above)		(143)
Depreciation c/f		(250)
Depreciation charge for year		(193)

(W4) Capital expenditure

Purchase of – leasehold	(500)	
– plant (W3)	(130)	
		(630)
Sale of – freehold	800	
– plant	75	875

(W5) Lease obligation

Balances b/f (30 + 60)	(90)
Additions (650 – 150)	(500)
Balances c/f (70 + 290)	360
Difference – capital repayment for $265,000 – $35,000 interest)	(230)

(b)   From the information in the question and the above statement of cash flows, the following observations can be made:

(i)   The (derived) operating profit of $176,000 is much the same as the cash generated from operations of $169,000. A closer inspection of the figures reveals a more worrying picture. The operating profit has been boosted by some non-recurring items: a large profit of $220,000 on the sale of the company's freehold and a profit of $18,000 on the sale of some plant. Without these items the operating profit of $176,000 would have been an operating loss of $62,000.

Overall the company's profitability should cause concern over the future prospects of the company.

(ii)   Despite there being positive cash flows from operations of $169,000, this figure is inadequate for the continued liquidity of the company. It is woefully insufficient to pay net interest costs of $30,000, a tax bill of $321,000 and the dividends to shareholders of $150,000. If the company had not sold its freehold for $800,000 and some investments for $177,000 its liquidity and solvency position would be very serious. Even with these sales the company's bank account has gone from a healthy balance of $125,000 to an overdraft of $45,000.

(iii)   Other factors that may also be an indication of cash flow difficulties are a move towards leasing rather than purchasing plant, a sizeable reduction in inventory levels (this may be welcomed provided it does not jeopardize future sales) and an increase in the level of trade payables.

In summary Pendant seems to have undertaken a number of measures that have improved both the current year's profit and cash flows, but most of these are unsustainable and do not bode well for the future.

57 CHARMER

Key answer tips

Read the question carefully. You may find it helpful to tick off items of information as you deal with them. Set out your workings clearly and cross reference them to your main answer.

Charmer statement of cash flows for the year to 30 September 20X1

Note: figures in brackets are in $000

	$000	$000
Cash flows from operating activities		
Net profit before interest and tax (3,198 – 1,479)		1,719
Adjustments for:		
Depreciation – buildings (W1)	80	
– plant (W1)	276	
Loss on disposal of plant (W1)	86	442
Amortization of government grants (W2)		(125)
Negligence claim previously provided		(120)
Operating profit before working capital changes		1,916
Increase in inventories (1,046 – 785)		(261)
Increase in accounts receivable (935 – 824)		(111)
Decrease in accounts payable (760 – 644)		(116)
Cash generated from operations		1,428
Interest paid (260 + 25 – 40)		(245)
Income tax paid (W4)		(368)
Dividends paid		(180)
Net cash from operating activities		635
Cash flows from investing activities		
Purchase of land and buildings (W1)	(50)	
Purchase of plant (W1)	(848)	
Purchase of non-current investments	(690)	
Purchase of treasury bills (120 – 50)	(70)	
Proceeds of sale of plant (W1)	170	
Receipt of government grant (W2)	175	
Investment income	120	
Net cash used in investing activities		(1,193)
Cash flows from financing activities		
Issue of ordinary shares (W3)		300
Net decrease in cash and cash equivalents		(258)
Cash and cash equivalents b/f		122
Cash and cash equivalents at the end of the period		(136)

Workings

(W1) Non-current assets

	$000
Land and buildings – cost/valuation	
Balance b/f	1,800
Revaluation surplus	150
Balance c/f	(2,000)
Difference cash purchase	(50)

Plant – cost	
Balance b/f	1,220
Disposal	(500)
Balance c/f	(1,568)
Difference cash purchase	(848)

Depreciation of non-current assets:

Building (760 – 680)	80
Plant (464 – (432 – 244))	276

The plant had a carrying value of $256,000 at the date of its disposal (500 cost – 244 depreciation). As there was a loss on sale of $86,000 (given in question), the sale proceeds must have been $170,000 (i.e. 256 – 86).

(W2) Government grant

	$000
Balances b/f – current	(125)
– non-current	(200)
Amortization credited to cost of sales	125
Balances c/f – current	100
– non-current	275
Difference cash receipt	175

(W3) Share capital and convertible loan stock

A reconciliation of share capital, share premium and the revaluation reserve shows the shares issued for cash:

	Share capital $000	Share premium $000	Revaluation reserve $000
Opening balance	(1,000)	(160)	(40)
Revaluation of land	Nil	Nil	(150)
Bonus issue 1 for 10	(100)	100	Nil
Conversion of loan stock (see below)	(100)	(300)	Nil
Closing balance	1,400	460	190
Difference issued for cash	200	100	nil

The 10% convertible loan stock had a carrying value of $400,000 at the date of conversion to equity shares. This would be taken as the consideration for the shares issued which would be 100,000 $1 shares (i.e. 400,000/100 × 25). This would increase issued share capital by $100,000 and share premium by $300,000.

(W4) **Income tax**

	$000
Tax provision b/f	(367)
Deferred tax b/f	(400)
Statement of comprehensive income tax charge	(520)
Tax provision c/f	480
Deferred tax c/f	439
	———
Difference cash paid	(368)
	———

58   PLANTER

Key answer tips

In this question, you are given the opening statement of financial position and the closing trial balance, but no statement of comprehensive income for the year. However, this should not present you with too many problems. Have the format for the statement of cash flows clear in your mind, and slot in the required figures in turn as with any other statement of cash flows question.

Statement of cash flows – Planter for the year to 31 March 20X4	$	$
Cash flows from operating activities		
Operating profit (per question)		15,600
Adjustments for:		
Depreciation – buildings (W1)	1,800	
– plant (W2)	26,600	
	———	28,400
Loss on sale of plant (W1)		4,200
Decrease in inventory (57,400 – 43,300)		14,100
Increase in receivables (50,400 – 28,600)		(21,800)
Decrease in payables (31,400 – 26,700)		(4,700)
		———
Cash generated from operations		35,800
Interest paid (1,700 – 300 accrued)		(1,400)
Income tax paid (8,900 + 1,100)		(10,000)
		———
Net cash from operating activities		24,400
Cash flows from investing activities		
Purchase of plant (W1)	(38,100)	
Purchase of land and buildings (W1)	(7,100)	
Investment income	400	
Sale of plant (W1)	7,800	
Sale of investments	11,000	
Net cash used in investing activities	———	(26,000)
Cash flows from financing activities		
Issue of ordinary shares (W2)	28,000	
Redemption of 8% loan notes	(3,400)	
Ordinary dividend paid	(26,100)	
Net cash used in financing activities	———	(1,500)
		———
Net decrease in cash and cash equivalents		(3,100)
Cash and cash equivalents at 1 April 20X3		1,200
		———
Cash and cash equivalents at 31 March 20X4		(1,900)
		———

Workings

(W1) **Non-current assets:**

	$
Land and buildings	
Valuation b/f	49,200
Revaluation surplus (18,000 – 12,000)	6,000
Acquisitions – balancing figure	7,100
Valuation c/f	62,300
Depreciation b/f	5,000
Charge for year – balancing figure	1,800
Depreciation c/f	6,800
Plant	
Cost b/f	70,000
Disposals at cost	(23,500)
Acquisitions – balancing figure	38,100
Cost c/f	84,600
Depreciation b/f	22,500
Disposals	(11,500)
Charge for year – balancing figure	26,600
Depreciation c/f	37,600
Disposal of plant:	
Net book value	12,000
Proceeds from question	(7,800)
Loss on sale	4,200

(W2) **Share capital and share premium:**

Ordinary shares b/f	25,000
Bonus issue 1 for 10 (from share premium)	2,500
Ordinary shares c/f	(50,000)
Difference issue for cash	22,500
Share premium b/f	5,000
Bonus issue	(2,500)
Share premium c/f	(8,000)
Increase is premium on cash issue	5,500
Total proceeds of issue is (22,500 + 5,500)	28,000

(W3) **Reconciliation of revaluation reserve**

Balance b/f	12,000
Difference revaluation of land	6,000
Balance c/f	18,000

59   CASINO

Key answer tips

Part (a) is a standard, although quite long, statement of cash flows question. Note that the starting point is an operating loss which then becomes a net cash outflow from operating activities. Take care when calculating the tax cash flow as you will need to include the opening and closing deferred tax balances as well as the balances for current tax.

(a)   **Statement of cash flows of Casino for the Year to 31 March 20X5:**

	$m	$m
Cash flows from operating activities		
Operating loss		(32)
Adjustments for:		
Depreciation – buildings (W1)	12	
– plant (W2)	81	
– intangibles (510 – 400)	110	
Loss on disposal of plant (from question)	12	215
Operating profit before working capital changes		183
Decrease in inventory (420 – 350)		70
Increase in trade receivables (808 – 372)		(436)
Increase in trade payables (530 – 515)		15
Cash generated from operations		(168)
Interest paid		(18)
Income tax paid (W3)		(81)
Net cash used in operating activities		(267)
Cash flows from investing activities		
Purchase of – land and buildings (W1)	(110)	
– plant (W2)	(60)	
Sale of plant (W2)	15	
Interest received (12 – 5 + 3)	10	
Net cash used in investing activities		(145)
Cash flows from financing activities		
Issue of ordinary shares (100 + 60)	160	
Issue of 8% variable rate loan	160	
Repayments of 12% loan (150 + 6 penalty)	(156)	
Dividends paid	(25)	
Net cash from financing activities		139
Net decrease in cash and cash equivalents		(273)
Cash and cash equivalents at beginning of period (120 + 75)		195
Cash and cash equivalents at end of period (125 – (32 + 15))		(78)

Interest and dividends received and paid may be shown as operating cash flows or as investing or financing activities as appropriate.

Workings (in $ million)

(W1) **Land and buildings**

Net book value b/f	420
Revaluation gains	70
Depreciation for year (balance after revaluation)	(12)
Net book value c/f	(588)
Difference is cash purchases	(110)

(W2) **Plant:**

Cost b/f	445
Additions from question	60
Balance c/f	(440)
Difference is cost of disposal	65
Loss on disposal	(12)
Proceeds	(15)
Difference accumulated depreciation of plant disposed of	38
Depreciation b/f	105
Less – disposal (above)	(38)
Depreciation c/f	(148)
Charge for year	(81)

(W3) **Taxation:**

Tax provision b/f	(110)
Deferred tax b/f	(75)
Statement of comprehensive income net charge	(1)
Tax provision c/f	15
Deferred tax c/f	90
Difference is cash paid	(81)

(W4) **Revaluation reserve:**

Balance b/f	45
Revaluation gains	70
Transfer to retained earnings	(3)
Balance c/f	112

(W5) **Retained earnings:**

Balance b/f	1,165
Loss for period	(45)
Dividends paid	(25)
Transfer from revaluation reserve	3
Balance c/f	1,098

(b)   The accruals/matching concept applied in preparing an statement of comprehensive income has the effect of smoothing cash flows for reporting purposes. This practice arose because interpreting 'raw' cash flows can be very difficult and the accruals process has the advantage of helping users to understand the underlying performance of a company. For example if an item of plant with an estimated life of five years is purchased for $100,000, then in the statement of cash flows for the five year period there would be an outflow in year 1 of the full $100,000 and no further outflows for the next four years. Contrast this with the statement of comprehensive income where by applying the accruals principle, depreciation of the plant would give a charge of $20,000 per annum (assuming straight-line depreciation). Many would see this example as an advantage of a statement of comprehensive income, but it is important to realize that profit is affected by many items requiring judgements. This has led to accusations of profit manipulation or creative accounting, hence the disillusionment of the usefulness of the statement of comprehensive income.

Another example of the difficulty in interpreting cash flows is that counter-intuitively a decrease in overall cash flows is not always a bad thing (it may represent an investment in increasing capacity which would bode well for the future), nor is an increase in cash flows necessarily a good thing (this may be from the sale of non-current assets because of the need to raize cash urgently).

The advantages of cash flows are:

–   it is difficult to manipulate cash flows, they are real and possess the qualitative characteristic of objectivity (as opposed to profits affected by judgements).

–   cash flows are an easy concept for users to understand, indeed many users misinterpret statement of comprehensive income items as being cash flows.

–   cash flows help to assess a company's liquidity, solvency and financial adaptability. Healthy liquidity is vital to a company's going concern.

–   many business investment decisions and company valuations are based on projected cash flows.

–   the 'quality' of a company's operating profit is said to be confirmed by closely correlated cash flows. Some analysts take the view that if a company shows a healthy operating profit, but has low or negative operating cash flows, there is a suspicion of profit manipulation or creative accounting.

60   TABBA

Key answer tips

The statement of cash flows has the usual standard calculations but take care with the government grant and finance leases which both have balances in both current and non-current liabilities. Part (b) requires an analysis of the company based on the information revealed in the statement of cash flows rather than by standard ratio analysis.

(a)   **Statement of cash flows of Tabba for the year ended 30 September 20X5:**

	$000	$000
Cash flows from operating activities		
Profit before tax	50	
Adjustments for:		
Depreciation (W1)	2,200	
Amortization of government grant (W3)	(250)	
Profit on sale of factory (W1)	(4,600)	
Increase in insurance claim provision (1,500 – 1,200)	(300)	
Interest receivable	(40)	
Interest expense	260	
	(2,680)	
Working capital adjustments:		
Increase in inventories (2,550 – 1,850)	(700)	
Increase in trade receivables (3,100 – 2,600)	(500)	
Increase in trade payables (4,050 – 2,950)	1,100	
Cash outflow from operations	(2,780)	
Interest paid	(260)	
Income taxes paid (W4)	(1,350)	
Net cash outflow used in operating activities		(4,390)
Cash flows from investing activities		
Sale of factory	12,000	
Purchase of non-current assets (W1)	(2,900)	
Receipt of government grant (from question)	950	
Interest received	40	
Net cash from investing activities		10,090
Cash flows from financing activities		
Issue of 6% loan notes	800	
Redemption of 10% loan notes	(4,000)	
Repayment of finance leases (W2)	(1,100)	
Net cash used in financing activities		(4,300)
Net increase in cash and cash equivalents		1,400
Cash and cash equivalents at beginning of period		(550)
Cash and cash equivalents at end of period		850

Note: interest paid may also be presented as a financing activity and interest received as an operating cash flow.

Workings ($000)

(W1) **Non-current assets:**

Cost/valuation b/f	20,200
New finance leases (from question)	1,500
Disposals	(8,600)
Acquisitions – balancing figure	2,900
	————
Cost/valuation c/f	16,000
	————
Depreciation b/f	4,400
Disposal	(1,200)
Depreciation c/f	(5,400)
	————
Charge for year – balancing figure	(2,200)
	————

Sale of factory:

Net book value	7,400
Proceeds (from question)	(12,000)
	————
Profit on sale	(4,600)
	————

(W2) **Finance lease obligations**

Balance b/f – current	800
– over 1 year	1,700
New leases (from question)	1,500
Balance c/f – current	(900)
– over 1 year	(2,000)
	————
Cash repayments – balancing figure	1,100
	————

(W3) **Government grant:**

Balance b/f – current	400
– over 1 year	900
Grants received in year (from question)	950
Balance c/f – current	(600)
– over 1 year	(1,400)
	————
Difference – amortization credited to statement of comprehensive income	250
	————

(W4) **Taxation:**

Current provision b/f	1,200
Deferred tax b/f	500
Tax credit in statement of comprehensive income	(50)
Current provision c/f	(100)
Deferred tax c/f	(200)
	————
Tax paid – balancing figure	1,350
	————

(W5) Reconciliation of retained earnings

Balance b/f	850
Transfer from revaluation reserve	1,600
Profit for period	100
	———
Balance c/f	2,550
	———

(b) Consideration of the statement of cash flows reveals some important information in assessing the change in the financial position of Tabba in the year ended 30 September 20X5. There is a huge net cash outflow from operating activities of $4,390,000 despite Tabba reporting a modest operating profit of $270,000. More detailed analysis of this difference reveals some worrying concerns for the future. Many companies experience higher operating cash flows than the underlying operating profit mainly due to depreciation charges being added back to profits to arrive at the cash flows. This is certainly true in Tabba's case, where operating profits have been 'improved' by $2.2 million during the year in terms of the underlying cash flows.

However, the major reconciling difference is the profit on the sale of Tabba's factory of $4.6 million. This amount has been credited in the statement of comprehensive income and has dramatically distorted the operating profit. If the sale and leaseback of the factory had not taken place, Tabba's operating profits would be in a sorry state showing losses of $4.33 million (4,600 – 270 ignoring any possible tax effects). When Tabba publishes its financial statements this profit will almost certainly require separate disclosure which should make the effects of the transaction more transparent to the users of the financial statements. A further indication of poor operating profits is that they have been boosted by $300,000 due to an increase in the insurance claim provision (again this is not a cash flow) and $250,000 amortization of government grants.

Many commentators believe that the net cash flow from operating activities is the most important figure in the statement of cash flows. This is because it is a measure of expected or maintainable future cash flows. In Tabba's case this highlights a very important point; although Tabba has increased its cash position during the year by $1.4 million, $12 million has come from the sale of its factory. Clearly this is a one off transaction that cannot be repeated in future years. If the drain on the operating cash flows continues at the current rates, the company will not survive for very long.

The tax position is worthy of comment. There is a small tax credit in the statement of comprehensive income, whereas the statement of cash flows shows that tax of $1.35 million has been paid during the year. This payment of tax is on what must have been a substantial profit for the previous year. This seems to confirm the deteriorating position of the company.

Another relevant point is that there has been a very small increase in working capital of $100,000 (700 + 500 – 1,100). However, underlying this is the fact that both inventories and trade receivables are showing substantial increases (despite the profit deterioration), which may indicate the presence of bad debts or obsolete inventories, and trade payables have also increased substantially (by $1.1 million) which may be a symptom of liquidity problems prior to the sale of the factory.

On the positive side there has been substantial investment in non-current assets (after stripping out the sale of the factory), but even this is partly due to leasing assets of $1.5 million (companies often lease assets when they do not have the resources to purchase them outright) and finance from a government grant of $950,000.

The company appears to have taken advantage of the proceeds from the sale of the factory to redeem the expensive 10% $4 million loan note (this has partly been replaced by a less expensive 6% $800,000 loan note).

In conclusion the statement of cash flows reveals some interesting and worrying issues that may indicate a bleak future for Tabba and serves as an illustration of the importance of a statement of cash flows to the users of financial statements.

61   PJ GAMEWRITERS

Key answer tips

The point of this question is that traditional financial statements (and traditional ratio analysis) sometimes tell users surprisingly little about an entity's 'true' financial performance and position. Read the scenario very carefully; the Examiner expects you to interpret the figures in the light of the additional information provided.

REPORT

To: The Finance Director of OPQ

Subject: Financial Performance and position of PJ Gamewriters

Date: 22 November 20X5

As requested, I have analysed the information provided from the financial statements of PJ Gamewriters. Calculations of key performance measures are set out in the attached Appendix.

(a)   **Profitability**

PJ Gamewriters is clearly a profitable operation.The statement of comprehensive income for the year ended 31 July 20X5 shows that revenue has risen by 26% and profit from operations has risen by 29% compared with the previous year.Gross profit margin is 55% and operating profit margin is 40%.Both these margins have risen slightly in the year. All costs except directors' remuneration have risen approximately in line with sales.

Return on capital employed (ROCE) is extremely high at 112%, although it has fallen from 122% in 20X4. One reason why ROCE is so high is that the assets of the business are understated. Non-current assets consist mainly of freehold property, which is stated at historical cost. Measuring the property at market value would reduce ROCE to approximately 83%. In addition, the assets actually used to generate revenues and profits are all intangible and have not been recognized. These assets consist of copyrights to the games and the technical skills of the two directors and the employees. The value of these intangibles is unknown and it is impossible to calculate a meaningful figure for ROCE without it.

Dividend payments in 20X5 are almost 43% higher than in 20X4. Because profits have risen, dividend cover is not significantly reduced. As most of the equity shares are owned by the two directors and their parents, the dividend can be seen partly as additional directors' remuneration and partly as a repayment of capital.

Financial position

The business does not appear to have any liquidity problems. The current ratio has risen from 1.26 in 20X4 to just over 2 in 20X5. Inventories and trade payables appear low when compared to revenue and cost of sales; as production is outsourced trade payables probably relate only to administrative overheads. The collection period for trade receivables has risen from 54 days to 60 days; this is fairly high but does not give any real cause for concern.

Despite the substantial dividend payment, there has been a net cash inflow of $196,000 (216 – 20) in the year. No additional finance has been raised and no assets appear to have been sold, so the additional cash must have been generated from operations. There is no long-term debt and the main liability is for income tax for the current year.

Conclusion

The extracts from the financial statements show that PJ Gamewriters is highly profitable and that revenue and profits are increasing. There are no apparent liquidity or gearing problems and the business had a healthy cash surplus at 31 July 20X5.

However, this analysis has been based on extremely limited information. The business has intangible assets which have not been recognized on the statement of financial position and which are used to generate sales. Therefore it is impossible to calculate any meaningful figure for return on capital employed or to make any judgement as to how efficiently the business is using its assets. As you will be aware, much more information is needed before any investment decision can be made.

Signed: Assistant

Appendix: Ratio calculations

	20X5	*20X4*
Gross profit margin	$\dfrac{1,523}{2,793} = 55\%$	$\dfrac{1,168}{2,208} = 53\%$
Operating profit margin	$\dfrac{1,108}{2,793} = 40\%$	$\dfrac{858}{2,208} = 39\%$
Employment costs/revenue	$\dfrac{700}{2,793} = 25\%$	$\dfrac{550}{2,208} = 25\%$
Production costs/revenue	$\dfrac{215}{2,793} = 8\%$	$\dfrac{160}{2,208} = 7\%$
Operating expenses/revenue	$\dfrac{415}{2,793} = 15\%$	$\dfrac{310}{2,208} = 14\%$
Return on capital employed (ROCE)	$\dfrac{1,108}{987} \times 100 = 112\%$	$\dfrac{858}{703} \times 100 = 122\%$
Return on capital employed (ROCE) based on market value of freehold	$\dfrac{1,108}{987 + 350} \times 100 = 83\%$	
Dividend cover	$\dfrac{784}{500} = 1.6$ times	$\dfrac{570}{350} = 1.6$ times
Current ratio	$\dfrac{744}{367} = 2{:}1$	$\dfrac{403}{320} = 1.26{:}1$
Receivables collection period	$\dfrac{460}{2,793} \times 365 = 60$ days	$\dfrac{324}{2,208} \times 365 = 54$ days

(b) **Limitations of the analysis**

The nature of the business and the way in which it operates mean that the financial statements alone cannot provide enough relevant information on which to assess the financial performance and position of the company.

- The business owns the copyrights to its existing computer games. These are a very significant intangible asset (one of its original games brings in a significant proportion of its revenue), but they have not been recognized on the statement of financial position. It will be necessary to value the copyrights, not only to assist in assessing PJ's financial performance but also in order to arrive at the purchase price should OPQ acquire the business.

- The business has another important intangible asset: the technical expertise of its directors and its games writers. However, this cannot be recognized on the statement of financial position because the business does not control its employees and cannot prevent them from leaving to work elsewhere. This type of business cannot operate without suitably qualified and talented staff. Any investment decision must take into account the fact that the business will lose the skills of the two directors (who wish to pursue other interests). It is also possible that some of the staff will leave. It will be necessary to assess the likelihood of staff moves and the possible long-term impact on revenue and the development of new products if key employees cannot be easily replaced.

- It is possible that the amounts included for employee costs are unrealistic. Directors' remuneration has remained constant, but the directors appear to have taken some of their remuneration in the form of dividends. Some of the games writers hold shares in the business; as a result they may have accepted salaries below the market rate. Information about staff salaries and directors' remuneration paid by competitors would be useful, given the importance of retaining or replacing key employees.

- There is no information about accounting policies. Information about revenue recognition would be particularly useful. Many software companies have adopted 'aggressive' policies that recognize revenue at the earliest possible stage, before it has been properly earned. It is possible that revenue is overstated.

- The business outsources the manufacture and distribution of the software. Information is needed about these operations and of their impact on the financial statements. It is possible that the distributor holds inventory on sale or return or consignment inventory or that there are other complex transactions. If so, the way in which these are treated may have affected reported revenue, production costs, operating expenses, receivables and inventories.It would be useful to compare PJ's financial statements with those of other small companies in the same sector to gain an idea of what is 'normal' for this type of business.

62   DM

Key answer tip

Look at your answer to part (a) for ideas for points to be included in part (b).

(a)   **REPORT**

To: A private shareholder

Subject: Performance and position of DM

Date: 24 May 20X5

As requested, I have analysed the performance and position of DM. My analysis is based on extracts from the financial statements for the year ended 31 December 20X4 with comparative figures for the year ended 31 December 20X3. A number of key measures have been calculated and these are set out in the attached Appendix.

Sales

The company has opened six new stores during the year. However, sales have only increased very slightly in 20X4 and annual sales per store have fallen. This may be because the new stores have only opened part way through the year and have therefore not contributed a full year's revenue. Alternatively, there may have been an increase in the level of sales tax.

Annual sales per store are still above the industry average. On the face of it, this is a good sign. However, it is possible that DM has large stores relative to the rest of the sector.

Profitability

Gross profit margin has increased very slightly during the year and this is a little above the industry average. However, although net profit margin has increased significantly during the year, this is still below the industry average. The increase in net profit margin has occurred because operating expenses have fallen by over a quarter in 20X4. The operating profit margin has risen from 3.8% in 20X3 to 4.5% in 20X4.

Given the information available, the most likely cause of this fall in operating expenses is the increase in asset lives and the resulting reduction in the depreciation expense. As might be expected, the company has a considerable investment in property, plant and equipment and depreciation would normally be a significant expense. An increase in asset lives is relatively unusual and it is possible that the directors have used this method to deliberately improve the operating and the net profit margins. (They may have been particularly concerned that the net profit margin has obviously been well below the industry average.) On the other hand, the directors may have carried out their review of asset lives in good faith or there could be another legitimate reason why operating expenses have fallen. For example, the 20X3 figure may have been inflated by a significant 'one off' expense.

It is impossible to prove that the profit figure has been manipulated on the basis of the very limited information available. Information about the reasons for the fall in operating expenses and the review of asset lives and about the property, plant and equipment held by the company would be extremely useful.

Other matters

Non-current asset turnover has improved slightly, but is still below the industry average. This suggests that the company uses its assets less efficiently than others in the same sector. However, increasing the asset lives will have reduced the ratio for 20X4; it is possible that the company's asset turnover would have approached the sector average had the review not been carried out. Given that six new stores have opened in 20X4, it is surprising that property, plant and equipment has only increased by $5 million in the year. It is possible that most of the investment in new property was made during 20X3.

The current ratio for both years is extremely low. Supermarkets often do have relatively low current and quick ratios, but no average figure for the industry is available, so it is difficult to tell whether this is normal for the type of operation. Short-term liquidity appears not to be a problem, because the company has a positive cash balance which has increased in the year. However, the appearance of the statement of financial position suggests that this has been achieved by delaying payment to suppliers. Trade and other payables have increased by nearly 9%, while revenue and cost of sales have only increased by approximately 3%.

The debt/equity ratio has fallen in the year and gearing does not appear to be a problem.

Conclusion

DM's profit margins appear to be reasonable for a company in its industry sector. Although its net profit margin is below the industry average, this is improving. There are no apparent short-term liquidity problems.

It is possible that at least some of this improvement has been achieved by deliberately reducing the operating expenses for the year. If, as seems likely, the directors wish to sell their interests in the company in the near future, improved results will help to secure a better price. However, it is impossible to be certain that this has happened without much more detailed information about the reason for the fall in operating expenses. There may be a legitimate explanation for the improvement in the company's profit margins.

Appendix: Ratio calculations

	20X4	*20X3*	*Key sector ratio*
Annual sales per store	$\dfrac{1,255}{42} = \$29.9m$	$\dfrac{1,220}{36} = \$33.9m$	$27.6m
Gross profit margin	$\dfrac{78}{1,255} \times 100\% = 6.2\%$	$\dfrac{75}{1,220} \times 100\% = 6.1\%$	5.9%
Operating profit margin	$\dfrac{57}{1,255} \times 100\% = 4.5\%$	$\dfrac{46}{1,220} \times 100\% = 3.8\%$	–
Net profit margin	$\dfrac{33}{1,255} \times 100\% = 2.6\%$	$\dfrac{23}{1,220} \times 100\% = 1.9\%$	3.9%
Non-current asset turnover	$\dfrac{1,255}{680} = 1.85$	$\dfrac{1,220}{675} = 1.81$	1.93
Current ratio	$\dfrac{105}{317} = 0.33{:}1$	$\dfrac{71}{309} = 0.23{:}1$	–
Debt/equity	$\dfrac{142}{301} \times 100\% = 47.2\%$	$\dfrac{140}{276} \times 100\% = 50.7\%$	–

(b)   **Limitations of the use of sector comparatives**

It can often be useful to compare ratios for an individual company with averages for the sector. However, this type of analysis has a number of limitations:

- Some accounting ratios can be calculated in different ways. Therefore a sector average may be based on ratios that have not been calculated consistently.

- The figures in the financial statements are affected by the accounting policies adopted and by accounting estimates. Accounting estimates (such as the useful lives of assets) require judgement. Some international accounting standards still allow a choice of accounting policies.

- Entities in the same sector may operate under different business environments. For example, DM operates in one of six provinces. Conditions may be very different in the other five; so DM's financial performance and position may not be strictly comparable with companies operating in other provinces.

- Sector comparatives are normally based on an average of several entities. The average can be distorted by one entity that is significantly out of line with the others. Also, the smaller the number of entities, the less reliable the average figure will be. For example, 12 entities is quite a small number.

- Published sector averages may exclude some important ratios. For example, it would be useful to know the average current ratio and debt/equity ratio for DM's industry sector.

63   EFG

(a)
Gross profit margin	$= 429/1{,}810 \times 100$	$= 23.7\%$
Operating profit margin	$= 193/1{,}810 \times 100$	$= 10.7\%$
Return on total capital employed	$= 193/(769 + 248) \times 100$	$= 19.0\%$
Gearing	$= 248/769 \times 100$	$= 32.2\%$

(b)   **Note 1**

The balance on revaluation reserve is $200,000 at 31 January 20X4 because each year the entity has transferred $10,000 from non-distributable to distributable reserves. The non-current assets total includes the depreciated balance of the revaluation element in property of $200,000. For the purposes of EFG's analysis, both the revaluation reserve and non-current assets should be reduced by $200,000. In addition, $10,000 should be added back to profit (and deducted from cost of sales) in respect of the current year's depreciation charge on the revalued element.

Note 2

This is a difference in an operating policy rather than in an accounting policy, but it is important to take it into account in estimating the return on capital employed that is potentially achievable in J. Operating expenses would be reduced by $46,000 ($96,000 − $50,000), and so operating profit and profit for the year would increase.

Note 3

Share capital should be reduced by $50,000 to $300,000 and long-term liabilities should be increased by the same amount to $298,000.

Note 4

J's inventories at 31 January 20X4 would increase by $17,000 if FIFO were adopted. Of this total, $11,000 ($208,000 − $197,000) would be reflected in retained earnings brought forward, and the remainder ($6,000) would be a deduction from cost of sales.

Summary of adjustments:

(figures in $000)

Cost of sales:	1,381 – 10 (note 1) – 6 (note 4)	=	1,365
Gross profit therefore:	1,810 – 1,365	=	445
Profit from operations:	193 + 10 (note 1) + 46 (note 2) + 6 (note 4)	=	255
Retained earnings:	219 + 17 (note 4) + 46 (note 2)	=	282
Total capital employed:	300 (note 3) + 282 + 298 (note 3)	=	880
Shareholders' funds:	300 (note 3) + 282	=	582

Recalculation of four key ratios after adjustments:

Gross profit margin: 445/1,810 × 100	=	24.6%
Operating profit margin: 255/1,810 × 100	=	14.1%
Return on total capital employed: 255/880	=	29.0%
Gearing: 298/582 × 100	=	51.2%

Advice to directors

Prior to the adjustments, none of the four key criteria were met. However, once the adjustments arising from alterations to accounting and operating policies are made, two out of the four criteria are met: operating margin now exceeds the requirement of 13% and return on total capital employed exceeds the requirement of 25%. In addition, it should be noted that gross profit margin falls only marginally short of the requirement. The significant problem lies in the gearing ratio, which is substantially in excess of the requirement. It appears that the acquisition of J should not, therefore, be pursued. However, given that (almost) three of the four criteria are met, the directors may wish to treat J as a borderline case, and subject it to further consideration.

(c)   The principal advantage of this approach to appraisal of acquisition opportunities is that it constitutes a fairly straightforward screening process. Investigating possible acquisitions requires a great deal of senior management time, and it makes sense to approach the initial analysis systematically so that unsuitable opportunities can be assessed and rejected quickly.

However, there are some significant drawbacks. This initial screening involves the calculation of only four key ratios. It is possible that the analysis is over-simplified, and will allow good investment opportunities to 'slip through the net' Specifically, the insistence on a relatively low level of gearing may be unhelpful. Many successful businesses operate at higher levels of gearing and, indeed, debt finance is often to be preferred as it tends to be cheaper than financing through equity.

In the specific case of J, the adjustment in respect of the operating policy on staff remuneration may be incomplete. While it may, indeed, be possible to save substantial sums on staff remuneration, members of the skilled sales team are likely to be unimpressed by the change in policy. EFG's directors should recognize that the implementation of such a policy would probably result in loss of skilled staff, and that there could be consequent reductions in sales. The adjustment made to profit for savings in staff bonus is probably over-optimistic.

64 BZJ GROUP

Key answer tip

The main difficulty here is not getting carried away with the calculations; practically every ratio you could calculate provides useful information and supports the overall picture: declining performance; and an attempt to expand the business which may or may not have succeeded. There are probably more calculations here than you would need to produce a good answer in the exam, but notice that some of them are particularly relevant to a private investor (e.g. dividend cover, dividend payout rate, return on shareholders' equity).

(a) **Earnings per share for the year ended 31 December 20X4**

$$\frac{3,676,000}{2,800,000} = 131.3c$$

Earnings per share for the year ended 31 December 20X5

$$\frac{2,460,000}{2,850,000} = 86.3c$$

Working: Weighted average number of shares in issue

$2,800,000 \times 10/12$	2,333,333
$3,100,000 \times 2/12$	516,667
	—————
	2,850,000
	—————

(b) **REPORT**

To: Investor in BJZ Group

Date: May 20X6

Subject: Performance and position of BJZ Group

As requested, I set out my comments on the performance and position of the BJZ Group as shown by its financial statements for the year ended 31 December 20X5. I have calculated a number of key ratios based on the financial statements and these are included in the attached Appendix.

Financial performance

The general impression is one of declining performance. Revenue has fallen by 0.8% between 20X4 and 20X5. This is surprising, given the effort that has apparently been made to increase market share and to develop new products. Gross profit margin and operating profit margin have both fallen. Some of this fall in profitability may have been caused by additional depreciation on the new non-current assets and there may have been additional costs connected with developing the new product line (this would be borne out by the slight increase in cost of sales). The comments in the Chairman's statement suggest that the group has gone through major changes in personnel and overall strategy during the year and the decline in profitability may be temporary. On the other hand, sales of new products and sales to new markets may mean that profit margins will continue to be lower than they were previously. This need not result in a permanent fall in overall earnings provided that sales increase in future periods.

Return on capital employed (ROCE) and return on shareholders' equity have both fallen very sharply. ROCE has fallen from 15.3% to 8.5% and return on shareholders' equity has fallen from 21.5% to 12%; a fall of nearly 50% in both cases. Some of this decrease will have been caused by the purchase of non-current assets during the year;

these are included in capital employed, but have probably not yet begun to generate significant increases in sales and profits. Non-current asset turnover shows that in 20X4 the non-current assets generated sales of nearly five times their value, while in 20X5 they generated only 2.76 times their value; another fall of almost 50%.

It is noticeable that interest payable has increased by 62%, which reduces the profit available for dividends. Interest cover has fallen from 7.3 times to 3.7 times but, on that basis, the company should still be able to meet interest payments reasonably easily. However, interest payable for 20X5 is only 4.8% (1,469 as % of (26,700 + 3,662)) of total borrowings at the year-end and total borrowings have almost doubled during the year. This suggests that the interest charge for 20X6 and subsequent years may be significantly higher. Unless sales or profit margins improve considerably, overall earnings may fall dramatically in future periods. Earnings are likely to be volatile in any case because the group is highly geared.

Financial position

As the Chairman's statement explains, the group has invested in new non-current assets during the year. Actual new assets appear to have cost approximately $17.3 million (there was also a revaluation during the year) and this investment was financed partly by a share issue that raised $1.5 million and partly by an increase of $10 million in long-term borrowings. This means that gearing (as measured by the debt/equity ratio) has increased from just under 63% to almost 82%. This is quite a high level of gearing and means that many people would consider equity shares in the group to be a risky investment. It may be difficult for the group to obtain further long-term finance if this is required in future periods.

In addition, the group has moved from having a small positive cash balance in 20X4 to having short-term borrowings of $3.7 million in 20X5. Presumably these have also been used to finance the additional capital investment and to meet other costs connected with the planned expansion. The current ratio has fallen from 1.73 to 1.44 and the acid test ratio has fallen from 0.68 to a worryingly low 0.41.

All the elements of working capital except receivables have increased during the year. Inventory turnover has risen from 97 days to 131 days. This may be because inventory levels are being deliberately built up in anticipation of orders but it may also be a sign that that the group is finding it difficult to sell its new product range. This seems to be borne out by the decrease in receivables days and the decrease in receivables. Both of these could have resulted from improved credit control during the year, but the fall in overall sales suggests that the more likely explanation is that sales fell towards the end of the year. Trade payables days have increased from 87 days to 111 days; a worrying increase which suggests that the group may be using suppliers as a source of finance.

The Chairman's comments

The Chairman's comments can be read as an attempt to put a positive 'spin' on the group's disappointing performance and to justify the reduction in dividends. Earnings per share, dividend per share and dividend payout rate (the proportion of profit for the year paid out as dividend) have all fallen and the dividend per share is less than half that of the previous year.

The increase in non-current assets and working capital shows that the group is actually attempting to expand its operations. The additional investment has not yet resulted in increased sales and profits.

According to the Chairman's statement, the replacement of directors took place in March 20X5 and the new storage systems went into production in September 20X5, only four months before the year end. Given these timings it is quite possible that the new product range was only just starting to be sold at the year-end. It is difficult to predict future results, but it is not impossible that performance will improve in 20X6 and subsequent periods. There are some positive signs: a successful share issue two months before the year-end suggests that investors are reasonably confident of the group's future.

However, in the meantime the group has potential liquidity problems and a high level of gearing. If the directors' new policies do not lead to improved profits within the next two or three years, the group will probably face severe financial difficulties.

Appendix: Ratio calculations

	20X5	*20X4*
Gross profit margin	$\dfrac{17,342}{120,366} \times 100\% = 14.4\%$	$\dfrac{19,065}{121,351} \times 100\% = 15.7\%$
Operating profit margin	$\dfrac{5,377}{120,366} \times 100\% = 4.5\%$	$\dfrac{6,617}{121,351} \times 100\% = 5.5\%$
Return on shareholders' equity	$\dfrac{3,908}{30,428 + 2,270} \times 100\% = 12.0\%$	$\dfrac{5,711}{24,623 + 1,947} \times 100\% = 21.5\%$
Return on capital employed	$\dfrac{5,377}{30,428 + 2,270 + 26,700 + 3,662} \times 100\% = 8.5\%$	
	$\dfrac{6,617}{24,623 + 1,947 + 16,700} \times 100\% = 15.3\%$	
Non-current asset turnover	$\dfrac{120,366}{43,575} = 2.76$	$\dfrac{121,351}{24,320} = 4.99$
Interest cover	$\dfrac{5,377}{1,469} = 3.7$	$\dfrac{6,617}{906} = 7.3$
Debt/equity	$\dfrac{26,700}{30,428 + 2,270} \times 100\% = 81.7\%$	$\dfrac{16,700}{24,623 + 1,947} \times 100\% = 62.9\%$
Current ratio	$\dfrac{52,030}{36,207} = 1.44{:}1$	$\dfrac{44,951}{26,001} = 1.73{:}1$
Acid test ratio	$\dfrac{14,922}{36,207} = 0.41{:}1$	$\dfrac{17,691}{26,001} = 0.68{:}1$
Inventory turnover	$\dfrac{37,108}{103,024} \times 365 = 131.5 \text{ days}$	$\dfrac{27,260}{102,286} \times 365 = 97.3 \text{ days}$
Receivables turnover	$\dfrac{14,922}{120,366} \times 365 = 45.2 \text{ days}$	$\dfrac{17,521}{121,351} \times 365 = 52.7 \text{ days}$
Trade payables turnover	$\dfrac{31,420}{103,024} \times 365 = 111.3 \text{ days}$	$\dfrac{24,407}{102,286} \times 365 = 87.1 \text{ days}$
Dividend per share	$\dfrac{155}{3,100} = 5\text{c}$	$\dfrac{364}{2,800} = 13\text{c}$
Dividend payout rate	$\dfrac{155}{2,460} \times 100\% = 6.3\%$	$\dfrac{364}{3,676} \times 100\% = 9.9\%$

65   ACQUIRER AND TARGET

Key answer tips

Make sure you leave enough time to write a proper answer to part (b). It represents 9 relatively easy marks.

(a)   **REPORT**

To: The Board of Directors of Acquirer

Subject: Comparison of Target with other companies

Introduction

I have prepared a schedule of accounting ratios calculated from the latest published financial statements of Target, showing how these ratios compare with the equivalent ratios for comparable entities.

The purpose of this report is to discuss the implications of these figures, pointing out their relevance to your decision on whether to launch a takeover bid for Target.

Profitability ratios

The gross profit margin of Target is towards the top end of the range of comparable entities, while the operating profit margin is towards the bottom end. This suggests that, while Target's operations have a good underlying profitability, there is lax control over operating expenses which have been allowed to grow to unacceptable levels. Curiously, this lack of control at present might actually be good news for us, since it suggests that we might easily be able to improve Target's reported profits without having to radically change its operations. We would need to impose the control over expenses that is currently absent.

Return on total capital employed for Target is around the average level achieved by the comparative group of entities. Since the ROCE is calculated as the product of the operating profit margin and the asset turnover, and we have already seen that the operating profit margin is low, this suggests that the asset turnover must be higher than average. This is another encouraging statistic: as long as we can impose the controls already discussed over expenses, then the high gross profit margin and the high asset turnover should generate attractive revenues and profits.

Gearing ratios

The statement of financial position gearing ratio at 52% is towards the top end of the range of comparative entities, and seems high also in absolute terms. As would be expected, this is accompanied by a gearing ratio in statement of comprehensive income terms (the interest cover) towards the bottom end of the range. High gearing means large finance costs that are only modestly covered by available profits. The gearing ratio is not of fundamental importance to our decision as to whether to bid for Target since, whatever the capital structure, we would be responsible for financing Target after we acquired it. However, if our existing group gearing ratio is already very high, then we should hesitate before taking on additional group borrowings.

Investor ratio

Target's dividend cover is higher even than the highest number seen in the comparative group, suggesting that very low dividends are currently being paid. Perhaps the past level of dividend payout is irrelevant to our decision to bid for the company, since we could insist on whatever dividends we wanted to be paid, if we acquire the company. However it is possible that low dividends are being paid currently due to severe liquidity problems at the company. We should research this possibility further.

Working capital ratios

The inventory turnover ratio of Target is towards the top end of the range of comparative entities, while the receivables days is towards the bottom end of the observed numbers. Both of these are indications of good control over working capital, ie low inventories being held, and low receivables at the reporting period end. These results are consistent with the high asset turnover of Target that was discussed earlier. Control over net assets appears to be sound.

Conclusion

The most important point identified above is the poor control over Target's operating expenses that appears to be in force at the moment. If we were to buy the company, we may be able to increase profitability substantially by imposing stronger controls over these expenses.

Please contact me if I can be of any further help to you in respect of this matter.

(b)   I have a number of reservations regarding the extent to which the provided ratios can contribute to an acquisition decision.

The ratios for Target have been calculated from the latest published financial statements, namely for the year ended 30 November 20X2. Are there any more recent figures available, perhaps interim figures for the first six months of the next year?

Companies may choose different accounting policies, which can affect the reported results materially. We are not told whether Target complies with IASs, or whether this is the accounting framework adopted by all the comparative enterprises, but even if all the companies concerned adopt IASs, there is still some potential for different accounting practices to be followed. For example, IAS 16 permits non-current assets to be measured either at depreciated cost or at revalued amount, a decision that can have an enormous impact on the ratios calculated. We must therefore ensure that all the companies are using the same accounting policies before we can effectively compare them.

Accounting ratios are concerned only with financial factors that are captured in a set of prepared financial statements. There are many non-financial factors that we should also consider. What is Target's reputation in the market-place? Does it have skilled employees and managers running the company? Does it have research and development activity that is not included in the statement of financial position but may generate future profits? We must investigate all of these matters before we launch a bid. Unfortunately, the published financial statements will be of little help, though the chairman's statement or chief executive officer's report may give some insight into the strengths of the company that are not recognized in the statement of financial position.

Finally, accounting ratios are only concerned with the past. When we buy a company, the past is largely irrelevant and we will be buying the future earnings stream. We must be looking for any indications of future results that Target expects to report. Perhaps, again, the chairman's statement in the annual report will indicate whether future results are expected to be higher or lower than currently achieved.

66 INVESTOR

Key answer tips

Before you answer part (a), look at the information given in the question. This tells you that the two sets of figures are not comparable because Alpha has entered into transactions with group companies while Beta has not, and this gives you one of the points for your answer.

(a) **Factors that should be considered when comparing the financial statements of two entities**

There are many reasons why the financial statements of two entities may not be strictly comparable, even when the entities carry out similar business operations.

Differences in the financial statements

- The amounts included in the financial statements often depend on the accounting policies adopted by the directors. A few accounting standards still allow a choice of accounting treatment (for example, most classes of non-current asset can be measured either at historic cost or at a valuation). There are still a few areas not covered by accounting standards (for example, there is no international accounting standard that deals specifically with reporting the substance of transactions).

- Even where two entities appear to be following the same accounting policies, management must make accounting estimates. This requires the exercise of judgement (for example, of the useful life and residual value of assets), which means that the resulting figures may be very different. In addition, accounting standards tend to be principles based, which means that they can be interpreted differently by similar entities.

Differences in the business environment

Entities in the same business sector may operate in very different ways and this may affect their profitability and financial position.

- An entity's profit margin may depend on the market that it serves. For example, a specialist dealing in precious stones will make relatively few sales at very high profit margins, while a high street jeweller will have a lower profit margin, but will compensate by making a high volume of sales.

- An entity that is part of a group is likely to operate in a different way from an entity that is independent. For example, it may exist to supply goods to other companies in the group. In this situation, it has a ready market for its goods and prices may be set artificially by the parent company. Therefore its results may not be strictly comparable with those of another entity that is not part of a group.

(b) **Adjustments to the earnings per share of Alpha**

- The interest on Alpha's long-term loans is provided by another group company at below the market rate. To make the financial statements of Alpha and Beta more comparable, Alpha's statement of comprehensive income should be charged with interest at the market rate. This increases interest payable by $210,000 (7 million × 3%).

- Alpha sells goods to Gamma at an artificially high margin. Revenue should be adjusted to show the price that Alpha could obtain for the goods in the open market.

	Per statement of comprehensive income	Adjusted	Difference
	$m	$m	$m
Revenue (adjusted 6 × 100/50)	15	12	3
Cost (15 × 40%)	(6)	(6)	Nil
	9	6	3

Pre-tax profit is reduced by $3 million.

- Alpha receives administrative services from its parent without charge. Alpha's profits should be reduced by $1.5 million to reflect the amount that would have been paid by Beta for management services.

Earnings per share calculation

Adjustments:

	$000
Loan interest	210
Intra-group sales	3,000
Management fee	1,500
Reduction in pre-tax profit	4,710
Tax at 30%	(1,413)
Reduction in post-tax profit	3,297
Published profit for the year	4,710
Less reduction	(3,297)
Adjusted profit for the year	1,413

Earnings per share: $\dfrac{1,413}{3,000} = 47.1c$

(c) **REPORT**

To: The directors of Investor

Subject: Differences between the earnings per share of Alpha and Beta

Date: 24 November 20X4

Both Alpha and Beta have had the same number of shares in issue throughout the year. Therefore the difference in earnings per share reflects their profits for the year.

According to the published statements of comprehensive income, Alpha's performance appears to be superior to that of Beta. However, the two statements of comprehensive income are not strictly comparable, because Alpha has entered into several transactions with its group companies and these are on more favourable terms than would be available to Beta.

Therefore the statement of comprehensive income of Alpha has been adjusted to make a more meaningful comparison possible. The analysis below is based on the adjusted figures. No statements of financial position have been provided and therefore it is only possible to comment on the two companies' profit margins. Calculations are set out in the Appendix.

The gross profit margin of Alpha, even after the adjustments, is slightly higher than that of Beta. However, Beta's operating profit margin is almost twice that of Alpha and its results both before and after tax are also superior to those of Alpha. The main reason for this appears to be Alpha's relatively high operating expenses. Without further information, such as statements of financial position and notes to the financial statements, the cause of this is not clear.

Appendix: Ratios

	Alpha		Beta	
Gross profit margin	$\dfrac{19,000}{42,000-3,000}$	= 48.7%	$\dfrac{19,500}{44,000}$	= 44.3%
Operating profit margin	$\dfrac{2,500}{42,000-3,000}$	= 6.4%	$\dfrac{5,500}{44,000}$	= 12.5%
Other operating expenses/revenue	$\dfrac{15,000+1,500}{42,000-3,000}$	= 42.3%	$\dfrac{14,000}{44,000}$	= 31.8%

Workings

Adjustments to the statement of comprehensive income of Alpha

	Gross profit	Profit from operations
	$000	$000
Per original statement of comprehensive income	22,000	7,000
Effect of favourable intra-group sales	(3,000)	(3,000)
Effect of management fee		(1,500)
Revised figures	19,000	2,500

67   PHOENIX

Key answer tips

Note that as the report is to the retailer's banker it should concentrate on liquidity.

REPORT

To: The bankers of Phoenix

Subject: Financial performance of Phoenix

As requested, this report analyses the financial performance of Phoenix for the three years ending 30 June 20X9, paying particular attention to the rapidly increasing level of bank lending. Calculations of relevant key accounting ratios are given in an appendix to this report.

Ratios 1 to 4 in the appendix show that, in profitability terms, the policy of offering credit facilities in order to maintain growth in revenue has been a success. Revenues have risen strongly while the profit margin has been maintained.

However, the effects of the policy on liquidity are not so happy. The gearing ratio is increasing rapidly while interest cover is falling. There have been large increases in inventories and trade receivables which have been largely financed by bank loans and other borrowings. Insufficient cash is being generated from operations to cover even the interest payments for the year, let alone pay tax or dividend amounts.

By 30 June 20X9 the level of bank loans had reached $610m, only $20m below the bank's maximum lending facility, which is why the company is now seeking an increase in the lending facility. But the likelihood must be, if an increase is granted without any conditions, that the level of bank lending will continue to increase rapidly, a source of unsecured exposure for the bank. A floating charge already exists over the assets of the company in favour of other lenders, so it is possible that the bank would suffer a significant loss if the company were to be wound up.

I recommend that, before the level of bank lending is increased, the bank should meet with the directors of the company to discuss the following points:

(i)   Why are the levels of inventory and receivables so high? For example, the level of trade receivables at 30 June 20X9 represents a whole year's credit sales.If these figures can be reduced, cash can be released to repay borrowings.

(ii)   Why have operating profits not increased despite the increases in revenue? It appears that operating costs have risen faster than would be expected.

Unless satisfactory answers are received to these queries, further bank lending should be refused. The fact that the existing bank loans are unsecured means that the bank must take this company's situation very seriously in view of a possible failure through illiquidity in the near future.

Please contact me again if I can be of any further help to you in this or any other matter.

Appendix

Phoenix – key accounting ratios

		20X7	20X8	20X9
1	Increase in total revenue	N/A	18.9%	13.6%
	Increase in credit sales	N/A	33.3%	50%
2	Profit margin $\left(\dfrac{50+45}{1,850}\right)$	5.1%	5.5%	5.6%
3	Return on capital employed $\left(\dfrac{50+45}{342+520}\right)$	11.0%	11.2%	10.9%
4	Asset turnover $\left(\dfrac{1,850}{342+520}\right)$	2.1 times	2.1 times	2.0 times
5	Gearing $\left(\dfrac{320+200}{342+520}\right)$	60.3%	67.2%	72.5%
6	Interest cover $\left(\dfrac{50+45}{25}\right)$	3.8 times	2.0 times	1.3 times
7	Inventory turnover $\left(\dfrac{1,250}{400}\right)$	3.1 times	2.8 times	2.8 times
8	Days credit sales outstanding $\left(\dfrac{492}{300}\times365\right)$	599 days	502 days	385 days

Tutorial note: When preparing a schedule of ratios such as the above, it is important to show the numbers you have used to calculate each ratio, since there can be more than one way to define certain ratios.

When calculating the days sales outstanding (ratio 8 above) a case could be argued to include the income from credit sales in the denominator of the ratio, since it will probably have been included in the receivables figure in the numerator. The trend over the three years would still be the same.

9   Cash generated from operations

	20X8	20X9
	$m	$m
Profit before tax	60	30
Add back: Interest payable	60	110
Depreciation	60	70
	—	—
	180	210
Increase in inventory	(140)	(80)
Increase in trade receivables	(58)	(83)
Increase in trade and other creditors	–	–
	——	——
Cash generated	(18)	47

68   EXPAND AGAIN

Key answer tips

Look carefully at the accounts of B when computing the adjustments in part (a). During the year excess depreciation of $1,000,000 has been transferred from the revaluation reserve to retained earnings. In other words, the depreciation charge for the year was $1,000,000 higher than it would have been if the properties had been valued at historic cost.

Part (c) is worth 7 marks, so your answer needs to do more than list the ways in which the ratios have changed following the adjustments.

(a)   **Adjustments**

Note 1   The substance of this transaction is not a sale but a loan. Therefore the following adjustments are necessary to reverse the effect of the sale:

Dr Revenue	$2,400,000	
Dr Inventories (2,400,000 × 100/160)	$1,500,000	
Cr Cost of sales		$1,500,000
Cr Loan		$2,400,000

Note 2   Expand needs to be able to make meaningful comparisons between the accounts of A and B. As far as possible, both sets of accounts should be based on the same accounting policies. The only practical way of achieving this is to restate the accounts of B so that both sets of properties are stated at historical cost:

Dr Revaluation reserve	$5,000,000	
Cr Property, plant and equipment		$5,000,000
Dr Retained earnings (excess depreciation)	$1,000,000	
Cr Cost of sales		$1,000,000

These adjustments affect the accounts as follows:

	Before $000	*Adjustment* $000	*After* $000
Company A			
Revenue	68,000	(2,400)	65,600
Cost of sales	(42,000)	1,500	(40,500)
Gross profit	26,000	(900)	25,100
Profit from operations	8,000	(900)	7,100
Borrowings (4,000 + 16,000)	20,000	2,400	22,400
Capital and reserves	23,500	(900)	22,600
Capital employed	43,500		45,000
Company B			
Revenue	66,000		66,000
Cost of sales	(45,950)	1,000	(44,950)
Gross profit	20,050	1,000	21,050
Profit from operations	6,050	1,000	7,050
Borrowings (6,000 + 18,000)	24,000		24,000
Capital and reserves	22,050	(5,000)	17,050
Capital employed	46,050		41,050

(b) **Ratios**

	A	B
Return on capital employed		
$\dfrac{\text{Profit from operations}}{\text{Capital employed}}$	$\dfrac{7,100}{45,000} = 15.8\%$	$\dfrac{7,050}{41,050} = 17.2\%$
Gross profit margin		
$\dfrac{\text{Gross profit}}{\text{Revenue}}$	$\dfrac{25,100}{65,600} = 38.3\%$	$\dfrac{21,050}{66,000} = 31.9\%$
Turnover of capital employed		
$\dfrac{\text{Revenue}}{\text{Capital employed}}$	$\dfrac{65,600}{45,000} = 1.5$	$\dfrac{66,000}{41,050} = 1.6$
Gearing		
$\dfrac{\text{Total borrowings}}{\text{Capital employed}}$	$\dfrac{22,400}{45,000} = 49.8\%$	$\dfrac{24,000}{41,050} = 58.5\%$

(c) **Evaluation**

The ratios based on the adjusted accounts show that A is not necessarily the better acquisition.

The adjustments have had the effect of reducing the profits of A and slightly improving the profits of B. Although A still clearly has the better gross profit margin, B now has the better return on capital employed. There appear to be two reasons for this:

- the turnover of capital employed ratio shows that B is slightly better at generating revenue from its capital base than A; and

- A has operating expenses of $4 million more than B, although both companies have similar levels of revenue.

For these reasons B may be the better company to acquire, particularly if the operating expenses of A cannot be reduced. B has significantly higher gearing than A, but this may not be a critical factor if Expand can change the capital structure or provide the company with additional finance.

Section 3

PILOT PAPER EXAM QUESTIONS

1   PUMICE

On 1 October 2005 Pumice acquired the following non-current investments:

−   80% of the equity share capital of Silverton at a cost of $13.6 million

−   50% of Silverton's 10% loan notes at par

−   1.6 million equity shares in Amok at a cost of $6.25 each.

The summarized draft balance sheets of the three companies at 31 March 2006 are:

	Pumice $000	Silverton $000	Amok $000
Non-current assets			
Property, plant and equipment	20,000	8,500	16,500
Investments	26,000	Nil	1,500
	46,000	8,500	18,000
Current assets	15,000	8,000	11,000
Total assets	61,000	16,500	29,000
Equity and liabilities			
Equity			
Equity shares of $1 each	10,000	3,000	4,000
Retained earnings	37,000	8,000	20,000
	47,000	11,000	24,000
Non-current liabilities			
8% loan note	4,000	Nil	Nil
10% loan note	Nil	2,000	Nil
Current liabilities	10,000	3,500	5,000
Total equity and liabilities	61,000	16,500	29,000

The following information is relevant:

(i) The fair values of Silverton's assets were equal to their carrying amounts with the exception of land and plant. Silverton's land had a fair value of $400,000 in excess of its carrying amount and plant had a fair value of $1.6 million in excess of its carrying amount. The plant had a remaining life of four years (straight-line depreciation) at the date of acquisition.

(ii) In the post acquisition period Pumice sold goods to Silverton at a price of $6 million. These goods had cost Pumice $4 million. Half of these goods were still in the inventory of Silverton at 31 March 2006. Silverton had a balance of $1.5 million owing to Pumice at 31 March 2006 which agreed with Pumice's records.

(iii) The net profit after tax for the year ended 31 March 2006 was $2 million for Silverton and $8 million for Amok. Assume profits accrued evenly throughout the year.

(iv) An impairment test at 31 March 2006 concluded that consolidated goodwill was impaired by $400,000 and the investment in Amok was impaired by $200,000.

(v) No dividends were paid during the year by any of the companies.

Required:

(a) Discuss how the investments purchased by Pumice on 1 October 2005 should be treated in its consolidated financial statements. **(5 marks)**

(b) Prepare the consolidated balance sheet for Pumice as at 31 March 2006. **(20 marks)**

(Total: 25 marks)

2 KALA

The following trial balance relates to Kala, a publicly listed company, at 31 March 2006:

	$000	$000
Land and buildings at cost (note (i))	270,000	
Plant – at cost (note (i))	156,000	
Investment properties – valuation at 1 April 2005 (note (i))	90,000	
Purchases	78,200	
Operating expenses	15,500	
Loan interest paid	2,000	
Rental of leased plant (note (ii))	22,000	
Dividends paid	15,000	
Inventory at 1 April 2005	37,800	
Trade receivables	53,200	
Revenue		278,400
Income from investment property		4,500
Equity shares of $1 each fully paid		150,000
Retained earnings at 1 April 2005		119,500
8% (actual and effective) loan note (note (iii))		50,000
Accumulated depreciation at 1 April 2005 – buildings		60,000
– plant		26,000
Trade payables		33,400
Deferred tax		12,500
Bank		5,400
	739,700	739,700

The following notes are relevant:

(i)   The land and buildings were purchased on 1 April 1990. The cost of the land was $70 million. No land and buildings have been purchased by Kala since that date. On 1 April 2005 Kala had its land and buildings professionally valued at $80 million and $175 million respectively. The directors wish to incorporate these values into the financial statements. The estimated life of the buildings was originally 50 years and the remaining life has not changed as a result of the valuation.

Later, the valuers informed Kala that investment properties of the type Kala owned had increased in value by 7% in the year to 31 March 2006.

Plant, other than leased plant (see below), is depreciated at 15% per annum using the reducing balance method. Depreciation of buildings and plant is charged to cost of sales.

(ii)   On 1 April 2005 Kala entered into a lease for an item of plant which had an estimated life of five years. The lease period is also five years with annual rentals of $22 million payable in advance from 1 April 2005. The plant is expected to have a nil residual value at the end of its life. If purchased this plant would have a cost of $92 million and be depreciated on a straight-line basis. The lessor includes a finance cost of 10% per annum when calculating annual rentals. (*Note:* you are not required to calculate the present value of the minimum lease payments.)

(iii)   The loan note was issued on 1 July 2005 with interest payable six monthly in arrears.

(iv)   The provision for income tax for the year to 31 March 2006 has been estimated at $28.3 million. The deferred tax provision at 31 March 2006 is to be adjusted to a credit balance of $14.1 million.

(v)   The inventory at 31 March 2006 was valued at $43.2 million.

Required:

Prepare for Kala:

(a)   An income statement for the year ended 31 March 2006.   **(10 marks)**

(b)   A statement of changes in equity for the year ended 31 March 2006.   **(4 marks)**

(c)   A balance sheet as at 31 March 2006.   **(11 marks)**

                                          (Total: 25 marks)

3   REACTIVE

Reactive is a publicly listed company that assembles domestic electrical goods which it then sells to both wholesale and retail customers. Reactive's management were disappointed in the company's results for the year ended 31 March 2005. In an attempt to improve performance the following measures were taken early in the year ended 31 March 2006:

–   a national advertising campaign was undertaken,

–   rebates to all wholesale customers purchasing goods above set quantity levels were introduced,

–   the assembly of certain lines ceased and was replaced by bought in completed products. This allowed Reactive to dispose of surplus plant.

Reactive's summarized financial statements for the year ended 31 March 2006 are set out below:

Income statement	$million
Revenue (25% cash sales)	4,000
Cost of sales	(3,450)
Gross profit	550
Operating expenses	(370)
	180
Profit on disposal of plant (note (i))	40
Finance charges	(20)
Profit before tax	200
Income tax expense	(50)
Profit for the period	150

Balance Sheet	$million	$million
Non-current assets		
Property, plant and equipment (note (i))		550
Current assets		
Inventory	250	
Trade receivables	360	
Bank	Nil	610
Total assets		1,160
Equity and liabilities		
Equity shares of 25 cents each		100
Retained earnings		380
		480
Non-current liabilities		
8% loan notes		200
Current liabilities		
Bank overdraft	10	
Trade payables	430	
Current tax payable	40	480
Total equity and liabilities		1,160

Below are ratios calculated for the year ended 31 March 2005.

Return on year end capital employed (profit before interest and tax over total assets less current liabilities)	28.1%
Net asset (equal to capital employed) turnover	4 times
Gross profit margin	17%
Net profit (before tax) margin	6.3%
Current ratio	1.6:1
Closing inventory holding period	46 days
Trade receivables' collection period	45 days
Trade payables' payment period	55 days
Dividend yield	3.75%
Dividend cover	2 times

Notes:

(i) Reactive received $120 million from the sale of plant that had a carrying amount of $80 million at the date of its sale.

(ii) The market price of Reactive's shares throughout the year averaged $3.75 each.

(iii) There were no issues or redemption of shares or loans during the year.

(iv) Dividends paid during the year ended 31 March 2006 amounted to $90 million, maintaining the same dividend paid in the year ended 31 March 2005.

Required:

(a) Calculate ratios for the year ended 31 March 2006 (showing your workings) for Reactive, equivalent to those provided above. **(10 marks)**

(b) Analyse the financial performance and position of Reactive for the year ended 31 March 2006 compared to the previous year. **(10 marks)**

(c) Explain in what ways your approach to performance appraisal would differ if you were asked to assess the performance of a not-for-profit organization. **(5 marks)**

(Total: 25 marks)

4 **PORTO**

(a) The qualitative characteristics of relevance, reliability and comparability identified in the IASB's Framework for the preparation and presentation of financial statements (Framework) are some of the attributes that make financial information useful to the various users of financial statements.

Required:

Explain what is meant by relevance, reliability and comparability and how they make financial information useful. **(9 marks)**

(b) During the year ended 31 March 2006, Porto experienced the following transactions or events:

(i) entered into a finance lease to rent an asset for substantially the whole of its useful economic life.

(ii) a decision was made by the Board to change the company's accounting policy from one of expensing the finance costs on building new retail outlets to one of capitalising such costs.

(iii)   the company's income statement prepared using historical costs showed a loss from operating its hotels, but the company is aware that the increase in the value of its properties during the period far outweighed the operating loss.

Required:

Explain how you would treat the items in (i) to (iii) above in Porto's financial statements and indicate on which of the Framework's qualitative characteristics your treatment is based.   **(6 marks)**

(Total: 15 marks)

5   BEETIE

IAS 11 *Construction contracts* deals with accounting requirements for construction contracts whose durations usually span at least two accounting period.

Required:

(a)   Describe the issues of revenue and profit recognition relating to construction contracts.
                                                            (4 marks)

(b)   Beetie is a construction company that prepares its financial statements to 31 March each year. During the year ended 31 March 2006 the company commenced two construction contracts that are expected to take more than one year to complete. The position of each contract at 31 March 2006 is as follows:

Contract	1	2
	$000	$000
Agreed contract price	5,500	1,200
Estimated total cost of contract at commencement	4,000	900
Estimated total cost at 31 March 2006	4,000	1,250
Agreed value of work completed at 31 March 2006	3,300	840
Progress billings invoiced and received at 31 March 2006	3,000	880
Contract costs incurred to 31 March 2006	3,900	720

The agreed value of the work completed at 31 March 2006 is considered to be equal to the revenue earned in the year ended 31 March 2006. The percentage of completion is calculated as the agreed value of work completed to the agreed contract price.

Required:

Calculate the amounts which should appear in the income statement and balance sheet of Beetie at 31 March 2006 in respect of the above contracts.

                                                            (6 marks)

(Total: 10 marks)

Section 4

ANSWERS TO PILOT PAPER EXAM QUESTIONS

1 PUMICE

(a) As the investment in shares represents 80% of Silverton's equity, it is likely to give Pumice control of that company. Control is the ability to direct the operating and financial policies of an entity. This would make Silverton a subsidiary of Pumice and require Pumice to prepare group financial statements which would require the consolidation of the results of Silverton from the date of acquisition (1 October 2005). Consolidated financial statements are prepared on the basis that the group is a single economic entity.

The investment of 50% ($1 million) of the 10% loan note in Silverton is effectively a loan from a parent to a subsidiary. On consolidation Pumice's asset of the loan ($1 million) is cancelled out with $1 million of Silverton's total loan note liability of $2 million. This would leave a net liability of $1 million in the consolidated balance sheet.

The investment in Amok of 1.6 million shares represents 40% of that company's equity shares. This is generally regarded as not being sufficient to give Pumice control of Amok, but is likely to give it significant influence over Amok's policy decisions (eg determining the level of dividends paid by Amok). Such investments are generally classified as associates and IAS 28 *Investments in associates* requires the investment to be included in the consolidated financial statements using equity accounting.

(b) **Consolidated balance sheet of Pumice at 31 March 2006**

	$000	$000
Non-current assets:		
Plant, property and equipment (w (i))		30,300
Goodwill (4,000 (w (ii)) – 400 impairment)		3,600
Investments – associate (w (iii))		11,400
– other ((26,000 – 13,600 – 10,000 – 1,000 intra-group loan note))		1,400
		46,700
Current assets (15,000 + 8,000 – 1,000 (w (iv)) – 1,500 current account)		20,500
Total assets		67,200

	$000	$000
Equity and liabilities		
Equity attributable to equity holders of the parent		
Equity shares of $1 each		10,000
Reserves:		
Retained earnings (w (v))		37,640
		47,640
Minority interest (w (vi))		2,560
Total equity		50,200
Non-current liabilities		
8% Loan note	4,000	
10% Loan note (2,000 – 1,000 intra-group)	1,000	5,000
Current liabilities (10,000 + 3,500 – 1,500 current account)		12,000
		67,200

Workings in £000

(i)   Property, plant and equipment

		$000	$000
Pumice			20,000
Silverton			8,500
Fair value	– land	400	
	– plant	1,600	2,000
Additional depreciation (see below)			(200)
			30,300

The fair value adjustment to plant will create additional depreciation of $400,000 per annum (1,600/4 years) and in the post acquisition period of six months this will be $200,000.

(ii)   Goodwill in Silverton:

	$000	$000
Investment at cost		13,600
Less – equity shares of Silverton (3,000 × 80%)	(2,400)	
– pre-acquisition reserves (7,000 × 80% (see below))	(5,600)	
– fair value adjustments (2,000 (w (i)) × 80%)	(1,600)	(9,600)
Goodwill on consolidation		4,000

The pre-acquisition reserves are:	
At 31 March 2006	8,000
Post acquisition (2,000 × 6/12)	(1,000)
	7,000

(iii) Carrying amount of Amok at 31 March 2006

Cost (1,600 × $6.25)	10,000
Share post acquisition profit (8,000 × 6/12 × 40%)	1,600
	11,600
Impairment loss per question	(200)
	11,400

(iv) The unrealized profit (URP) in inventory is calculated as:

Intra-group sales are $6 million of which Pumice made a profit of $2 million. Half of these are still in inventory, thus there is an unrealized profit of $1 million.

(v) Consolidated reserves:

Pumice's reserves	37,000
Silverton's post acquisition (((2,000 × 6/12) – 200 depreciation) × 80%)	640
Amok's post acquisition profits (8,000 × 6/12 × 40%)	1,600
URP in inventory (see (iv))	(1,000)
Impairment of goodwill – Silverton	(400)
– Amok	(200)
	37,640

(vi) Minority interest

	$000
Equity shares of Silverton (3,000 × 20%)	600
Retained earnings ((8,000 – 200 depreciation) × 20%)	1,560
Fair value adjustments (2,000 × 20%)	400
	2,560

ACCA marking scheme		Marks
(a)	1 mark per relevant point	5
(b)	Balance sheet:	
	Property, plant and equipment	2½
	Goodwill	3½
	Investments – associate	3
	– other	1
	Current assets	2
	Equity shares	1
	Retained earnings	3
	Minority interest	1½
	8% Loan notes	½
	10% Loan notes	1
	Profit and loss account	1
	Maximum	20
Total		**25**

2   KALA

(a)   **Kala – Income statement – Year ended 31 March 2006**

	$000	$000
Revenue		278,400
Cost of sales (w (i))		(115,700)
Gross profit		162,700
Operating expenses		(15,500)
		147,200
Investment income– property rental	4,500	
– valuation gain (90,000 × 7%)	6,300	10,800
Finance costs – loan (w (ii))	(3,000)	
– lease (w (iii))	(7,000)	(10,000)
Profit before tax		148,000
Income tax expense (28,300 + (14,100 – 12,500))		(29,900)
Profit for the period		118,100

(b)   **Kala –Statement of changes in equity – Year ended 31 March 2006**

	Equity shares	Revaluation reserve	Retained earnings	Total
	$000	$000	$000	$000
At 1 April 2005	150,000	Nil	119,500	269,500
Profit for period (see (a))			118,100	118,100
Revaluation of property (w (iv))		45,000		45,000
Equity dividends paid			(15,000)	(15,000)
At 31 March 2006	150,000	45,000	222,600	417,600

(c) **Kala – Balance sheet as at 31 March 2006**

	$000	$000
Non-current assets		
Property, plant and equipment (w (iv))		434,100
Investment property (90,000 + 6,300)		96,300
		530,400
Current assets		
Inventory	43,200	
Trade receivables	53,200	96,400
Total assets		626,800
Equity and liabilities		
Equity (see (b) above)		
Equity shares of $1 each		150,000
Reserves:		
Revaluation	45,000	
Retained earnings	222,600	267,600
		417,600
Non-current liabilities		
8% loan note	50,000	
Deferred tax	14,100	
Lease obligation (w (iii))	55,000	119,100
Current liabilities		
Trade payables	33,400	
Accrued loan interest (w (ii))	1,000	
Bank overdraft	5,400	
Lease obligation (w (iii)) – accrued interest	7,000	
– capital	15,000	
Current tax payable	28,300	90,100
Total equity and liabilities		626,800

Workings in brackets in $000

(i) Cost of sales:

	$000
Opening inventory	37,800
Purchases	78,200
Depreciation (w (iv)) – buildings	5,000
– plant: owned	19,500
leased	18,400
Closing inventory	(43,200)
	115,700

(ii) The loan has been in issue for nine months. The total finance cost for this period will be $3 million (50,000 × 8% × 9/12). Kala has paid six months interest of $2 million, thus accrued interest of $1 million should be provided for.

(iii)   Finance lease:

	$000
Net obligation at inception of lease (92,000 – 22,000)	70,000
Accrued interest 10% (current liability)	7,000
Total outstanding at 31 March 2006	77,000

The second payment in the year to 31 March 2007 (made on 1 April 2006) of $22 million will be $7 million for the accrued interest (at 31 March 2006) and $15 million paid of the capital outstanding. Thus the amount outstanding as an obligation over one year is $55 million (77,000 – 22,000).

(iv)   Non-current assets/depreciation:

Land and buildings:

At the date of the revaluation the land and buildings have a carrying amount of $210 million (270,000 – 60,000). With a valuation of $255 million this gives a revaluation surplus (to reserves) of $45 million. The accumulated depreciation of $60 million represents 15 years at $4 million per annum (200,000/50 years) and means the remaining life at the date of the revaluation is 35 years. The amount of the revalued building is $175 million, thus depreciation for the year to 31 March 2006 will be $5 million (175,000/35 years). The carrying amount of the land and buildings at 31 March 2006 is $250 million (255,000 – 5,000).

Plant: owned

The carrying amount prior to the current year's depreciation is $130 million (156,000 – 26,000). Depreciation at 15% on the reducing balance basis gives an annual charge of $19.5 million. This gives a carrying amount at 31 March 2006 of $110.5 million (130,000 – 19,500).

Plant: leased

The fair value of the leased plant is $92 million. Depreciation on a straight-line basis over five years would give a depreciation charge of $18.4 million and a carrying amount of $73.6 million.

	$000
Summarising the carrying amounts:	
Land and buildings	250,000
Plant (110,500 + 73,600)	184,100
Property, plant and equipment	434,100

ACCA marking scheme		Marks
(a)	Income statement	
	Revenue	½
	Cost of sales	4½
	Operating expenses	½
	Investment income	1½
	Finance costs	1½
	Taxation	1½
	Maximum	10

(b)	Movement in share capital and reserves	
	Brought forward figures	1
	Revaluation	1
	Profit for period	1
	Dividends paid	1
	Maximum	4
(c)	Balance sheet	
	Land and buildings	2
	Plant and equipment	2
	Investment property	1
	Inventory and trade receivables	1
	8 % Loan	½
	Deferred tax	½
	Lease obligation:	
	Interest and capital one year	1
	Capital over one year	1
	Trade payables and overdraft	1
	Accrued interest	½
	Income tax provision	½
	Maximum	11
Total		**25**

3 REACTIVE

(a)   *Note:* figures in the calculations are in $million

Return on year end capital employed	32.3%	220/(1,160 – 480) × 100
Net asset turnover	5.9 times	4,000/680
Gross profit margin	13.8%	(500/4,000) × 100
Net profit (before tax) margin	5.0%	(200/4,000) × 100
Current ratio	1.3:1	610:480
Closing inventory holding period	26 days	250/3,450 × 365
Trade receivables' collection period	44 days	360/4,000 – 1,000) × 365
Trade payables' payment period (based on cost of sales)	45 days	(430/3,450) × 365
Dividend yield	6.0%	(see below)
Dividend cover	1.67 times	150/90

The dividend per share is 22.5 cents (90,000/(100,000 × 4 i.e. 25 cents shares). This is a yield of 6.0% on a share price of $3.75.

(b)   Analysis of the comparative financial performance and position of Reactive for the year ended 31 March 2006

Profitability

The measures taken by management appear to have been successful as the overall ROCE (considered as a primary measure of performance) has improved by 15% (32.3 – 28.1)/28.1). Looking in more detail at the composition of the ROCE, the reason for the improved profitability is due to increased efficiency in the use of the company's assets (asset turnover), increasing from 4 to 5.9 times (an improvement of 48%). The improvement in the asset turnover has been offset by lower profit margins at both the gross and net level. On the surface, this performance appears to be due both to the company's strategy of offering rebates to wholesale customers if they achieve a set level of orders and also the beneficial impact on sales revenue of the advertising campaign. The rebate would explain the lower gross profit margin, and the cost of the advertising has reduced the net profit margin (presumably management expected an increase in sales volume as a compensating factor). The decision to buy complete products rather than assemble them in house has enabled the disposal of some plant which has reduced the asset base. Thus possible increased sales and a lower asset base are the cause of the improvement in the asset turnover which in turn, as stated above, is responsible for the improvement in the ROCE.

The effect of the disposal needs careful consideration. The profit (before tax) includes a profit of $40 million from the disposal. As this is a 'one-off' profit, recalculating the ROCE without its inclusion gives a figure of only 23.7% (180m/(1,160 – 480m + 80m (the 80m is the carrying amount of plant)) and the fall in the net profit percentage (before tax) would be down even more to only 4.0% (160m/4,000m). On this basis the current year performance is worse than that of the previous year and the reported figures tend to flatter the company's underlying performance.

Liquidity

The company's liquidity position has deteriorated during the period. An acceptable current ratio of 1.6 has fallen to a worrying 1.3 (1.5 is usually considered as a safe minimum). With the trade receivables period at virtually a constant (45/44 days), the change in liquidity appears to be due to the levels of inventory and trade payables. These give a contradictory picture. The closing inventory holding period has decreased markedly (from 46 to 26 days) indicating more efficient inventory holding. This is perhaps due to short lead times when ordering bought in products. The change in this ratio has reduced the current ratio, however the trade payables payment period has decreased from 55 to 45 days which has increased the current ratio. This may be due to different terms offered by suppliers of bought in products.

Importantly, the effect of the plant disposal has generated a cash inflow of $120 million, and without this the company's liquidity would look far worse.

Investment ratios

The current year's dividend yield of 6.0% looks impressive when compared with that of the previous year's yield of 3.75%, but as the company has maintained the same dividend (and dividend per share as there is no change in share capital), the 'improvement' in the yield is due to a falling share price. Last year the share price must have been $6.00 to give a yield of 3.75% on a dividend per share of 22.5 cents. It is worth noting that maintaining the dividend at $90 million from profits of $150 million gives a cover of only 1.67 times whereas on the same dividend last year the cover was 2 times (meaning last year's profit (after tax) was $180 million).

Conclusion

Although superficially the company's profitability seems to have improved as a result of the directors' actions at the start of the current year, much, if not all, of the apparent improvement is due to the change in supply policy and the consequent beneficial effects of the disposal of plant. The company's liquidity is now below acceptable levels and would have been even worse had the disposal not occurred. It appears that investors have understood the underlying deterioration in performance as there has been a marked fall in the company's share price.

(c)   It is generally assumed that the objective of stock market listed companies is to maximize the wealth of their shareholders. This in turn places an emphasis on profitability and other factors that influence a company's share price. It is true that some companies have other (secondary) aims such as only engaging in ethical activities (e.g. not producing armaments) or have strong environmental considerations. Clearly by definition not-for-profit organizations are not motivated by the need to produce profits for shareholders, but that does not mean that they should be inefficient. Many areas of assessment of profit oriented companies are perfectly valid for not-for-profit organizations; efficient inventory holdings, tight budgetary constraints, use of key performance indicators, prevention of fraud etc.

There are a great variety of not-for-profit organizations; e.g. public sector health, education, policing and charities. It is difficult to be specific about how to assess the performance of a not-for-profit organization without knowing what type of organization it is. In general terms an assessment of performance must be made in the light of the stated objectives of the organization. Thus for example in a public health service one could look at measures such as treatment waiting times, increasing life expectancy etc, and although such organizations do not have a profit motive requiring efficient operation, they should nonetheless be accountable for the resources they use. Techniques such as 'value for money' and the three Es (economy, efficiency and effectiveness) have been developed and can help to assess the performance of such organizations.

ACCA marking scheme		
		Marks
(a)	1 mark per ratio	10
(b)	1 mark per valid point	10
(c)	1 mark per valid point	5
Total		**25**

4 PORTO

(a) **Relevance**

Information has the quality of relevance when it can influence, on a timely basis, users' economic decisions. It helps to evaluate past, present and future events by confirming or perhaps correcting past evaluations of economic events. There are many ways of interpreting and applying the concept of relevance, for example, only material information is considered relevant as, by definition, information is material only if its omission or misstatement could influence users. Another common debate regarding relevance is whether current value information is more relevant than that based on historical cost. An interesting emphasis placed on relevance within the Framework is that relevant information assists in the predictive ability of financial statements. That is not to say the financial statements should be predictive in the sense of forecasts, but that (past) information should be presented in a manner that assists users to assess an entity's ability to take advantage of opportunities and react to adverse situations. A good example of this is the separate presentation of discontinued operations in the income statement. From this users will be better able to assess the parts of the entity that will produce future profits (continuing operations) and users can judge the merits of the discontinuation i.e. has the entity sold a profitable part of the business (which would lead users to question why), or has the entity acted to curtail the adverse affect of a loss making operation.

Reliability

The Framework states that for information to be useful it must be reliable. The quality of reliability is described as being free from material error (accurate) and a faithful representation of that which it purports to portray (i.e. the financial statements are a faithful representation of the entity's underlying transactions). There can be occasions where the legal form of a transaction can be engineered to disguise the economic reality of the transaction. A cornerstone of faithful representation is that transactions must be accounted for according to their substance (i.e. commercial intent or economic reality) rather than their legal or contrived form. To be reliable, information must be neutral (free from bias). Biased information attempts to influence users (perhaps to come to a predetermined decision) by the manner in which it is presented. It is recognized that financial statements cannot be absolutely accurate due to inevitable uncertainties surrounding their preparation. A typical example would be estimating the useful economic lives of non-current assets. This is addressed by the use of prudence which is the exercise of a degree of caution in matters of uncertainty. However prudence cannot be used to deliberately understate profit or create excessive provisions (this would break the neutrality principle). Reliable information must also be complete, omitted information (that should be reported) will obviously mislead users.

Comparability

Comparability is fundamental to assessing an entity's performance. Users will compare an entity's results over time and also with other similar entities. This is the principal reason why financial statements contain corresponding amounts for previous period(s). Comparability is enhanced by the use (and disclosure) of consistent accounting policies such that users can confirm that comparative information (for calculating trends) is comparable and the disclosure of accounting policies at least informs users if different entities use different policies. That said, comparability should not stand in the way of improved accounting practices (usually through new Standards); it is recognized that there are occasions where it is necessary to adopt new accounting policies if they would enhance relevance and reliability.

(b) (i)   This item involves the characteristic of reliability and specifically reporting the substance of transactions. As the lease agreement is for substantially the whole of the asset's useful economic life, Porto will experience the same risks and rewards as if it owned the asset. Although the legal form of this transaction is a rental, its substance is the equivalent to acquiring the asset and raising a loan. Thus, in order for the financial statements to be reliable (and comparable to those where an asset is bought from the proceeds of a loan), the transaction should be shown as an asset on Porto's balance sheet with a corresponding liability for the future lease rental payments. The income statement should be charged with depreciation on the asset and a finance charge on the 'loan'.

(ii)   This item involves the characteristic of comparability. Changes in accounting policies should generally be avoided in order to preserve comparability. Presumably the directors have good reason to be believe the new policy presents a reliable and more relevant view. In order to minimize the adverse effect a change in accounting policy has on comparability, the financial statements (including the corresponding amounts) should be prepared on the basis that the new policy had always been in place (retrospective application). Thus the assets (retail outlets) should include the previously expensed finance costs and income statements will no longer show a finance cost (in relation to these assets whilst under construction). Any finance costs relating to periods prior to the policy change (i.e. for two or more years ago) should be adjusted for by increasing retained earnings brought forward in the statement of changes in equity.

(iii)   This item involves the characteristic of relevance. This situation questions whether historical cost accounting is more relevant to users than current value information. Porto's current method of reporting these events using purely historical cost based information (i.e. showing an operating loss, but not reporting the increases in property values) is perfectly acceptable. However, the company could choose to revalue its hotel properties (which would subject it to other requirements). This option would still report an operating loss (probably an even larger loss than under historical cost if there are increased depreciation charges on the hotels), but the increases in value would also be reported (in equity) arguably giving a more complete picture of performance.

ACCA marking scheme		
		Marks
(a)	3 marks each for relevance, reliability and comparability	9
(b)	2 marks for each transaction ((i) to (iii)) or event	6
Total		**15**

5 BEETIE

(a) The correct timing of when revenue (and profit) should be recognized is an important aspect of an income statement showing a faithful presentation. It is generally accepted that only realized profits should be included in the income statement. For most types of supply and sale of goods it is generally understood that a profit is realized when the goods have been manufactured (or obtained) by the supplier and satisfactorily delivered to the customer. The issue with construction contracts is that the process of completing the project takes a relatively long time and, in particular, will spread across at least one accounting period-end. If such contracts are treated like most sales of goods, it would mean that revenue and profit would not be recognized until the contract is completed (the 'completed contracts' basis). This is often described as following the prudence concept. The problem with this approach is that it may not show a faithful presentation as all the profit on a contract is included in the period of completion, whereas in reality (a faithful representation), it is being earned, but not reported, throughout the duration of the contract. IAS 11 remedies this by recognising profit on uncompleted contracts in proportion to some measure of the percentage of completion applied to the estimated total contract profit. This is sometimes said to reflect the accruals concept, but it should only be applied where the outcome of the contract is reasonably foreseeable. In the event that a loss on a contract is foreseen, the whole of the loss must be recognized immediately, thereby ensuring the continuing application of prudence.

(b) **Beetie**

Income statement

	Contract 1	Contract 2	Total
	$000	$000	$000
Revenue recognized	3,300	840	4,140
Contract expenses recognized (balancing figure contract 1)	(2,400)	(720)	(3,120)
Expected loss recognized (contract 2)		(170)	(170)
Attributable profit/(loss) (see working)	900	(50)	850

	Contract 1 $000	Contract 2 $000	Total $000
Balance sheet			
Contact costs incurred	3,900	720	4,620
Recognized profit/(losses)	900	(50)	850
	4,800	670	5,470
Progress billings	(3,000)	(880)	(3,880)
Amounts due from customers	1,800		1,800
Amounts due to customers		(210)	(210)

Workings (in $000)

Estimated total profit:

	Contract 1	Contract 2
Agreed contract price	5,500	1,200
Estimated contract cost	(4,000)	(1,250)
Estimated total profit/(loss)	1,500	(50)

Percentage complete:

Agreed value of work completed at	
31 March 2006	3,300
Contract price	5,500
Percentage complete at 31 March 2006	
$(3,300/5,500 \times 100)$	60%
Profit to 31 March 2006 $(60\% \times 1,500)$	900

At 31 March 2006 the increase in the expected total costs of contract 2 mean that a loss of $50,000 is expected on this contract. In these circumstances, regardless of the percentage completed, the whole of this loss should be recognized immediately.

ACCA marking scheme		Marks
(a)	1 mark per valid point to maximum	4
(b)	Revenue (½ mark for each contract)	1
	Profit/loss (½ mark for each contract)	1
	Amounts due from customers (contract 1)	2
	Amounts due to customers (contract 2)	2
	Maximum	6
Total		**10**